YES,

BUT WHY?

Teaching for understanding in mathematics

Sara Miller McCune founded SAGE Publishing in 1965 to support the dissemination of usable knowledge and educate a global community. SAGE publishes more than 1000 journals and over 800 new books each year, spanning a wide range of subject areas. Our growing selection of library products includes archives, data, case studies and video. SAGE remains majority owned by our founder and after her lifetime will become owned by a charitable trust that secures the company's continued independence.

Los Angeles | London | New Delhi | Singapore | Washington DC | Melbourne

YES, BUT WHY?

Teaching for understanding in mathematics

ED SOUTHALL

@solvemymaths

Los Angeles | London | New Delhi
Singapore | Washington DC | Melbourne

Los Angeles | London | New Delhi
Singapore | Washington DC | Melbourne

SAGE Publications Ltd
1 Oliver's Yard
55 City Road
London EC1Y 1SP

SAGE Publications Inc.
2455 Teller Road
Thousand Oaks, California 91320

SAGE Publications India Pvt Ltd
B 1/I 1 Mohan Cooperative Industrial Area
Mathura Road
New Delhi 110 044

SAGE Publications Asia-Pacific Pte Ltd
3 Church Street
#10-04 Samsung Hub
Singapore 049483

Editor: James Clark
Assistant editor: Rob Patterson
Production editor: Tom Bedford
Copyeditor: Andy Baxter
Proofreader: Camille Bramall
Marketing manager: Dilhara Attygalle
Cover design: Sheila Tong
Typeset by: C&M Digitals (P) Ltd, Chennai, India
Printed in the UK by Bell & Bain Ltd, Glasgow

Library of Congress Control Number: 2016947798

British Library Cataloguing in Publication data

A catalogue record for this book is available from the British Library

ISBN 978-1-4739-4895-2
ISBN 978-1-4739-4896-9 (pbk)

MIX
Paper from responsible sources
FSC® C007785

Contents

About the Author

Ed Southall is a teacher trainer in mathematics working for Huddersfield University. He also teaches mathematics in a local 11–16 comprehensive school. Ed has worked in education for 13 years in a variety of roles, starting as a teacher of computing before taking up senior roles leading departments for both computing and mathematics, and working as an Assistant Headteacher. He has also worked abroad in the Middle East as a mathematics education consultant and teacher trainer.

Author blog

Visit Ed's blog *Solve My Maths* at solvemymaths.com where you'll discover an array of maths problems to solve, tips for teachers, engaging opinions and mesmerising animations. Ed also tweets @solvemymaths.

Praise for this Book

'I am currently in my 12th year of teaching maths, and it scares me just how little I really understand about the subject I love. Why are eleven and twelve not called one-teen and two-teen? Why does a negative times a negative equal a positive? Why can I just flip the second fraction over and change to a multiply when I want to divide? Why does the Venn diagram method produce the highest common factor and lowest common multiple of two numbers? Why is the volume of a pointed shape equal to a third of the volume of the full shape? I kind of know the answer to these, and I can carry out the skills relatively comfortably myself (unless it is a really nasty fraction, of course), but that is no real help when I am trying to introduce the topic to students and they are asking me why. Now, thanks to Ed's book, I have the answers and a whole lot more besides. For this is not just a book packed full of fascinating facts. Scattered through the pages are practical teaching tips that can be used straightaway in the classroom. Having read the book, I don't just have more answers to students' questions, I also have new ways of introducing and extending topics, and a much more in-depth knowledge of a subject I thought I knew pretty well. Personally, I would make this book compulsory for all trainee teachers, all NQTs, all maths teachers, all heads of department, and all senior leaders. Basically, everyone. I just wish I had negotiated some kind of commission deal!'

Craig Barton, Maths Teacher, TES Maths Adviser and Creator of www.mrbartonmaths.com and www.diagnosticquestions.com

'Ed Southall's new book is the most interesting mathematics education book that I have read in a long time. It is packed full of fascinating nuggets of information, pedagogical advice and suggestions for the classroom. The author's meticulous research is clear throughout, as is his consideration to correct pedagogy. In my opinion, this book should be required reading for all trainee maths teachers, and even the most experienced teachers will, no doubt, learn something.'

Tom Bennison, Maths Teacher

'This is the book that we've all been waiting for! I thoroughly enjoyed reading it and was astonished by how much new stuff I learnt. This book makes mathematical concepts crystal clear. It provides fascinating insights and helpful teaching tips for a comprehensive range of topics. This book has given me a fresh burst of enthusiasm for teaching our wonderful subject! It's a must buy for all new and experienced maths teachers.'

Jo Morgan, Maths Teacher, Writer of resourceaholic.com and SCITT Teacher Trainer

Introduction

I was never a keen mathematician as a child. When I first started school, I was good at maths, but I never really understood it. I followed algorithms, and churned out answers that matched those of the teacher, but I was never satisfied with the process. I knew how to check if things were correct, but it was the steps to get there that bothered me. I didn't understand them, and they were left to my imagination to try and explain. Mathematics gradually became a mysterious entity, whose rules and steps I was expected to unquestioningly memorise – which I dutifully did. However, the process of storing numerous algorithms and their quirky properties became increasingly tedious, and I fell out of love with the subject that once intrigued and excited me. It still felt important though. I continued to study it alongside other subjects right through to my graduation from university, and went on to become a teacher of ... computing, although, my skillset inevitably brought me back into the maths classroom. I was determined not to teach mathematics the way it had been taught to me. I revisited the various topics on the curriculum with a determination to understand everything. Every detail. Getting the right answers wasn't enough. Where did they come from? What was the point of each step for each solution? I wasn't interested in stating formulae, I was interested in deriving them. I wasn't satisfied with being told there were three types of average (there are more, I was lied to), I wanted to know *why*, I wanted to know who decided upon them as standard measures and I wanted to know about the struggles that people endured to make people listen the first time these ideas were mooted. Who was Pythagoras? Why do so many things have such bizarre names? Surds? Quadratics? Where do these words come from?

I needed to know. I wanted students to know. I wanted them to have the opportunity to genuinely understand, rather than passively accept mathematics.

As a teacher, this knowledge has transformed the way in which I teach. Concepts have origins, stories, logic, connections and intuitiveness – rather than being isolated sorcery. The feeling when a student gets the right answer is incomparable to when they say 'that makes *sense*'.

As a student, this additional understanding is transformational. Answers begin to *look* right, methods can be adapted and applied to different contexts, and students no longer need to rely on the memorisation of hundreds of disparate facts. Each concept is suddenly connected and the sophisticated beauty of mathematics becomes clear. Perhaps even more importantly, mathematics becomes a joyful experience.

This book is intended as a complement to your existing subject knowledge. It is written with an underlying assumption that you are already familiar with many of the algorithms used to solve maths problems – and although time is spent revisiting those procedures, the emphasis here is on *how* they work, *where* mathematical rules come from and *why* they're important.

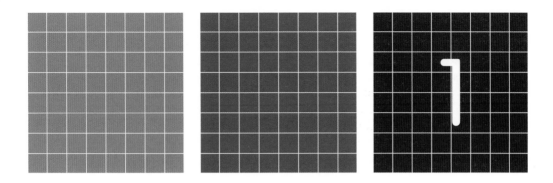

Types of Numbers (Part 1)

It feels sensible enough to start at what is arguably the most intuitive element of mathematics – counting. We can all do it. Furthermore, alongside many other animals, we are instinctively able to do a kind of counting called **subitising**. Subitising is an intuitive sense of comparison of quantity, without a need for symbols. A basic ability to subitise small numbers has allowed us, and everything else in the food chain, to check whether all of our children are still around, or to count the number of predators near our next meal. This ability is apparent very early on too. Children who have not yet learnt to speak, or indeed stand, will still show surprise when one of a small number of identical objects is removed without replacement when they aren't looking.

Counting is slightly different. It is both the ability to order numbers in sequence, but also an ability to total a quantity. Where subitising may allow us to sense which size is bigger, counting allows us to say how many of each thing there is (Figure 1.1).

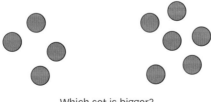

Which set is bigger?
Do you need to count them?

Figure 1.1 Subitising is the ability to instantly recognise small quantities without counting

Counting is the simplest sequence there is, but what we perhaps don't appreciate, is how the English language has conveniently made it easier for us. Our number language is systematic and highly structured. There is a clear pattern in sets of ten that can be picked up quickly by anyone looking at it for the first time. However, the Chinese perhaps have the most straightforward number system:

The Chinese language of number (Table 1.1)

Table 1.1   The Chinese number system is more intuitive than our own

Decimal	Chinese	Literal translation	Decimal	Chinese	Literal translation
1	Yi	One	7	Qi	Seven
2	Er	Two	8	Ba	Eight
3	San	Three	9	Jiu	Nine
4	Si	Four	10	Shi	Ten
5	Wu	Five	11	Shi Yi	Ten One
6	Liu	Six	12	Shi Er	Ten Two

That's pretty clear and sensible. And if we were inventing words for numbers in English all over again I'd probably opt for that structure for clarity. So what about our own language?

The English language of number

At first glance we don't fare too badly:

'one' 'two' 'three' … 'twenty-one' … 'thirty-two' … 'forty-three'.

There is a sound structure in place, allowing us to understand quite easily the quantity being portrayed by the words themselves.

Alas, there are a few peculiarities. One to ten are quite straightforward, but then we get to eleven. What's wrong with eleven? Well for a start, it doesn't crop up again until we count a further hundred numbers forward. In fact, the whole set of numbers between eleven and nineteen are a bit of a pain if you think about it. So why aren't they called 'ten-one', 'ten-two', 'ten-three' and so on? That would at least fit into the pattern of the other ninety numbers before we reach one hundred. Also why does the pattern reset itself after every ten? Why not after every five? Or sixteen?

Why are eleven and twelve such misfits?

Eleven and twelve are arguably the most peculiar, ill-fitting names for numbers in our number system. Their names originate from German. English as a language is largely Germanic, and German, like English, is fairly unique in having the rather awkward 'eleven' (*elf* in German) and 'twelve' (*zwolf*). And if you go back to *Old German*, these words effectively mean 'ten-and-one' (*ein-lif*), and 'ten-and-two' (*zwo-lif*). So once upon a time they *did* fit in with a conventional, sensible structure. Over time, as with most words, they have evolved and changed a bit, and hence feel a little unsuitable in their current format. But it could be worse – we have historically used quite a few peculiar alternative names for numbers such as 'four score and eight' or 'four and twenty'. Spare a thought then for our Welsh friends, who say 'nineteen on twenty' (literally translated) to describe thirty-nine, or the Danes who say 'two-and-a-half times twenty, and four' for fifty-four. Suddenly eleven, twelve and the teens don't seem so bad after all.

Unique descriptions of numbers in English

couple	(2)
pair	(2)
brace	(2)
dozen	(12)
baker's dozen	(13)
score	(20)
gross	(144)
myriad	(10,000)

Teacher tip

Get students to create their own number systems. They can create their own words and symbols. See if they start to create a logical system (or guide them towards doing so). Does their system repeat its structure to mimic our own? Does it repeat its structure in a different way? You could encourage students to try a different base under the guise of an alien number system. Perhaps they could create new symbols that more accurately represent the quantities they represent. For example three might become 'o_o_o'. This kind of activity can help students understand and appreciate our number system and the logical structure it follows.

Why do we count in base-10?

Base-10 is known as the **decimal system**. We have ten digits that we use in organised combinations for all numbers: 0–9. The reason we use base-10 is incredibly likely to be because we have 10 fingers. The Simpsons therefore, should count in base-8, as they have 8 fingers. That would mean going from 1 to 7 and then straight to 10. Which would mean ... 8. The mind boggles. Binary and hexadecimal are other examples of number systems in different bases. Binary is base-2 (zeroes and ones), and hexadecimal uses letters (A–F) to continue the symbols past 0–9 to create a base-16 system (Table 1.2). Both are used in computing.

Table 1.2   The numbers 1–16 in base-10, base-2 and base-16

Decimal	Binary	Hexadecimal	Decimal	Binary	Hexadecimal
1	1	1	9	1001	9
2	10	2	10	1010	A
3	11	3	11	1011	B
4	100	4	12	1100	C
5	101	5	13	1101	D
6	110	6	14	1110	E
7	111	7	15	1111	F
8	1000	8	16	10000	10

Teacher tip

To help students understand and appreciate the decimal system (and what alternative systems could look like), get them to tape two fingers together on one or both hands. Role-play the idea that the students are now cartoon characters with a different number system. See if they can accurately count in a new base system.

Odd and even numbers

Once children get familiar with counting, the next step is often to introduce the first example of *categorisation* in our number system – odd and even numbers.

Odd numbers (a number of **odd parity**) always end in a 1, 3, 5, 7 or a 9. Contrastingly, even numbers (a number of **even parity**) end in a 2, 4, 6, 8 or 0. However, these facts alone do not make a particularly good definition. For example, 3 is odd, but would 3.0 be even? Of course not. What about 3.2? Is that even or odd? Let's look a little deeper.

Why do we categorise odd and even numbers?

To answer this we must first appreciate two things – the usefulness of categorisation in mathematics, and the properties of odd and even numbers. Mathematicians have a love of categorising. If a set of numbers has a special property, then categorising helps us identify, describe and study them. Odd and even numbers are perhaps the simplest example of categorisation in maths. There are also several other types of numbers that students are exposed to at school, such as prime numbers, square numbers and negative numbers. Each of these is categorised due to its own unique properties. We'll look at them later.

What are the properties of odd and even numbers?

Even numbers can be represented pictorially (Figure 1.2).

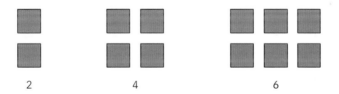

Figure 1.2   Even numbers pictorially are even ended

As you can see, they are always nicely *even* ended.
Odds however …

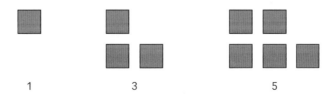

Figure 1.3   Odd numbers pictorially are uneven

have an awkward (some might say … odd) bump (Figure 1.3).

By drawing odd and even numbers in this way, we can answer some other puzzling questions quite easily.

Why do two even numbers always sum to make another even number?

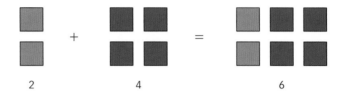

Figure 1.4   The addition of two even numbers sums to an even number

You can see from Figure 1.4 that any two even numbers added together would always result in a larger, but still rectangular shape, which is even.

Why do two odd numbers always add to make an even number?

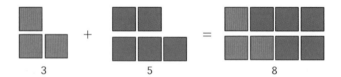

Figure 1.5   The addition of two odd numbers sums to an even number

This time, we can see that two odd shapes equal an even (rectangular) shape, by rotating one of the odd shapes 180° (Figure 1.5).

Why do an odd and an even number always add to make an odd number?

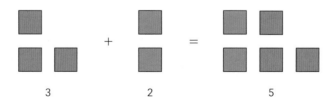

Figure 1.6   The addition of an odd and an even number sums to an odd number

Here we have our only odd answer when adding two numbers. You can see how an odd and even shape will never yield an even rectangle when adding (Figure 1.6).

What are the multiplicative properties of odd and even numbers?

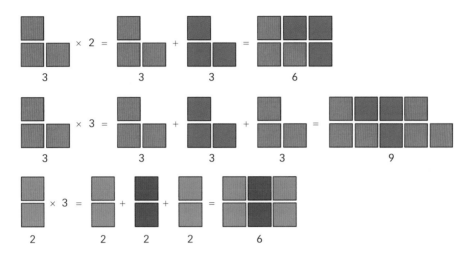

Figure 1.7 The multiplicative properties of odd and even numbers

Again, with careful observation of the shape of even and odd numbers, you can see in Figure 1.7 how only an odd number multiplied by another odd number will produce an odd answer.

We're getting closer to a nice mathematical definition of odd or even numbers, but first let us consider fractions and decimals, which incidentally are neither odd nor even.

Why are fractions and decimals neither odd nor even?

While it is quite understandable why one might assume that *anything* ending in an odd number is odd, or ending in an even number is even, the idea breaks down the more you analyse it.

Let us start with fractions. Would we assume that if the numerator is odd, then the fraction is odd? If we did, then $\frac{3}{5}$ would be odd. But $\frac{3}{5}$ is equivalent to 0.6, which ends in an even number, so it must be even, mustn't it? Furthermore, $\frac{3}{5}$ is equivalent to $\frac{6}{10}$. So now would it be considered even? Quite simply, the odd/even argument doesn't work when we use fractions.

Now let us consider decimals. Assuming a number ending in an even digit is even, and a number ending in an odd digit is odd, then 0.3 would be odd. However, 0.3 is the same as 0.30, which would be even. Not convinced? Here's another problem: recall the rules we established earlier about odd numbers added to odd numbers (they always make an even number). Now consider:

$$1.5 + 1.5 = 3$$

Well, either our rules are ruined, or decimals shouldn't be in the club.

Let us conclude then, with an appropriate definition of odd and even numbers:

An even number is an integer of the form $n = 2k$, *where k is also an integer*. Use Table 1.3 if you need help visualising the algebra.

Table 1.3

Value for n	Value for k	$n = 2k$
0	$k = 0$	$0 = 2 \times 0$
2	$k = 1$	$2 = 2 \times 1$
4	$k = 2$	$4 = 2 \times 2$
6	$k = 3$	$6 = 2 \times 3$

An odd number therefore, is simply any integer that is *not* even. That is, an integer of the form $n = 2k + 1$, where k is (still) an integer (Table 1.4).

Table 1.4

Value for n	Value for k	$n = 2k + 1$
1	$k = 0$	$1 = (2 \times 0) + 1$
3	$k = 1$	$3 = (2 \times 1) + 1$
5	$k = 2$	$5 = (2 \times 2) + 1$
7	$k = 3$	$7 = (2 \times 3) + 1$

Since we're throwing in terms like **integer** now, we should probably visit some of the other broad categories in our number system (Table 1.5, Figure 1.8).

Yes, But Why? Teaching for Understanding in Mathematics

Table 1.5 Symbols for types of numbers and their meanings

Category	Description
Natural numbers, ℕ	Natural numbers are all of the **positive whole numbers**. 1, 2, 3, …
	They are sometimes referred to as 'counting numbers', and, depending on your definition, can be considered either exclusive or inclusive of the number zero (there is no universal agreement on whether it should be included, as it is 'non-negative' so loosely fits with some definitions)
Integers, ℤ (The Z stands for **Zahlen** meaning 'numbers' in German)	Integers are all the **whole numbers**. Integers are inclusive of negative numbers *and* zero
Rational numbers, ℚ (the Q stands for **quotient**, meaning the result when dividing one quantity by another)	In our ever expanding net, rational numbers are inclusive of **integers *and* fractions**
Irrational numbers ℝ\ℚ (meaning real numbers excluding rational numbers)	Irrational numbers *cannot* be expressed as fractions, π being a famous example
Real numbers, ℝ	This is the net that catches all of the above. Real numbers includes everything apart from imaginary and complex numbers, but let's not worry about those here

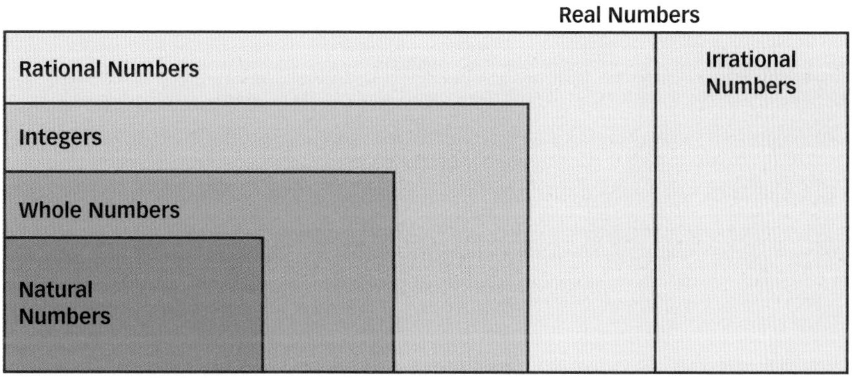

Figure 1.8 Broad categories of our number system

Zero (part 1)

Zero is one of the younger numbers in the number system. It has a long and trouble-some history as a bit of a rebel but was a significant breakthrough in the world of maths. Put simply, zero changed the way we use mathematics forever.

Why did zero arrive so late?

Zero simply wasn't a consideration for most cultures in ancient times. There was no real need for a specific number or symbol to explain *the absence* of something. For example, 'There are no cows in this field' does not require the number zero to convey understanding. Before zero, the typical structure of numerical symbolism was to use new symbols or symbol repetition as you ascended the number line. Roman numerals are a great example. X is ten, L is 50, etc. Romans used a logical structure to their number system, which was based around seven key symbols: I (1), V (5), X (10), L (50), C (100), D (500) and M (1000). Each number could be represented using a combination of those symbols, in descending order from left to right (occasionally with subtraction to avoid writing the same symbol several times, e.g. 4 is IV – 'one less than five', indicated by having a smaller number in front of

Table 1.6 Numbers and their Roman numeral equivalents

Decimal number	Roman numeral	Decimal number	Roman numeral	Decimal number	Roman numeral
1	I	51	LI	91	XCI
2	II	52	LII	92	XCII
3	III	53	LIII	93	XCIII
4	IV	54	LIV	94	XCIV
5	V	55	LV	95	XCV
6	VI	56	LVI	96	XCVI
7	VII	57	LVII	97	XCVII
8	VIII	58	LVIII	98	XCVIII
9	IX	59	LIX	99	XCIX
10	X	60	LX	100	C

a larger one (Table 1.6). Strangely, this convention didn't quite follow into modern clock faces, which often have 4 written as IIII instead of IV).

A major downside to doing things this way around, is that eventually you begin to use ridiculously long combinations of symbols for relatively small numbers.

For example: LXXXVIII is 88, and MCMLXXXVII is 1987. Worse still, imagine how addition would work in the Roman numeral system. Mental addition would be fine for small numbers, but to work out bigger sums would take a lot of tedious work, cross-referencing and symbol exchanging. In fact, Romans used to use a combination of an abacus and their Roman numeral system to essentially convert from one to the other, then back again.

What is strange, is that the idea of a placeholder (which eventually became 'zero') arose *before* Roman numerals, but was not used by the Romans. Evidence of the conceptual beginnings of zero can be found on ancient Babylonian tablets circa 2000 BC where empty spaces were used to indicate place value. So the difference between 1, 101 and 1001 would be the size of the gap between the 1's. However, this is a rather poor system, as different people could interpret gaps differently, and only context could help someone differentiate between 1 and 100.

So it was a bit of a stroke of genius when someone started using a *symbol* to represent this gap, and it came from a fairly unlikely source. Some 5000 years ago, traders in Mesopotamia began using double dashes, like //, to mean 'nothing goes here' when writing out large numbers. Who needs famous mathematicians? The use of the actual '0' symbol developed in India, where some of the first written uses of zero can still be seen today. India was the first country to truly conceptualise the idea of zero and see the benefits of it as part of the number system.

This breakthrough suddenly allowed people to write 101 as '1 // 1' instead of 1 1. The brilliant consequence of this, is that suddenly a mere nine numerical symbols, plus some dashes (so … ten symbols) are required to represent any whole number. Pretty handy, especially considering that up to this point, deciphering the difference between 11, 101 or 1001 was surprisingly tricky.

Place value

The adoption of zero, or any other symbol acting as a zero, allowed for a coherent and effective place-value system. But what *is* place value? Well, it is the notion that any digit in a number has a specific quantity attached to it, and that quantity differs depending on *where* the digit resides.

Consider 2, 20 and 200. Each number contains the digit 2, but the value of 2 means something quite different in each example.

2 = two units

20 = two tens and zero units

200 = two hundreds, zero tens and zero units.

You can see how zero is playing its part beautifully. It is creating a specific place for the 2 to go each time. Younger students often struggle with aligning these digits. As such, it is common to provide columns as in Figure 1.9.

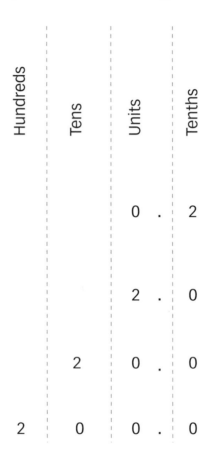

Figure 1.9 Digits aligned in columns

Our base-10 system ensures that each place in a number is an increase in value of a power of ten.

Hence:

$$20 = 2 \times 10 = 2 \times 10^1$$

$$200 = 2 \times 10 \times 10 = 2 \times 10^2$$

$$2000 = 2 \times 10 \times 10 \times 10 = 2 \times 10^3$$

$$\ldots$$

$$3480 = (3 \times 10 \times 10 \times 10) + (4 \times 10 \times 10) + (8 \times 10) + 0$$

These powers can continue infinitely, but place value also allows us to write numbers *between* integers with **decimal places**.

Decimal places

The use of a decimal point '.' differentiates whole number values from decimal values (confusingly, it is sometimes written as a comma ',' rather than a dot). As before, these ascend in powers of ten (ten hundredths are equivalent to one tenth, etc.) (Figure 1.10).

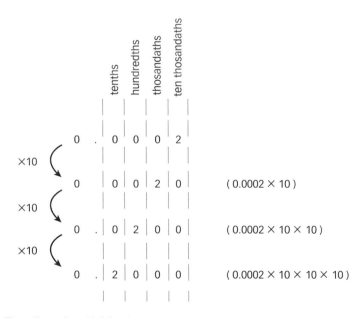

Figure 1.10   The effect of multiplying by ten

Try to avoid discussing 'adding a zero' when multiplying by ten. It only clouds what is actually happening mathematically. A set of stacked paper cups can be an excellent way to show the place value of different digits in a number and start a deeper conversation about multiplying and dividing by multiples of ten (Figure 1.11).

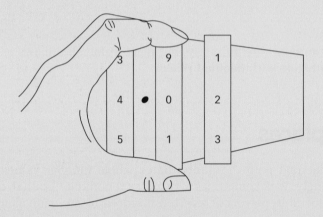

Figure 1.11   Using cups to visually demonstrate place value

Decimals are frequently used in measurements (measurement is discussed in Chapter 6), and often students are required to *round* a decimal to the nearest whole number, or tenth, or hundredth, etc. Rounding is a fairly straightforward task. One must simply determine whether a number is closer to a, or to b.

For example:

3.266 to the **nearest tenth** will either be 3.2 or 3.3. But which is it closer to? Let us use a number line to visualise it (Figure 1.12).

We can see that it is closest to 3.3, which is therefore our answer.

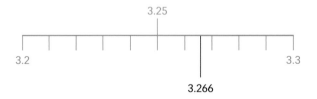

Figure 1.12   A visual demonstration of rounding to the nearest tenth

Visualising the problem on a number line makes this example easier – but what if the original number was 3.25?

This sits equidistant from 3.2 and 3.3. So rounding 3.25 to the *nearest* tenth (1 decimal place) can't be done can it? Well, we say it rounds to 3.3.

Why do we round 'up'?

Well, this is known as a tie-breaking scenario. There is no definitive 'closer' number. The general rule is to 'round up' *towards* positive infinity simply because we need convention to allow for consistency. So for example, 4.55 would round 'up' by default to 4.6 to the nearest tenth. However, it would be perfectly acceptable to round down to 4.5 if one were specifically instructed to 'round down'.

Incidentally, this causes an interesting case with *negative* numbers. Considering −4.55, we would in fact round 'up to the nearest tenth' to −4.5 by default as this is *closer to positive infinity*.

Other types of rounding

Some less common but equally valid rounding strategies are given in Table 1.7.

Table 1.7 The results of rounding when using different conventions

Decimal	Round half towards zero	Round half away from zero	Round half to even	Round half to odd
0.4	0	0	0	0
1.5	1	2	2	1
0.6	1	1	1	1
−0.5	0	−1	0	−1
−0.4	0	0	0	0

Before we move on, there is one further point to make about types of decimals (pun intended).

Rounding 0.9 to the nearest whole number will give an answer of 1. As will 0.99, and 0.999. But all of these values themselves (prior to rounding) are actually **less than 1** (see the number line in Figure 1.13).

Figure 1.13 0.999 is very close to 1

However, the *recurring* decimal 0.9999 … (symbolised in mathematics as $0.\dot{9}$ is in fact **equal to 1**.

What is a recurring decimal?

A recurring decimal is the opposite of a **terminating decimal**. Recurring decimals continue infinitely, but with a recurring pattern of numbers. This could be a single digit, like with a third:

$$0.\dot{3} = 0.333333...$$

Or a sequence of digits such as:

$$0.\dot{1}2\dot{3} = 0.123123123123...$$

Why is $0.\dot{9}$ equal to 1?

Well, let us first consider the whole number 5. We can rewrite 5 as 5.0, or indeed 5.00 – in fact, we can write 5 as $5.\dot{0}$. And it is still just 5.

The point here is that we are simply changing the notation for the same number. This is the same as $0.\dot{9}$ and 1.

We can, of course, prove it with maths:

Let

$$m = 0.\dot{9}$$

Therefore

$$10m = 9.\dot{9}$$
$$9m = 10m - m = 9.\dot{9} - 0.\dot{9} = 9$$
$$9m = 9$$
$$m = 1$$

So, somewhat counter-intuitively, the number $349.\dot{9}$ will round to 400 as the nearest 100.

Zero (part 2)

Zero has another fundamental purpose beyond being a convenient placeholder. Zero is also the gatekeeper between positive numbers and negative numbers – which in itself makes it an *even* number.

Why is zero an even number?

Take a look at the number line in Figure 1.14.

Figure 1.14   Zero is neither positive nor negative

Zero is cushioned between odd numbers, and must therefore be even. Notice that this number line also reveals another unique property of zero. It is the only number that is neither positive nor negative.

Teacher tip

Do not abandon number lines. They are incredibly useful for visualising numbers, estimations, place value, negatives, quantities and numerical operations. Sadly they often get dismissed as 'juvenile' later on in school. Nothing could be further from the truth.

Zero the rebellious rule breaker

Let's take a closer look at the bizarre properties of zero that made its adoption into mathematics a rather bumpy ride.

Addition and subtraction seem to stop working properly

$3 + 1 = 4$ Our answer got bigger.

$3 + (-1) = 2$ Our answer got smaller.

$3 + 0 = 3$ Addition did nothing!

Multiplication and division seem to stop working properly

$$0 \times 6 = 0$$

$$0 \times 7 = 0$$

Normally, if we multiply something by different numbers, we get different answers – but not with zero! Zero is not playing by the rules. No other numbers get these kinds of nutty results.

This particular oddity is easier to see if we switch to algebra:

$$ab = d$$

$$ac = d$$

$$\text{but } b \neq c$$

When it comes to division by zero, you may have heard about how you simply cannot do it, and it's often attributed to apocalyptic consequences. Ever wondered why?

Why is dividing by zero undefined?

It would make a degree of sense to assume that anything divided by zero equals zero. That may feel intuitive, but in fact, when we look at division as an inverse operation of multiplication, it quickly becomes apparent that dividing by zero simply doesn't work.

Take 2×3 for example:

$$2 \times 3 = 6$$

$$6 \div 3 = 2$$

By rearranging, we can see that 2 must be 6 divided by 3 by use of inverse operations. One effectively undoes the other.

This can be generalised as follows:

$$a \times b = c$$

$$c \div b = a$$

Taking this principle and applying it to division by zero would imply that, for example, $3 \div 0$ can be multiplied by some unknown number x, which will magically bring us back to 3.

In other words:

$$3 \div 0 = x$$

$$\therefore x \times 0 = 3$$

If you find a number that works for the above, do let me know! It simply doesn't work. As such, dividing by zero is not defined.

Now that we've covered counting, and zero, it makes sense to discuss counting beyond zero towards *negative infinity*.

Negative numbers

Relatively speaking, negative numbers took a long time to enter the world of maths. Counting has always had its place, and despite zero not originally being a necessity to count objects, it eventually fitted in quite nicely because of its ability to create place value and help perform written calculations. Negatives on the other hand, were simply not required. I cannot count 'negative two' loaves of bread, or subtract more physical objects than there are to begin with. At least, not practically speaking. However, negative numbers eventually found their way into maths via a concept all too familiar with many of us, *debt*. At some point most of us have happily noted our bank balance looked healthier than expected, only to be disappointed when we noticed the DR next to it. DR is a polite version of a negative symbol, i.e. you are overdrawn and you owe the bank money. The concept of negative numbers can be traced back to China and India in slightly different guises (around 200 BC and 300 AD, respectively) long before Europe adopted them. Negative numbers seem to perplex many (many!) students and it is quite understandable to see why. They do not feel intuitive, and although the concept makes a degree of sense – particularly when describing temperatures (pun intended) and bank balances. But the behaviour of negative numbers when being used in addition, subtraction, multiplication and division can start to feel a little unpredictable and, particularly for students, difficult to understand conceptually.

Adding and subtracting from a negative number

When we add or subtract a positive number *from* a negative number, the results are quite intuitive, particularly if we use a number line. For example:

$$-2 + 1 = -1$$

$$-2 - 1 = -3$$

What is going on in the sums shown above? Let's look at a simple case of adding 1 to a number, using a number line (Figure 1.15).

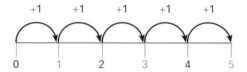

Figure 1.15   Adding 1 on a number line

Now if we extend our number line to include negative numbers, the process remains the same (Figure 1.16).

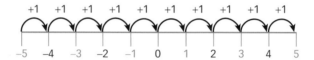

Figure 1.16   Adding 1 on a number line including negative numbers

We are moving along the number line towards infinity ('up' the number line) by adding 1. Already you may begin to see how this gets complicated for students. It's easy to start talking about the number getting 'bigger' or 'larger'. But which is 'bigger': −500 or 2? If we're talking about debt, a debt of £500 feels intuitively 'bigger' than £2 credit, especially if you're picturing the actual cash. Yet when we use inequalities (more on those later), 2 is 'greater than' −500. 'Bigger' suddenly starts to feel like a fuzzy term.

When we subtract *positive 1* from a number, the pattern of moving 'down' the number line remains the same whether starting at a point greater or less than zero (Figure 1.17).

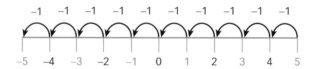

Figure 1.17   Subtracting 1 will eventually take you past zero into negative numbers

Adding and subtracting a negative number

Things start getting a little weird when we add or subtract a *negative* number:

$$3 + (-1) = 2$$
$$3 - (-1) = 4$$

These examples begin to make more sense if we think of them as adding and subtracting *debt*. For $3 + (-1)$, I am *adding a debt* of 1. Therefore, I *owe* 1, and am left with 2. Similarly for $3 - (-1)$, I am *removing a debt* of 1. Therefore, I *am owed* 1, and I am left with 4.

But analogies of negative numbers as debt only take us so far. With a little mathematical thinking, the behaviour of negative numbers makes even more sense. Consider these sequences:

$$3 + 3 = 6$$
$$3 + 2 = 5$$
$$3 + 1 = 4$$
$$3 + 0 = 3$$
$$3 + (-1) = ?$$

$$3 - 3 = 0$$
$$3 - 2 = 1$$
$$3 - 1 = 2$$
$$3 - 0 = 3$$
$$3 - (-1) = ?$$

When presented in this way, it's unthinkable to consider anything other than the correct answer. It's *intuitive*.

Teacher tip

Get into the habit of referring to negative numbers as 'negative one, negative two, negative three', etc., rather than 'minus one, minus two, minus three', and similarly 'subtract' rather than 'minus'. Students can easily get confused trying to recall that 'a minus and a minus make a plus'; and this oversimplification of a complex topic does not help when presented with something like $(-3)-5$, which is often mistakenly assumed to be 8 or 2. Furthermore, the interchangeability of 'minus' meaning negative, and 'minus' meaning subtract is confusing for experts, let alone students just beginning to get to grips with the topic!

Not convinced? Read this out loud using only 'minus', 'three' and 'two'

$$(-3) - (-2) -2 - (-3)$$

Multiplying and dividing a negative number by a positive number

Again, when starting with negative numbers, but applying operations that involve positive numbers, the results are a little more intuitive:

$$(-3) \times 4 = -12$$

This can be thought of as four groups of -3, or more specifically:

$$(-3) \times 4 = (-3) + (-3) + (-3) + (-3) = -12$$

All that is needed here is an appreciation of integer multiplication being addition in disguise!

Division is perhaps a little trickier:

$$(-10) \div 2 = -5$$

$(-10) \div 2$ can be thought of as a debt of 10 shared equally between 2. Each share therefore must be a debt of 5 (which is represented as -5).

Multiplying and dividing a negative number by a negative number

This seems to be one of the harder things for students to master, probably because it isn't supported particularly well with any meaningful metaphor. In fact metaphors here will likely mislead students and confuse them. We will have to rely on good old mathematical reasoning, by considering the following sequence:

$$(-1) \times 3 = -3$$
$$(-1) \times 2 = -2$$
$$(-1) \times 1 = -1$$
$$(-1) \times 0 = 0$$
$$(-1) \times (-1) = ?$$

The sequence logically implies that $-1 \times -1 = 1$, which is true.

For division, which is the inverse of multiplication, it is perhaps clearer to consider rearranging the division to become multiplication.

For example, we know already that:

$$(-1) \times 1 = -1$$

Therefore, by rearranging the sum:

$$-1 \div -1 = 1$$

We have deduced a relatively abstract fact about negative numbers using a little manipulation of multiplication. It's important that time is well spent discussing these concepts in depth. Declaring the rules simply as fact without explanation is an assured way to bypass understanding of a difficult topic.

Interesting number systems around the globe

Huli

Huli (spoken in Papua New Guinea) uses a base-15 system. The number 16 translates to '15 and 1', 31 translates to '15 × 2 + 1' and so forth.

Tongan

The Tongan number system utilises repetition of the numbers 0–9. For example, 12 would be '1 2', and 20 would be '2 0'.

Georgian

The Georgian number system is in base-20. The number 30 translates to '20 and 10', 51 translates to '2 × 20 and 1 more than 10' and so forth.

Hindi

Strictly speaking, Hindi is a base-10 number system. However, in reality it acts as a base-100 system, as each number up to 100 has a unique pronunciation.

Oksapmin

Oksapmin (spoken in Papua New Guinea) has a base-27 number system, utilising 27 body parts to count from(!). In fact, the words for the numbers 1–27 are the same as the words for the body parts. Would you like a '*thumb* of carrots'? Possibly not.

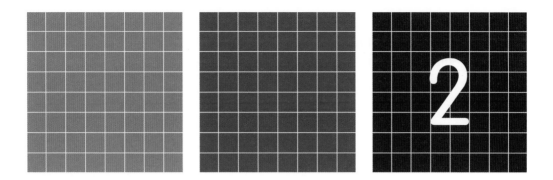

The Four Operations

Here we will discuss in depth the nature of addition, subtraction, multiplication and division. We will look at the properties of each operation, and the ways in which they can be manipulated without breaking any mathematical rules. We will look at the importance of number bonds, the order of operations and why standard methods of multiplying, dividing, adding and subtracting actually work.

We'll start with a brief history of notation.

The addition and subtraction symbols

The 'plus' symbol, +, is used to signify addition, and is in fact an abbreviation of the Latin *et* meaning 'and'. It is believed to have appeared in print for the first time in around 1350 in a manuscript written by a French philosopher called Nicole d'Oresme. The origin of the subtraction symbol is less clear, although it was not always the preferred symbol to indicate subtraction. What we now use as the division symbol, ÷, was once used for subtraction in Germany, for example. Ironically, Germany is also the place of origin for the first printed use of the more familiar − symbol to represent subtraction, in 1481.

The multiplication symbol

The multiplication symbol, ×, was first used by English mathematician William Oughtred in 1631. Oughtred also invented the slide rule, a tool to help aid multiplication and division. In some early texts, the symbol is referred to as the St Andrew's

Cross, however other symbols were also introduced to represent multiplication at around the same time, and are still in use today:

$$6 \times 2 = 12$$
$$6 \cdot 2 = 12$$
$$6 * 2 = 12$$

Dots were used so as not to confuse people between the letter x and the symbol ×, although nowadays, you could say the same about a dot for multiplication, and a dot for a decimal place. Incidentally, the dot we now use to indicate a decimal place was once a line above the number:

$$34.5 = 34\overline{5}$$

In continental Europe, a decimal point is often represented as a comma to avoid confusion with dot notation for multiplication.

The division symbol

The symbol for division, ÷, is called an **obelus**, meaning 'pointed pillar' (closely related to *obelisk*). As mentioned previously, it was originally used as a symbol for subtraction, but was first applied as a division symbol by Swiss mathematician Johan Rahn in around 1659. Before that, division was usually indicated using a colon:

4:3 meant 4 ÷ 3

Division was also sometimes written using a single bracket. For example:

3)42 meant 42 ÷ 3

A vinculum was later introduced to group together the division more clearly:

3)$\overline{42}$

Which evolved into the division symbol (which has no name) that we recognise today as:

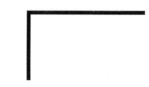

The equals sign

The symbol = to mean 'is equal to' was first introduced in 1557 by Welsh mathematician Robert Recorde. He reasoned that the symbol would save time, rather than writing 'is equal to', and chose the symbol as it represented two parallel lines, about which he stated 'no two things can be more equal'.

Addition

The process of addition is to sum together two quantities or numbers. In real-world terms, this will result in an increase in quantity. For example, if I have three cats, and I add more cats, the number of cats I have will increase. However, in abstract terms, my final amount will depend entirely on whether what I am adding to my original number is positive or negative. The properties of negative numbers are dealt with in more depth in Chapter 1.

Figure 2.1 gives a visual representation of the process of addition.

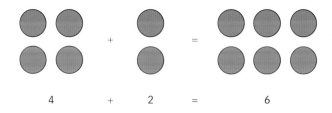

Figure 2.1   An array demonstrating the process of addition

Numbers being added together are called **addends** and their total is called their **sum**.

In this section we will mostly concern ourselves with the addition of positive numbers. Addition of integers can be thought of as an efficient method of counting. When we begin to count, we inevitably do so in increments of 1 – in fact, often you may spot students reverting to counting in 1's to perform addition operations, sometimes on their fingers as a visual aid. Be mindful that this does not become a reactionary exercise that students become dependent on, as it can bypass more efficient (but also more difficult) methods of adding numbers and developing numeracy.

As a student advances their knowledge of numbers and addition, they begin to develop strategies to add larger quantities than 1 in a single step. The beginnings of this process often take the form of **number bonds**.

Number bonds

Number bonds are simply pairs of numbers that form a total. The first bonds that a student encounters are those that sum to 10 (Figure 2.2):

$$10 + 0$$
$$9 + 1$$
$$8 + 2$$
$$7 + 3$$
$$6 + 4$$
$$5 + 5$$

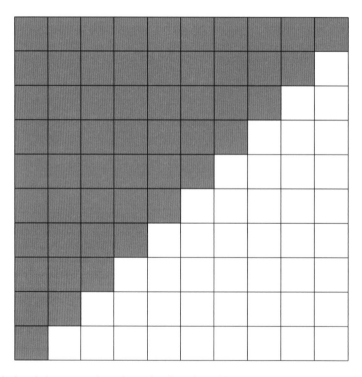

Figure 2.2 A visual demonstration of number bonds to 10

Why are number bonds to 10 so important?

Whilst recognition and utilisation of these simple number facts may seem trivial, the skill is a foundation tool to use standard addition algorithms and improve mental

Yes, But Why? Teaching for Understanding in Mathematics

arithmetic. Furthermore, we use a *decimal* system that is structurally built around sets of 10 – they are simply intrinsic to our language of numbers.

Other particularly important number bonds are those to 12, 24 and 60 (for time), 90, 180 and 360 (for angles), and bonds to 100, 1000, 10,000, etc.

Visual representations of addition

As with most areas of mathematics, teaching the abstract should come only when more visual and physical elements (manipulatives) have been explored. The use of counters, for example, is a great way to allow students to count objects before delving into written symbolism. There are many ways to highlight the process of addition visually. Figure 2.3 gives just a few.

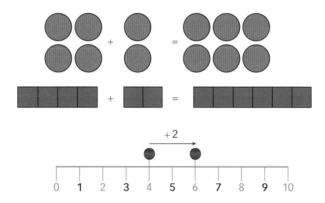

Figure 2.3 Addition can be demonstrated visually in many ways

Teacher tip

Whilst the use of manipulatives may seem like a step backwards for some older students, it is in fact one of the easiest ways to enable understanding of concepts. Manipulatives, when used correctly, can reduce any misunderstanding of what you are communicating. Similarly, a simple sketch of a number line can save you a lot of time too.

Laws of addition

There are three fundamental laws of addition that are key to being able to manipulate addition sums: the **associative** law, the **commutative** law and the **distributive** law.

Understanding of, and exploitation of these laws is key to a deeper understanding of how mathematics works, both in younger and older maths students.

The associative law

The associative law states:

$$(a + b) + c = a + (b + c)$$

For example:

$$(2 + 4) + 3 = 2 + (4 + 3)$$

Again we can demonstrate this visually (Figure 2.4).

Figure 2.4 A visual demonstration of the associative law of addition

In other words, it doesn't matter how we group the numbers in an addition sum. The answer will always be the same.

This law helps students with manipulating sums to make them more manageable. Take the following for example:

$$9 + 14 + 6$$

It is much simpler to attempt it as:

$$9 + (14 + 6)$$

rather than:

$$(9 + 14) + 6$$

The commutative law

The commutative law states that:

$$a + b = b + a$$

For example:

$$2 + 3 = 3 + 2$$

which we can represent visually, and convincingly as in Figure 2.5.

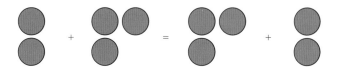

Figure 2.5   A visual representation of the commutative law of addition

The name has roots, unsurprisingly, in the Latin word *commutare* meaning 'exchange'. The law applies to any amount of numbers being added together:

$$3 + 4 + 5 = 3 + 5 + 4 = 4 + 3 + 5 = 4 + 5 + 3 = 5 + 4 + 3 = 5 + 3 + 4$$

Put simply, when we're only working with addition, the order of addition makes no difference to the outcome.

This knowledge, combined with number bonds, is vitally important to help students develop their mental maths skills. For example, if a student were faced with the following sum:

$$17 + 6 + 3 + 9 + 4 + 1$$

Students tend to work, as with reading, from left to right.

However, 17 + 6 is a fairly ugly sum, and 23 is not a nice number to work with compared to say, a round 10, 20 or 30.

If we study the sum briefly before attempting it, you'll see we can move things around to make it much simpler to solve:

$$17 + 6 + 3 + 9 + 4 + 1$$

$$= 17 + 3 + 9 + 1 + 6 + 4$$

Often we imply this property rather than explicitly teaching it. For example, when we teach students about *collecting like terms* in algebra, we're applying the commutative law:

$$3a + 2b + 5a + b = 3a + 5a + 2b + b = 8a + 3b$$

Yet without explicitly investigating this property, the above can seem quite a strange idea, and sums may be approached in far more difficult ways than necessary. There is no shame in manipulating the commutative law to make sums easy. It's simple efficiency!

The distributive law

The distributive law states that:

$$a(b + c) = ab + ac$$

As this law deals with the combined use of addition and multiplication, it will be discussed under the heading 'multiplication' later.

Breaking down numbers

The ability to break a number down into smaller components (sometimes referred to as number-splitting) is another key skill in being competent at mental arithmetic. You may have noticed in our earlier examples of manipulating the commutative law, we were fortunate enough to have a set of numbers that included several number bonds to 10. However, there is every chance that a student will face a set of numbers that do not have such handy conveniences. In which case, the laws will still become very handy, but it may be necessary to break down different numbers to effectively *create* number bonds.

For example:

$$23 + 18 + 14$$

This is an ugly sum, but with a little manipulation, we find it's not so bad after all:

$$23 + 18 + 14$$
$$= (20 + 2 + 1) + (10 + 8) + (10 + 2 + 2)$$
$$= (20 + 10 + 10) + (8 + 2) + (2 + 2 + 1)$$
$$= 55$$

Seeing that this is possible, and preferable, takes practice – but it is worth the investment.

The column method of addition

The formal method of addition for large numbers is known as the *column method*. To use this method, students stack each number on top of one another and line each digit up with its appropriate place value as in Figure 2.6 for:

$$34 + 105$$

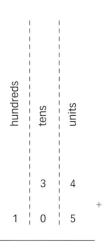

Figure 2.6   The column method of addition

The sum of each column is placed underneath in between the lines (Figure 2.7).

Figure 2.7 Summing the columns

And so we have calculated that:

$$34 + 105 = 139$$

When a column total is more than a single digit (i.e. greater than 9), then we 'carry' the first digit of our total to the next column along, to be used as an extra addend (Figure 2.8).

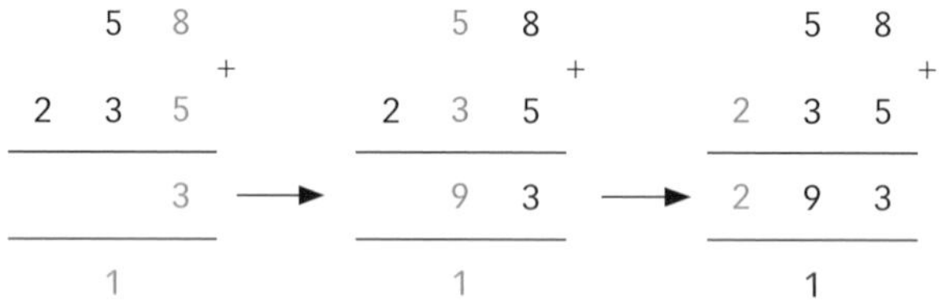

Figure 2.8 'Carrying' digits to the next column

As shown in the figure, at the second stage along, we have $5 + 3$, but we need to also account for the extra 1 carried over from the first addition. Hence, we get a column total of 9 rather than 8.

Why does the column addition method work?

To understand what is happening mathematically, we need to utilise our laws of addition. We are effectively transforming our sum (in the example above) from:

$$58 + 235$$

To:

$$(8 + 5) + (50 + 30) + 200$$

Whilst we have split the numbers into different parts (namely the separated values of the units, tens and hundreds), the answer will remain the same.

Yes, But Why? Teaching for Understanding in Mathematics

When the units are added, we find that their total is 13 units. 13 units is **equivalent** to 1 ten, and 3 units. By splitting the column total into *tens and units*, our method continues to appear in **decimal format** – keeping each column in single digits, which is exactly how the decimal system works.

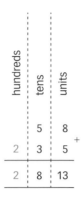

Figure 2.9 The answer as a collection of quantities

If we do not split our column total into tens and units, it would look like Figure 2.9. Our answer is *no longer in decimal format*. It is a collection of quantities (2 hundreds, 8 tens and 13 units), rather than a decimal number. It would make more sense in this format as place-value counters (Figure 2.10).

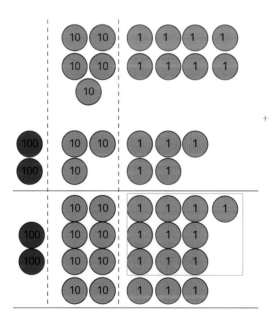

Figure 2.10 Using place-value counters can help students visualise the ways in which numbers are manipulated in column addition

The highlighted 1's show why we need to exchange them into 1 ten, which will make our answer read correctly as a decimal number.

Subtraction

Subtraction is the process of reducing one number or quantity by another. The word subtraction stems from the Latin *subtractionem* meaning 'removal'.

Below is a simple subtraction:

$$4 - 2 = 2$$

which we can represent more visually in several ways (Figure 2.11).

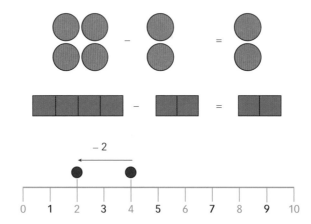

Figure 2.11   Subtraction can be demonstrated visually in many different ways

The number we are subtracting from is referred to as the **minuend** (from the Latin *minuere* meaning 'diminished') and the number being subtracted is referred to as the **subtrahend** (from the Latin *subtrahere* meaning 'to be taken away'). Subtraction can also be thought of as the difference between two numbers. In some ways this is a more useful perspective, as it makes certain manipulations make more sense, as we will see shortly.

The laws of subtraction

Subtraction is *not* commutative:

$$4 - 3 \neq 3 - 4$$

However, when we subtract several numbers in sequence like this:

$$20 - 3 - 4 - 5 - 6$$

then the **subtrahends** *are* commutative:

$$20 - 3 - 4 - 5 - 6 = 20 - 4 - 5 - 3 - 6 \dots \text{etc.}$$

This is because subtracting several numbers is the same as subtracting a group of numbers *added together* (and addition is commutative). Look at Figure 2.12 for clarity:

$$20 - 3 - 4 - 5 = 20 - (3 + 4 + 5)$$

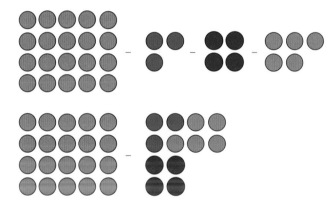

Figure 2.12 The subtrahends in subtraction can be added together without altering the outcome

Subtraction is *not* associative:

$$(10 - 3) - 2 \neq 10 - (3 - 2)$$

This is because we would effectively be reducing the size of the subtrahend(s) before subtracting them, and wrongly converting subtrahends into minuends (Figure 2.13).

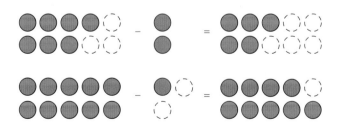

Figure 2.13 Subtraction is not associative

Manipulating subtraction using shifts

One of the most effective ways to manipulate subtraction to make it easier, is to view it as finding the difference between two numbers. As such, it becomes apparent that if you *shift* both the subtrahend and the minuend by the same amount, the difference between them will remain the same. The shift can be either an addition:

$$8 - 5 = (8 + 2) - (5 + 2)$$

or a subtraction:

$$8 - 5 = (8 - 2) - (5 - 2)$$

The reason why this works can be seen more clearly on a number line (Figure 2.14).

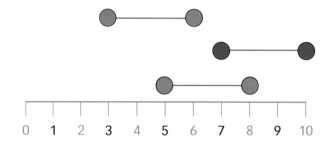

Figure 2.14   Visualising subtraction as 'finding the difference' makes shifting more intuitive

It's particularly useful for subtractions where neither the minuend nor the subtrahend is a nice round number:

$$23 - 7$$

We can alter this to:

$$26 - 10$$

Much nicer! The answer is 16.

The column method of subtraction

Although the column method of subtraction has much the same structure visually as the column method for addition, it is actually a lot more complex in terms of what is going on mathematically. We still stack each number, and line them up based on place value (Figure 2.15).

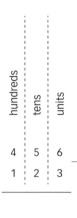

Figure 2.15 The column method of subtraction

And, like before, we subtract each column in turn (Figure 2.16).

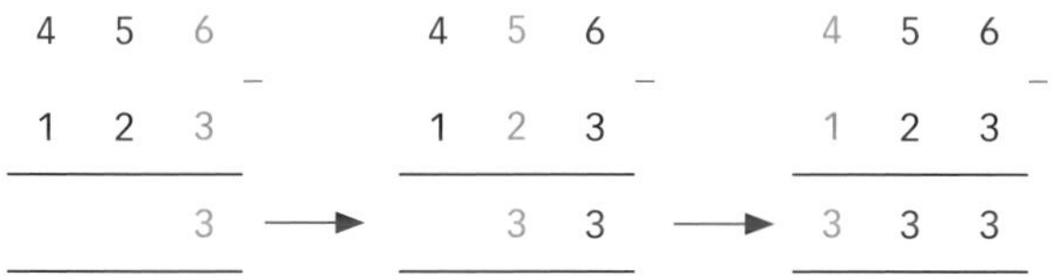

4	5	6				4	5	6				4	5	6	
1	2	3				1	2	3				1	2	3	
		3	→				3	3	→			3	3	3	

Figure 2.16 Subtracting each column in turn

However, the method needs adapting when we find ourselves subtracting a unit that is greater than the one above it. For example, Figure 2.17.

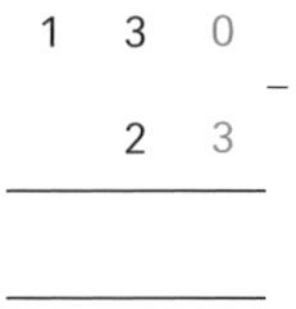

1	3	0
	2	3

Figure 2.17 This subtraction will need additional work

If we do not adapt our method, we will find a rather confusing answer presents itself (Figure 2.18).

$$
\begin{array}{ccc}
1 & 3 & 0 \\
& 2 & 3 \\
\hline
1 & 1 & -3 \\
\hline
\end{array}
$$

Figure 2.18 The answer not in decimal form

Clearly our answer is *not* in decimal form. However, it *does* make sense if you know what you're looking at. It's telling us that our answer is:

$$100 + 10 - 3 = 107$$

Funnily enough, we *do* adapt the method so that our answer *is* in decimal form, and no further interpretation is required (Figure 2.19).

Figure 2.19 The answer in decimal form

Suddenly our nice method looks messy and complicated – because it is! What's going on here?

Breaking down in subtraction

The column method of subtraction involves a process of *breaking down* higher place-value digits to their equivalent value of lower place-value digits. Take the number 100, for example. We can write quantities equivalent to 100 in several ways (Table 2.1).

At each row, we have broken down either a hundred into 10 tens, or a ten into 10 units. The last row can be thought of as either breaking down a hundred into 100 units, or breaking down 10 tens into 100 units. Every single row is **equal**. Appreciating this fact is key to understanding what is happening with the concept of breaking numbers down during column subtraction.

Yes, But Why? Teaching for Understanding in Mathematics

Table 2.1

Hundreds	Tens	Units
1	0	0
0	10	0
0	9	10
0	8	20
0	7	30
0	6	40
0	5	50
0	4	60
0	3	70
0	2	80
0	1	90
0	0	100

Teacher tip

Avoid using terms like 'borrowing' when discussing this method with students. Borrowing is misleading for several reasons, and you may end up inadvertently implying that a number can be altered in all sorts of (erroneous) ways to suit the subtraction. It's always a good idea to refer to each digit as its true value too. For example, rather than talking about 'the six' in 630, call it the 'six hundreds', as that is its value. This just reinforces that the digits are all part of a single number, rather than somehow separated, and helps contextualise the breaking down of hundreds into tens, tens into units and so on.

If we go back to our original example (Figure 2.20).

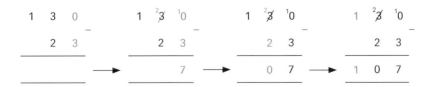

Figure 2.20   Subtracting 3 from 0 in the units column would give us a negative answer

Subtracting 3 from 0 in the units column would give us a negative answer, which would prevent our final answer being in decimal form.

To avoid this, we can instead break down '30' into 2 tens and 10 units (Figure 2.21).

$$\begin{array}{ccc} 1 & {}^2\cancel{3} & {}^1 0 \\ & 2 & 3 \\ \hline & & 7 \\ \hline \end{array}$$

Figure 2.21 Now we have a positive output

Now we have a positive output, and the value of the minuend has *not* changed. We have simply regrouped it as 1 hundred, 2 tens and 10 units, instead of 1 hundred, 3 tens and 0 units.

The rest of the columns do not require any more breaking down, and so are straightforward (Figure 2.22).

$$\begin{array}{ccc} 1 & {}^2\cancel{3} & {}^1 0 \\ & 2 & 3 \\ \hline 1 & 0 & 7 \\ \hline \end{array}$$

Figure 2.22 The rest of the columns are straightforward

Incidentally you can avoid this process altogether by applying the concept of **shifting** discussed previously (Figure 2.23).

$$\begin{array}{ccc} 1 & 3 & 0 \\ & 2 & 3 \\ \hline & & \\ \hline \end{array} \longrightarrow \begin{array}{ccc} 1 & 3 & 7 \\ & 3 & 0 \\ \hline & & 7 \\ \hline \end{array} \longrightarrow \begin{array}{ccc} 1 & 3 & 7 \\ & 3 & 0 \\ \hline & 0 & 7 \\ \hline \end{array} \longrightarrow \begin{array}{ccc} 1 & 3 & 7 \\ & 3 & 0 \\ \hline 1 & 0 & 7 \\ \hline \end{array}$$

Figure 2.23 Applying the concept of shifting

Multiplication

Multiplication of positive whole numbers can be visualised as repeated addition. Whilst this idea does not quite encompass more complicated examples of multiplication, it is a nice way into making sense of the basic premise. For example:

$$3 \times 4 = 3 + 3 + 3 + 3$$

3×4 can be thought of as adding together a set of four 3's, or adding together a set of three 4's (Figure 2.24).

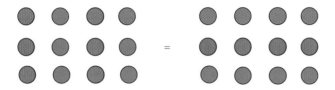

Figure 2.24   How do you see 3×4?

However, the first number is referred to as the **multiplier**, and the second the **multiplicand** (Figure 2.25). This means, technically speaking, the implied meaning of 3×4 is $4 + 4 + 4$ rather than $3 + 3 + 3 + 3$. But I'm not convinced anyone really cares.

Figure 2.25   Technical terms in multiplication

The laws of multiplication

The laws of multiplication are exactly the same as the laws of addition. Multiplication is commutative:

$$4 \times 5 = 5 \times 4$$

We can visualise each combination using arrays. For example, the different ways you can order $4 \times 3 \times 2$ are shown in Figure 2.26.

Multiplication is also associative:

$$(2 \times 3) \times 4 = 2 \times (3 \times 4)$$

In other words, we can associate any two terms rather than work strictly from left to right.

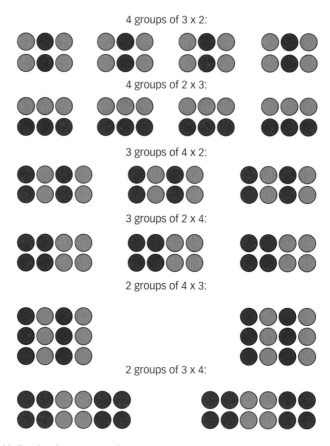

Figure 2.26 Multiplication is commutative

Also, as mentioned earlier, multiplication and addition are **distributive**. That is, multiplication **distributes over addition**:

$$a(b + c) = ab + ac$$

e.g.:

$$2(3 + 4) = 2 \times 3 + 2 \times 4$$

Similarly:

$$a(b - c) = ab - ac$$

Yes, But Why? Teaching for Understanding in Mathematics

Distribution is arguably the most interesting property of multiplication and addition, and the most useful.

Take for example, the following:

$$26 \times 8$$

As written, it's difficult to calculate mentally. However, with some manipulation:

$$26 \times 8 = 20 \times 8 + 6 \times 8$$

It's now a little easier. We could make it even easier by further distribution:

$$20 \times 8 + 6 \times 8 = 10 \times 8 + 10 \times 8 + 6 \times 8$$

Playing around with multiplication in this way is a really important task for students to undertake, as it is an effective way of helping them understand how we can manipulate difficult multiplication to make it much more manageable.

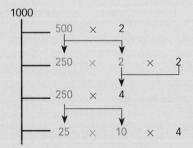

Figure 2.27   Methodically finding multiplication sums that equal the same number is useful practice for students

The column method of multiplication

As with the column methods for addition and division, the visual structure of multiplication is the same, with each digit laid out carefully in columns of place value (Figure 2.28).

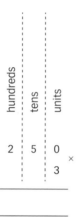

Figure 2.28   The column method of multiplication

Again, we work from units upwards (right to left) and multiply each column in turn. Just like with addition, if any column total is greater than 9, then we reconstruct it accordingly (in Figure 2.29, 15 tens is reconstructed into 1 hundred and 5 tens).

Figure 2.29   Column multiplication utilises the law of distribution

Mathematically, column multiplication utilises the law of distribution. What we are doing in the above example is redistributing the problem as follows:

$$250 \times 3 = 0 \times 3 + 50 \times 3 + 200 \times 3$$

Whilst it may feel like we're calculating $0 \times 3 + 5 \times 3 + 2 \times 3$, we aren't. The value of each column's digit is very different.

Long multiplication is slightly more complicated, but again it is based around manipulating the laws of multiplication. Let's look at a single example, 123×45 (Figure 2.30).

$$
\begin{array}{ccccc}
 & 1 & 2 & 3 & \\
 & & 4 & 5 & \times \\
\hline
 & 6_1 & 1_1 & 5 & \\
 & & & & + \\
4 & 9_1 & 2 & 0 & \\
\hline
5 & 5 & 3 & 5 & \\
\hline
\end{array}
$$

Figure 2.30   Long multiplication

It may seem odd that seemingly out of nowhere we've turned our multiplication into a problem involving addition, but if we analyse what this method is actually doing, all becomes clear.

Underneath our first line, we have performed two operations: 123×5 and 123×40 (Figure 2.31).

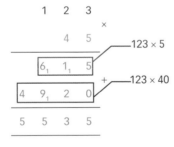

Figure 2.31   Utilising the law of distribution

Again, this is utilising the law of distribution. We have redistributed as follows:

$$123 \times 45 = 123 \times 5 + 123 \times 40$$

It may not be clear to students that we have multiplied by 40 at all, as quite often they fall into the misleading idea that they are 'placing a zero' before multiplying by 4. The idea itself makes no sense as a stand-alone explanation for what is happening. Why zero? Why there? What for? Why not 2 zeroes, or 5? It can be explained clearly by highlighting how we are once again manipulating a specific part of the question:

$$123 \times 40 = 123 \times 4 \times 10$$

The grid method of multiplication

Another popular method of performing multiplication is to split both the multiplicand and the multiplier into their respective digit place values, across from each other in a grid layout. For example, 123 would become 100, 20 and 3; and 45 would become 40 and 5 (Figure 2.32).

	100	20	3
40	4000	800	120
5	500	100	15

```
4000
 800
 120
 500  +
 100
  15
-----
5535
```

Figure 2.32   The grid method of multiplication

Each component is then multiplied by one another, and the sum of each of those gives us our answer.

Once again, this is the distributive law at work:

$$123 \times 45 = 123 \times 40 + 123 \times 5$$
$$= 100 \times 40 + 20 \times 40 + 3 \times 40 + 100 \times 5 + 20 \times 5 + 3 \times 5$$

Division

Division is the inverse operation of multiplication. Integer division is the sharing of an amount into equal parts. Division can be represented in several ways, but typically we use either the obelus symbol, $\div$, or we write division in fraction notation, $\frac{a}{b}$, to mean $a \div b$

A simple example could be written as:

$$8 \div 2$$

This means 'divide 8 into 2 equal parts'. Division is often easier to understand if we use a more visual approach (Figure 2.33).

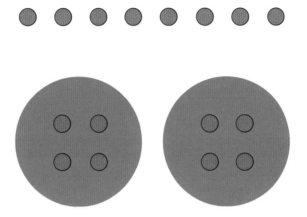

Figure 2.33   A visual demonstration of division

In the figure, 8 has been split equally into two parts, and each part is 4. Therefore

$$8 \div 2 = 4$$

Division involves a **divisor** and a **dividend**, and the result is referred to as the **quotient** (Figure 2.34). Dividend is a term also used in finance, as company shareholders are often paid a *dividend* each financial year – a share of the profits. The term quotient stems from the Latin *quotiens* meaning 'how many times?'.

Figure 2.34   The technical language of division

Division, like subtraction, does not obey the commutative law:

$$10 \div 2 \neq 2 \div 10$$

This is logical, as if it were commutative, then by implication the following would always have to be true:

$$\frac{a}{b} = \frac{b}{a}$$

Which is madness.

However, if there is more than one divisor, the divisors can be thought of as commutative:

$$20 \div 2 \div 5 = 20 \div 5 \div 2$$

This is because dividing by several divisors is the same as dividing by the *product* of those divisors. So we can rewrite them as a multiplication (which we know is commutative) using brackets (Figure 2.35):

$$20 \div 2 \div 5 = 20 \div (2 \times 5) = 20 \div (5 \times 2) = 20 \div 5 \div 2$$

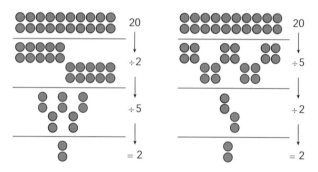

Figure 2.35   *Divisors are commutative*

This property can also be manipulated to make division easier. For example:

$$480 \div 16$$

This sum is not very accessible as it stands; however, we can manipulate it:

$$480 \div 16 = 480 \div 4 \div 4 = 480 \div 2 \div 2 \div 2 \div 2$$

Halving is pretty easy, so now we just perform a series of halvings to finally arrive at the answer, 30.

Division is not associative either:

$$(20 \div 2) \div 5 \neq 20 \div (2 \div 5)$$

In this example, we would end up with 2 = 50, which is clearly nonsense.

Note that whilst we may instinctively believe that division will always make our answer smaller than our dividend, if we divide by a number between 0 and 1, our answer actually gets bigger. This is easier to comprehend if we consider rephrasing, say, '5 divided by 0.2' as 'how many 0.2's are there in 5?' or by visualising the inverse operation:

$$5 \div 0.2 = b$$
$$0.2 \times b = 5$$
$$b = 5 \div 0.2$$
$$b = 25$$

The 'bus stop' method of division

This method is often referred to as the 'bus stop' method because the 'division symbol' (sadly it hasn't got a fun name) resembles a bus stop. Figure 2.36 is a typical use of the bus stop method to calculate $456 \div 3$.

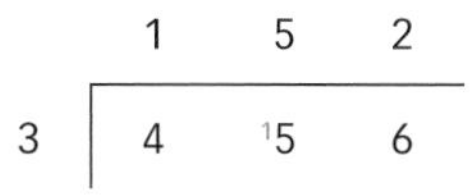

$$3 \overline{\smash{\big)}\, 4 \ {}^1 5 \ 6} \quad = 1 \ 5 \ 2$$

Figure 2.36 'Bus stop' division

What is interesting here, is that for the first time, we're working from left to right, rather than right to left. As we'll see in a moment, working right to left would require a lot of going backwards and forwards which would be a bit of a nightmare.

Initially then, we would ask ourselves 'how many 3's go into 4?', the answer is 1, with 1 remaining, which is carried over to the next digit. However, what have we really done mathematically?

Well, at each stage of the calculation, what we've written is that there is '1 group of **one hundred 3's**' in 400, leaving a remainder of 100 (Figure 2.37).

Figure 2.37 1 group of one hundred 3's in 400

In the next column, we have observed that there are '5 groups of **ten 3's**' in 150 (Figure 2.38),

Figure 2.38   5 groups of ten 3's in 150

and finally, there are two **3's** in 6 (Figure 2.39).

Figure 2.39   Two 3's in 6

Two digit division

When the divisor has more than one digit, division is more difficult. Figure 2.40 is an example, using the exact same bus stop method as before.

```
          0    3    8
      ┌─────────────────
12    │  4   ⁴5   ⁹6
```

Figure 2.40   Two digit division using the 'bus stop' method

The only difference here is that the calculations are a little more difficult as the numbers are bigger. Another popular strategy to tackle two digit divisors is a method known as **chunking**, which rest assured does not involve being sick.

Chunking

Division by chunking is a relatively intuitive method of division (arguably more so than the standard bus stop method, although less efficient).

Effectively, it is the process of partitioning the dividend into manageable chunks informed by knowledge of basic multiplication facts.

```
12   │   4    5    6
     │ −  1    2    0        12 × 10 = 120
     │ ───────────────
     │    3    3    6
     │ −  1    2    0        12 × 10 = 120
     │ ───────────────
     │    2    1    6
     │ −  1    2    0        12 × 10 = 120
     │ ───────────────
     │         9    6
     │ −       9    6        12 × 8 = 96
     │ ───────────────
     │              0
```

Figure 2.41   Division using the chunking method

In Figure 2.41, we use knowledge of multiplication to deduce that if $12 \times 10 = 120$, then there must be at least ten 12's in 456. 120 therefore is our first chunk. We continue utilising the fact that $12 \times 10 = 120$ until we reach a remainder of 96. At this point, we now know there are at least thirty 12's in 456. We then use the fact that $12 \times 8 = 96$, and 96 is our final chunk, and so overall our answer must be $10 + 10 + 10 + 8 = 38$

Remainders

Remainders are quantities that are 'left over' when a division does not give an exact integer answer. For example, $404 \div 8 = 50$ *remainder* 4.

To rewrite the answer as a decimal, you can continue the division algorithm by extending the dividend past the decimal point, or alternatively you can also interpret the remainder as a fraction where the numerator is the remainder, and the denominator is the divisor (Figure 2.42).

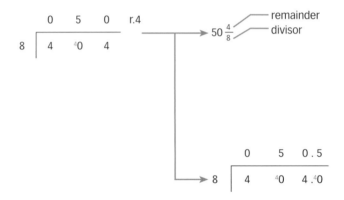

Figure 2.42   The different interpretations of a remainder

The order of operations

In a string of various operations, the order in which we tackle each one matters immensely. Take for example:

$$3 + 2 \times 4$$

If we work left to right, we get:

$$3 + 2 = 5$$
$$5 \times 4 = 20$$

However, if we multiply first:

$$2 \times 4 = 8$$
$$3 + 8 = 11$$

We have two completely different answers from the same starting point. Hence, we need a convention for how to approach written maths – which is known as the **order of operations**. Whilst it may sound like a strange cult, it is simply an agreed standard that dictates which operations take precedence over others.

The order of operations is this:

Brackets – indices – division and multiplication – addition and subtraction

Note that division and multiplication are clumped together, as are addition and subtraction. To differentiate which to do first between division and multiplication, or between addition and subtraction, we simply work from *left to right*. However, this is *not* clear from the popular acronym BIDMAS (or any similar acronyms) and so it will need to be explicitly taught. Note also that operations such as the square root fall under the category of 'indices' as they can be written in index notation ($\sqrt{2} = 2^{\frac{1}{2}}$)

For example:

$$3^2 + (6 - 4) - 2 \times 3 \div 2$$

We would work out the brackets first:

$$3^2 + 2 - 2 \times 3 \div 2$$

Then the indices:

$$9 + 2 - 2 \times 3 \div 2$$

Then the multiplication (it comes before division working from left to right):

$$9 + 2 - 6 \div 2$$

Then the division:

$$9 + 2 - 3$$

Then addition, followed by subtraction (left to right):

$$11 - 3 = 8$$

Some mathematical surprises using multiplication

$$1 \times 1 = 1$$
$$11 \times 11 = 121$$
$$111 \times 111 = 12321$$
$$1111 \times 1111 = 1234321$$
$$11111 \times 11111 = 123454321$$
$$111111 \times 111111 = 12345654321$$
$$1111111 \times 1111111 = 1234567654321$$
$$11111111 \times 11111111 = 123456787654321$$
$$111111111 \times 111111111 = 12345678987654321$$

$$0 \times 9 + 1 = 1$$
$$1 \times 9 + 2 = 11$$
$$12 \times 9 + 3 = 111$$
$$123 \times 9 + 4 = 1111$$
$$1234 \times 9 + 5 = 11111$$
$$12345 \times 9 + 6 = 111111$$
$$123456 \times 9 + 7 = 1111111$$
$$1234567 \times 9 + 8 = 11111111$$
$$12345678 \times 9 + 9 = 111111111$$

$$12345679 \times 9 = 111111111$$
$$12345679 \times 18 = 222222222$$
$$12345679 \times 27 = 333333333$$
$$12345679 \times 36 = 444444444$$
$$12345679 \times 45 = 555555555$$
$$12345679 \times 54 = 666666666$$
$$12345679 \times 63 = 777777777$$
$$12345679 \times 72 = 888888888$$
$$12345679 \times 81 = 999999999$$

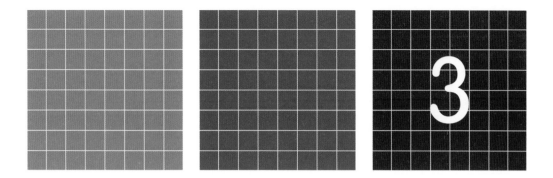

Angles and Shapes

In this chapter we will look at the properties of different types of shapes in both two and three dimensions. We'll look at the definitions of different classifications of shapes, and the vocabulary associated with them. We'll get a few essentials out of the way first.

Common symbols

Figure 3.1   Common notation for lines of equal length

Lines of **equal length** are represented using a single dash. In instances where there are two sets of equal sized lines, but each set is different, then double dashes are used to differentiate them (as shown in Figure 3.1).

SAGE would like to acknowledge that most figures in this chapter were created with GeoGebra (www.geogebra.org).

Figure 3.2   Common notation for parallel lines

Lines that are **parallel** to one another are shown using a single arrow (or double arrows to differentiate between two different pairs of parallel lines) (Figure 3.2).

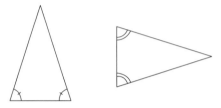

Figure 3.3   Common notation for identical angles

Angles that are identical can be identified using a single dash through the angle, or by using a pair of curved lines (as shown in Figure 3.3).

What is an angle?

An angle is the amount of rotation at a vertex (corner) needed to get one side into the position of the other. Angle derives from *angulus* – which is Latin for 'little bending'. Angles are usually measured in *degrees*, which are denoted using the ° symbol. Degrees were created by the Ancient Babylonians, who probably created a reference point of 360° for a full circle, based on the 360-day Babylonian year.

Types of angle

Acute angle

Any angle less than 90° is referred to as an acute angle (Figure 3.4). The word acute simply means 'sharp'.

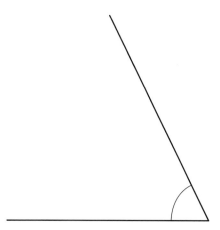

Figure 3.4   An acute angle

Right angle

An angle that is exactly 90°. This is the only angle that has a different symbol to other angles. We call it a right angle because it is upright (not because it is correct, or in a particular direction!) (Figure 3.5).

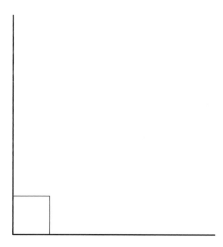

Figure 3.5   A right angle

Lines that are at right angles to one another are said to be **perpendicular**, and two angles that sum to equal 90° are called **complementary angles** (Figure 3.6).

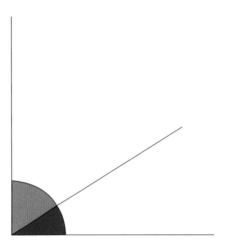

Figure 3.6   Complementary angles

Obtuse angle

Any angle that is greater than 90° but less than 180° is called an obtuse angle (which means 'blunted') (Figure 3.7).

Figure 3.7   An obtuse angle

Straight angle

This is an angle that creates a straight line, which is 180° (half a full circle/turn) (Figure 3.8).

Figure 3.8   A straight angle

Yes, But Why? Teaching for Understanding in Mathematics

Two angles that sum to 180° are called **supplementary angles** (Figure 3.9).

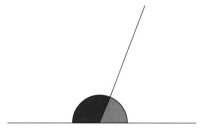

Figure 3.9   Supplementary angles

Reflex angle

A reflex angle is any angle that is greater than 180° and less than 360° (Figure 3.10).

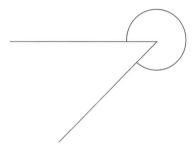

Figure 3.10   A reflex angle

Full angle

A 360° angle is known as a full angle, or full turn. It can also be referred to as a **perigon** (meaning 'enclosing angle') (Figure 3.11).

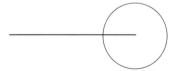

Figure 3.11   A full angle

Angles on intersecting lines

Using the fact that supplementary angles sum to 180°, it should be clear that **opposite angles** on intersecting lines must therefore be equal (Figure 3.12).

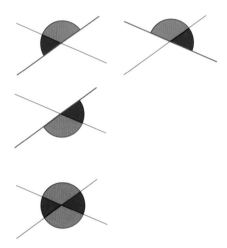

Figure 3.12   Angles on intersecting lines

Angles on a transversal

Parallel lines are lines that never intersect, and are the same distance apart at all points. A line passing through two (or more) parallel lines is called a transversal, and passes through them at the same angle (Figure 3.13).

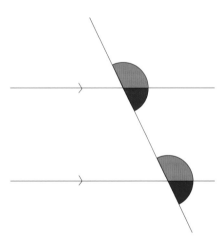

Figure 3.13   Supplementary angles on a transversal

Combining this concept with angles on intersecting lines, we can deduce Figure 3.14.

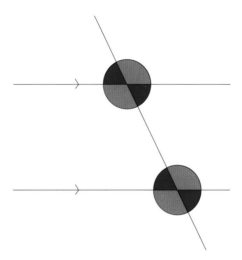

Figure 3.14   Angles on a transversal

Hence, **co-interior** angles sum to 180º (Figure 3.15).

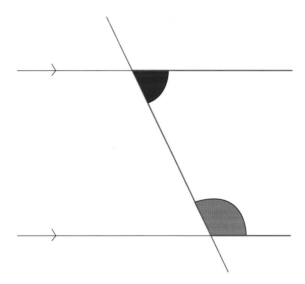

Figure 3.15   Co-interior angles

Alternate angles are equal (Figure 3.16).

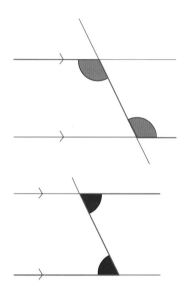

Figure 3.16 Alternate angles

and **corresponding angles** are equal (Figure 3.17).

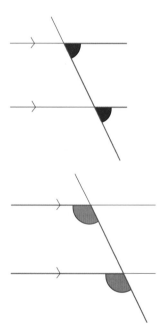

Figure 3.17 Corresponding angles

Yes, But Why? Teaching for Understanding in Mathematics

Bearings

Bearings are a navigational method to describe the position of a point relative to another (fixed) point. For standardisation purposes, these are always read clockwise from North, and have three figures, even if the angle itself is only two digits. For example, a bearing of 30° would be written as 030°.

Bearings always have three figures so that any bearing communicated to someone could not be misinterpreted. For example, a spoken bearing of 234° could be misheard as 23° or 24°, or 34° and writing 20 could be misconstrued as 200. However, as the standard is three figures, a recipient would expect to hear or see three figures, and therefore would ask for a repeated transmission or question the accuracy should they receive only two.

So in Figure 3.18, point B is at a bearing of 050° from point A, and point A is at a bearing of 230° from point B.

Note that the two North lines are parallel, and so when dealing with bearings problems we can utilise the same properties we looked at previously.

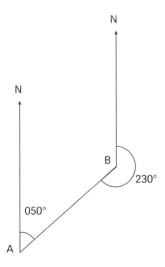

Figure 3.18   Bearings

Shapes

One definition of a shape is a geometric figure with a complete boundary made up of a set of points connected by straight lines. This type of shape can be generalised as a **polygon** (which literally means 'many angled').

The smallest number of sides a polygon can have is three (the triangle), although there is a *degenerate* polygon known as a *digon* which is just a straight line, but we'll leave that one alone. **Degenerate** in mathematics means 'limiting', in other words, degenerate cases are those at the extreme ends of a definition.

Polygons have a **perimeter**, which literally means 'the measure around' and is defined as the length of the boundary of the shape (in other words, the sum of its side lengths), **vertices** (corners, where two sides meet at a point) and an **area** (the space inside the shape – discussed in depth in Chapter 7).

The triangle

Unsurprisingly the word triangle literally means three (tri) angled – which implies three lines (sides). Triangles are special in that they get a whole host of sub-categories under their broad 'triangle' umbrella. Before we look at each sub-category of triangles, there is one ~~more property that applies to all triangles~~.

Why do polygons have interior angles that sum to 180°

This is part of a wider pattern of interior angles of polygons which we will explore shortly; however, we can prove this particular case using the properties of angles in parallel lines from earlier (Figure 3.19).

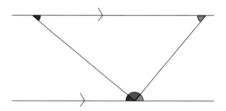

Figure 3.19 A visual proof that the angles in a triangle sum to 180°

You can see from Figure 3.19, that the green angles are equal (they are alternate angles), and the red angles are also equal (they are also alternate angles), and the sum of the red, green and blue angles must be equal to 180° as they lie on a straight line. Hence, the interior angles of the triangle must be equal to 180°.

Acute triangles

An acute triangle is a triangle whose interior angles are all acute angles (Figure 3.20).

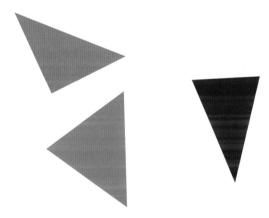

Figure 3.20   A selection of acute triangles

Obtuse triangles

An obtuse triangle is a triangle that has one obtuse interior angle (Figure 3.21).

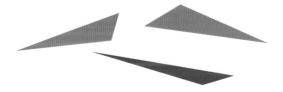

Figure 3.21   A selection of obtuse triangles

Right-angled triangles

A right-angled triangle has an interior angle of 90°. This particular type of triangle has 'legs' (the shortest two sides) and a hypotenuse (the longest side, which is opposite the right angle) (Figure 3.22).

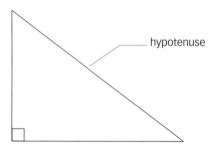

Figure 3.22   A right-angled triangle

This type of triangle is associated with the Pythagorean Theorem, which is discussed in depth in Chapter 10.

Equilateral triangles

An equilateral triangle has three sides of equal length, and therefore all three interior angles are equal (60°) (Figure 3.23).

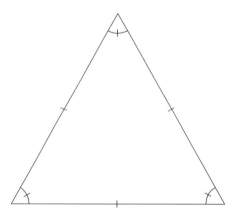

Figure 3.23   An equilateral triangle

An equilateral triangle is an acute triangle. Any shape with equal side lengths (and therefore equal sized interior angles) is part of a broader family of shapes called **regular** shapes. Equilateral simply means 'equal sides'.

Isosceles triangles

An isosceles triangle is a triangle with at least two equal side lengths (Figure 3.24).

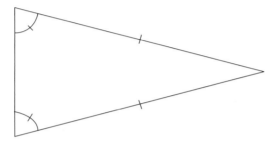

Figure 3.24   An isosceles triangle

This also means that two internal angles must be equal. The word isosceles means 'equal legs'.

Isosceles triangles are not an isolated group. We can have isosceles right-angled triangles, for example (Figure 3.25).

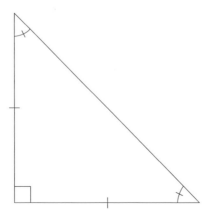

Figure 3.25   An isosceles right-angled triangle

In fact, an equilateral triangle is also a special type of isosceles triangle (it has 'at least two equal sides').

Scalene triangles

Finally, we have a scalene triangle. Scalene triangles have three unequal sides (and therefore, three unequal interior angles) (Figure 3.26).

Figure 3.26   A selection of scalene triangles

Again, there can be cross-over here. We can have scalene obtuse triangles, scalene acute triangles and scalene right-angled triangles. The word scalene means 'uneven'.

Quadrilaterals

A quadrilateral is a four-sided shape (quad means 'four', lateral means 'sided'). As with triangles, there are several sub-categories of quadrilaterals and some surprising overlaps between them. All quadrilaterals share two common properties. The first is that they have four sides, and the second is that their interior angles sum to 360° (Figure 3.27). You may be spotting a pattern about internal angles of shapes, but we'll get to that shortly.

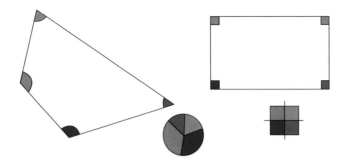

Figure 3.27   The interior angles of a quadrilateral sum to 360°

Kites

A kite is a quadrilateral with two pairs of equal length **adjacent** sides (Figure 3.28).

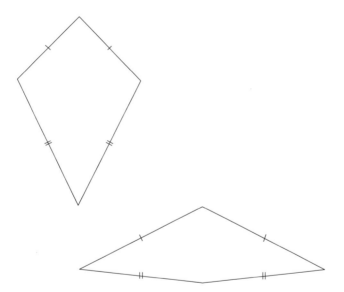

Figure 3.28   Kites

Trapeziums

A trapezium (confusingly referred to as a trapezoid in the US) means 'little table' and has two sides that are parallel (Figure 3.29).

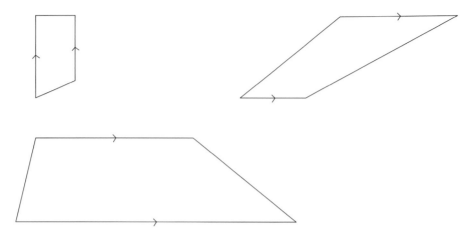

Figure 3.29 Trapeziums

Note that the definition does not explicitly imply that the two remaining sides are *not* parallel. Therefore, technically speaking, any quadrilateral with at least two parallel sides is a trapezium (including rectangles and squares). There is also an **isosceles trapezium** whose non-parallel sides are equal in length (Figure 3.30).

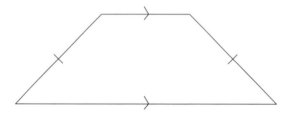

Figure 3.30 An isosceles trapezium

Parallelograms

A **parallelogram** is a quadrilateral with opposite sides that are parallel to one another (Figure 3.31).

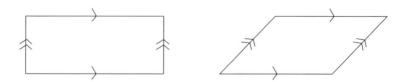

Figure 3.31 Parallelograms

You'll notice that a rectangle is, technically, a parallelogram. There are a lot of cross-overs when categorising quadrilaterals. But it would be a brave student who named a rectangle a parallelogram in an examination, despite it being technically correct.

Rhombi

A **rhombus** is a quadrilateral with opposite sides that are parallel to one another, *and* all sides are equal (Figure 3.32).

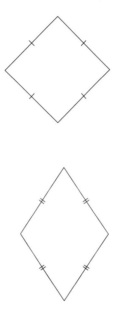

Figure 3.32   Rhombi

Again, there is plenty of cross-over here. The upper shape in the figure is a square. Squares fit into almost all categories of quadrilaterals as we'll see shortly.

Rectangles

A **rectangle** is a quadrilateral with opposite sides of equal length, and all interior angles are 90° (Figure 3.33). We can call this property **equiangular**.

Figure 3.33 A rectangle

Squares

A **square** is a regular quadrilateral, with four sides of equal length, and all interior angles are 90° (Figure 3.34). We can say a square is **equilateral** and **equiangular**.

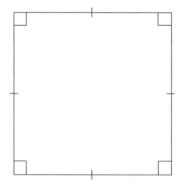

Figure 3.34 A square

Cross-overs

Here's the fun bit.

Technically speaking, a square is always a rectangle (it has opposite sides of equal length) and a rhombus (it has parallel opposite sides, and all sides are of equal length), and a parallelogram (opposite sides are parallel), and a trapezium (it has two sides that are parallel) and a kite (it has two pairs of equal length adjacent sides).

Similarly, a rectangle is always a special type of parallelogram and a special type of trapezium.

Finally, a parallelogram is always a special type of trapezium.

Well I'm sure that's very clear now. There are two more types of quadrilateral whilst we're here.

Concave quadrilaterals

All the quadrilaterals we've looked at so far have been **convex**; however, shapes such as a dart are **concave** quadrilaterals, which always include one interior reflex angle (Figure 3.35).

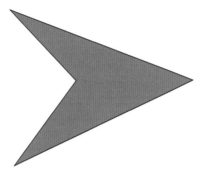

Figure 3.35   A dart shape is a concave quadrilateral

Crossed quadrilaterals

A crossed quadrilateral (sometimes referred to as a complex quadrilateral) is one where the sides cross-over, creating what looks like a six-sided shape, but is still technically a quadrilateral (it is created by connecting four distinct points with four straight lines). In Figure 3.36, you can see that the green line joins two distinct points, as does the black line.

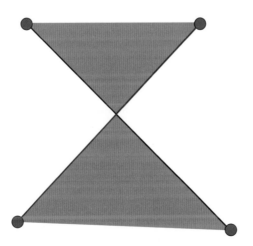

Figure 3.36   A crossed quadrilateral

Crossed shapes are curious wonders, but probably best left as an aside rather than something to potentially confuse younger students.

Regular polygons

A regular polygon is a two-dimensional shape with equal length sides, and equal interior angles. The first eight regular shapes are shown in Figure 3.37.

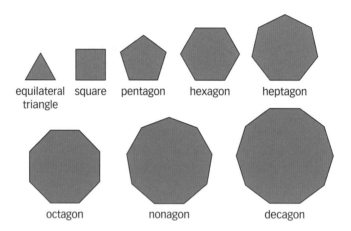

Figure 3.37   Regular polygons

Most shapes follow the convention of a Greek prefix for the number of sides, and 'gon' at the end, meaning 'angled'. As such, 'octagon' simply means 'eight-angled' and so forth.

Curiously, the quadrilateral and triangle escaped this convention, probably because they were named before the other shapes and before any desire for convention kicked in. Although trigon and tetragon are both valid names too. Quadrilateral is the oddest name though, as it does not mean literally 'four-angled', but rather, 'four-sided'.

Symmetry

Lines of reflective symmetry mean that an imaginary line could be drawn to halve the shape, and each half would be a reflection of the other. For example, an equilateral triangle has three distinct lines of reflective symmetry (Figure 3.38).

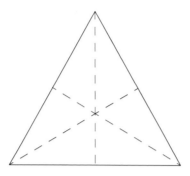

Figure 3.38   Lines of reflective symmetry

In fact, all regular shapes have as many lines of reflective symmetry as they have sides.

Rotational symmetry on the other hand, refers to how many times a shape is identical in appearance during a full 360° rotation about its centre. For example, a square has rotational symmetry of order four (the dot is purely for illustrative purposes) (Figure 3.39).

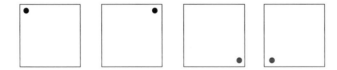

Figure 3.39   Rotational symmetry

Regular shapes with n sides, have rotational symmetry of order n.

Irregular polygons

An irregular polygon is a shape that does **not** have equal length sides, and therefore does not have equal interior angles (Figure 3.40).

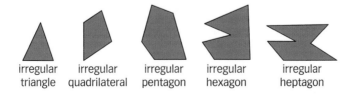

irregular triangle   irregular quadrilateral   irregular pentagon   irregular hexagon   irregular heptagon

Figure 3.40   Irregular polygons

Whilst irregular polygons still have the same sum of interior angles as their regular counterparts, individual interior angles will not all be equal to one another.

Interior angles of polygons

We have teased with the idea of a pattern regarding the interior angles of polygons so far. We saw that triangles have an interior angle sum of 180°, and quadrilaterals 360°, respectively. If we map the interior angle sums out as a sequence, you may indeed spot the pattern (Table 3.1).

Table 3.1 Table of interior angles of *n*-gons

Number of sides	3	4	5	6	7	8
Sum of interior angles	180°	360°	540°	720°	900°	1080°

What we have is an arithmetic sequence (discussed in more detail in Chapter 7), which increases by 180 each time. If we call the number of sides n, we can deduce the nth term of this sequence as

$$180n - 360$$

$$= 180 (n - 2)$$

And, should we wish, we can calculate the size of each interior angle (for a regular shape, as they're all equal) by dividing the sum of the interior angles by the number of sides (which is the same as the number of interior angles):

$$\frac{180(n-2)}{n}$$

Why does this pattern exist?

To understand *why* the sum of interior angles of polygons increases in this way, we need to visualise how each iteration is, essentially, the addition of a triangle to the previous version. In Figure 3.41 you can see how adding a triangle is effectively adding a side, and adding 180° to the interior angles.

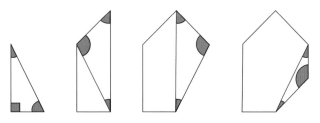

Figure 3.41   Adding a side to a polygon adds 180° to the sum of the interior angles

All polygons with n sides can be divided into a minimal set of $(n - 2)$ triangles (Figure 3.42).

Figure 3.42   All n-gons can be divided into $n - 2$ triangles

Exterior angles of a polygon sum to 360°

We define an exterior angle of a polygon as the supplementary angle to the interior angle (Figure 3.43).

Figure 3.43   Exterior angles of polygons sum to 360°

Why does every polygon have an exterior angle sum of 360°?

As each exterior angle is the supplementary angle to the interior angle, we can write the sum, S, of exterior angles of a triangle whose internal angles are x_1, x_2 and x_3 as:

$$S = (180 - x_1) + (180 - x_2) + (180 - x_3)$$
$$= 3(180) - (x_1 + x_2 + x_3)$$

Generalising for any shape with n sides, we have:

$$S = 180n - (x_1 + x_2 + \ldots + x_n)$$

We also know the internal angles of a polygon can be written as $180(n-2)$:

$$S = 180n - 180(n - 2)$$
$$S = 360$$

Tessellation

Certain shapes have the ability to tessellate with one another. Tessellation means a set of shapes can be fitted together such that there are no gaps. Figure 3.44 gives examples of tessellating (blue), and non-tessellating (red) shapes.

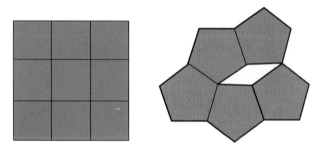

Figure 3.44   Tessellating and non-tessellating shapes

Only three regular shapes tessellate on their own: equilateral triangles, squares and hexagons.

Why is it that some shapes tessellate and others don't?

Tessellation requires a complete 360° closure around a point, without any overlap. As such, only shapes with interior angles that sum, collectively, to exactly 360° on a point will tessellate.

Yes, But Why? Teaching for Understanding in Mathematics

For example, squares have an interior angle of 90°. As such, when placed around a point, we have four squares whose interior angles at that point all sum to exactly 360° (Figure 3.45).

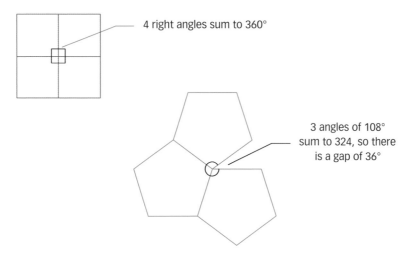

4 right angles sum to 360°

3 angles of 108° sum to 324, so there is a gap of 36°

Figure 3.45 Tessellating shapes must have complete 360° closure around a point

With some clever thinking it is possible to find other combinations of shapes that tessellate; for example, Figure 3.46.

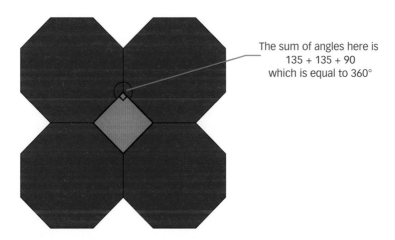

The sum of angles here is 135 + 135 + 90 which is equal to 360°

Figure 3.46 Tessellating with a combination of different shapes

Three-dimensional shapes

Shapes in three dimensions still have sides and vertices, but they also have depth, and **faces** (Figure 3.47).

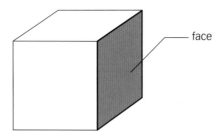

Figure 3.47 A cube is a three-dimensional shape

Three-dimensional (3-D) shapes also have **volume** and **surface area** (covered in Chapter 6).

Some typical 3-D shapes are shown in Figure 3.48.

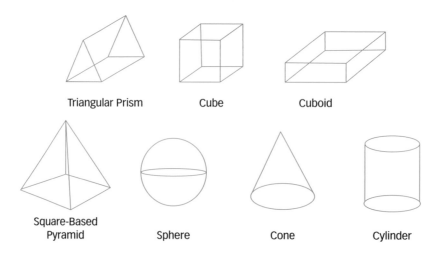

Figure 3.48 3-D shapes

3-D shapes can be represented in two dimensions as a flattened **net** that you could fold to create a model. Shapes such as cubes can have several different workable nets (11 to be exact). Figure 3.49 shows two possibilities.

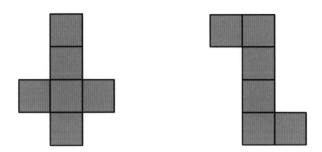

Figure 3.49   Two possible nets for a cube

Platonic solids

The platonic solids are a special group of 3-D shapes (platonic, in this sense, is a distant relative to the 'we're just friends' meaning, although both stem from the Greek philosopher Plato). They have identical regular-shaped faces, and the same number of faces meet at each vertex. There are only five of them (Figure 3.50).

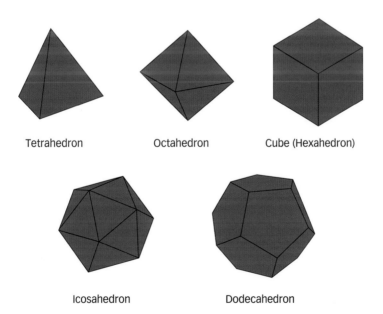

Tetrahedron   Octahedron   Cube (Hexahedron)

Icosahedron   Dodecahedron

Figure 3.50   The five platonic solids

To understand why there are no more than five platonic solids (we'd all like more, they make cool paperweights), we need to study the nets of the shapes. Three of our platonic solids are made from equilateral triangles. The tetrahedron has three around a point, the octahedron has four around a point and the icosahedron has five around a point. Why not have six? Well, compare the nets around a point of five and six triangles (Figure 3.51).

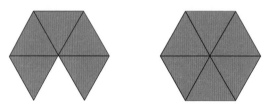

Figure 3.51   The net of a point on a platonic solid must leave a gap

There is a distinct gap when we have five triangles around a point, which allows for the net to be folded into a 3-D shape. However, with six triangles, there is no gap, and so no room to fold it into a concave shape. It is simply flat. Similarly, three squares around a point leave a 90° gap, and three pentagons around a point leave a gap of 36°. All other possible regular shapes will either be exactly, or greater than 360° around a point. Hence, they cannot be folded to become a platonic solid.

Similar shapes

Two shapes are said to be similar if they are proportionately the same. In other words, one is an **enlargement** of the other. Technically, two shapes that are identical

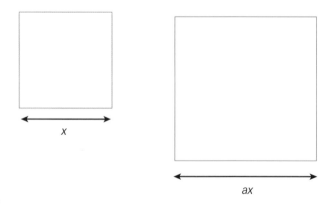

Figure 3.52   Similar shapes are proportionate to each other

are also similar shapes, but they are generally referred to as **congruent**. All regular shapes with n sides are similar to any other regular n-sided shape no matter what size they are. For example, all squares are similar to each other, mathematically. They have the same proportions (Figure 3.52).

However, it's trickier to identify similarity between two irregular shapes (Figure 3.53).

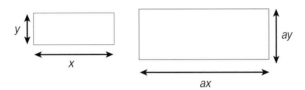

Figure 3.53 Similar irregular shapes

The two rectangles in the figure are similar because the second is proportionately the same as the first, but enlarged by a **scale factor** a. We can test similarity by dividing the corresponding sides of each shape by one another. If the result is always the same, then the shapes are similar. In the above example, this would be:

$$\frac{ax}{x} = a$$

$$\frac{ay}{y} = a$$

You can even divide two sides of one shape by each other, and you will still get an identical result if you do the same to the corresponding sides of the other shape (if they are similar):

$$\frac{y}{x}$$

$$\frac{ay}{ax} = \frac{y}{x}$$

Similar triangles

By extension, similar triangles are deducible by any of the following properties:

1. *Two angles are identical.* By extension, the third must also be identical. Hence, both triangles have the same interior angles (AAA). Therefore, the sides must be proportionately the same.

2. *Two sides are similar and their encompassing angle is the same* (SAS). If two sides are similar, and have the same angle at their vertex, then the third side is already determined. It cannot vary and is identifiable.

3. *All three sides are in the same proportion* (SSS)

Curved shapes

Shapes with curves in them are not polygons. They belong to a family simply known as curves. Common curved shapes are shown in Figure 3.54.

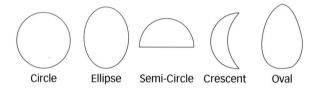

Circle   Ellipse   Semi-Circle   Crescent   Oval

Figure 3.54   Curved shapes

Circles are a special kind of ellipse, whereas 'oval' is a broad term meaning 'egg-shaped'.

Circles

Circles have been a thing of interest for mathematicians for many, many years. There are Japanese Sangaku puzzles (circle puzzles) in temples dating back to the 17th Century, which are painfully difficult to solve, and Archimedes, the famous Ancient Greek mathematician was also somewhat obsessed with them. They are technically defined as the set of points equidistant from a fixed point. That might not have been what you were expecting! When you think about it though, it makes sense. The fixed point is the centre of the circle, and the 'equidistant points' are all a radius length away from the centre.

Figure 3.55 shows a set of points equidistant from a fixed point (the centre). There are only 26 points here. Imagine 10,000. Imagine more. You can see how it would, at its limit, become a circle.

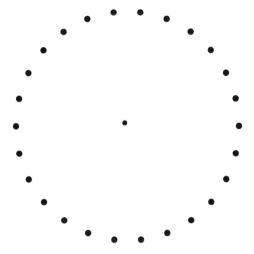

Figure 3.55   Equidistant points from a centre point

How many sides does a circle have?

This is not an easy question to answer! Whilst you may instinctively think it has one curved side, you need to ask yourself, what does 'side' mean? Up to this point, we've been using the term 'side' exclusively for polygons. And a side was a straight line joining two points in a polygon. Are there any straight sides in a circle? If not, then maybe it has zero sides? Does an open curve have sides? Does it have to be closed? Does a single point have sides? If not, then surely a circle

Figure 3.56   An icosagon looks similar to a circle

has no sides, as it is a set of points by definition. Does a semi-circle have two sides if a circle has none? We inevitably begin to blur the meaning of the word side to fit our context. Perhaps a circle has *infinite* sides, as it could be argued to be the limit of regular polygons. Figure 3.56 shows a 20-sided regular polygon (an icosagon).

Figure 3.57   A dihectagon looks very similar to a circle

It looks very similar to a circle. Figure 3.57 shows a 200-sided shape (a dihectagon).
It looks very much like a circle now, but it isn't. Imagine a regular polygon with 20,000 sides. As it approaches infinity, is that a circle? At this point your head probably hurts. Well, there's no definitive answer I'm afraid. The number of sides on a circle depends largely on your definition of a side. That's your answer! It makes for a great debate in class.

Labelling a circle (Figure 3.58)

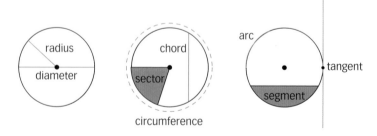

Figure 3.58   Labelled circles

Yes, But Why? Teaching for Understanding in Mathematics

Radius

The radius of a circle is the distance from the centre point to the edge. Radius actually means 'rod', which makes the most sense if you imagine the spokes in a wheel. The word *radio* shares the same roots, which makes less sense.

Diameter

The diameter of a circle is the distance from one edge to another, passing through the centre point.

Sector

A circle sector is the area contained by an arc and two adjoining radii.

Circumference

The circumference is the length of the border of the circle (the perimeter).

Chord

A chord is a line joining two points on a circle, without passing through the centre point.

Arc

An arc is a fraction of the circumference of a circle.

Tangent

A circle tangent is a straight line that touches the circle at a single point, but does not pass through it.

Segment

A segment is the area contained by an arc and the adjoining chord.

π

One of the most famous irrational numbers, and the symbol perhaps most associated with circles, is π (pi). The Greek symbol has become synonymous with circles and the number 3.14. However, π is not exactly 3.14, and where does it come from exactly?

The origins of π

π is a constant. It is irrational, meaning that it has infinite non-repeating digits, and as such cannot be written as a whole number or fraction. Hence, we use the Greek symbol π, or shorten it to 3.14.

It is the ratio of any circle's circumference, C, to its diameter, d:

$$\pi = \frac{C}{d}$$

Hence, the value of π is constant. It does not vary with different circles. We can therefore use π to calculate either the circumference or diameter of a circle with a simple rearranging of the ratio:

$$d = \frac{C}{\pi}$$

And:

$$C = \pi d$$

We can rewrite this formula using the radius, which is half of a diameter:

$$C = \pi(2r) = 2\pi r$$

The area of a circle also uses π and is discussed in depth in Chapter 6.

Circle theorems

There are many angle facts relating to circles, but there are a core of seven angle facts that students are taught at school. Here we will take each in turn and prove them.

#1 Angles inscribed in a semi-circle are always 90°

The term *inscribed* here means that the angle must be contained exactly within a semi-circle, as in Figure 3.59.

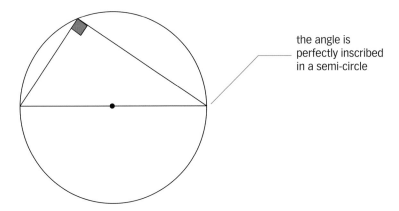

the angle is
perfectly inscribed
in a semi-circle

Figure 3.59   Angles inscribed in a semi-circle equal 90°

Why is this true?

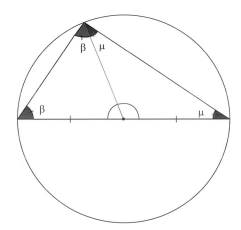

Figure 3.60   A visual proof

By drawing a third radius (in red) we can create two isosceles triangles (Figure 3.60). Now picture the original, largest triangle:

$$\beta + (\beta + \mu) + \mu = 180°$$

$$2\beta + 2\mu = 180°$$

$$\therefore \mu + \beta = 90°$$

#2 Opposite angles in a cyclic quadrilateral sum to 180°

A cyclic quadrilateral is simply a quadrilateral inscribed within a circle (Figure 3.61).

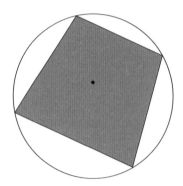

Figure 3.61   A cyclic quadrilateral

Why is this true?
Again, we can explain why this is true using isosceles triangles (Figure 3.62).

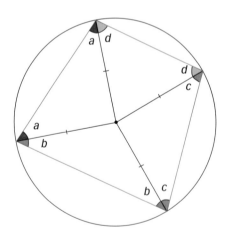

Figure 3.62   A cyclic quadrilateral has opposite angles that sum to 180°

$$2a + 2b + 2c + 2d = 360°$$

$$\therefore a + b + c + d = 180°$$

(Opposite angles in the diagram are all $a + b + c + d$.)

#3 The angle at the centre of a circle is twice the angle at the circumference

This can be visualised as in Figure 3.63.

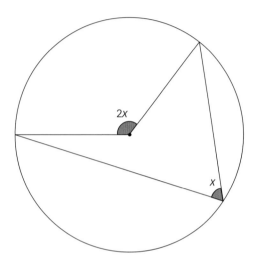

Figure 3.63 The angle at the centre of a circle is twice the angle at the circumference

Why is this true?

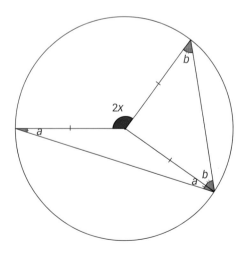

Figure 3.64 A visual proof

$$2x + (180° - 2a) + (180° - 2b) = 360°$$
$$2x - 2a - 2b + 360° = 360°$$
$$2x - 2a - 2b = 0$$
$$2x = 2a + 2b$$
$$x = a + b$$

(Figure 3.64).

#4 The angles at the circumference subtended by the same arc are equal

This can be visualised as in Figure 3.65.

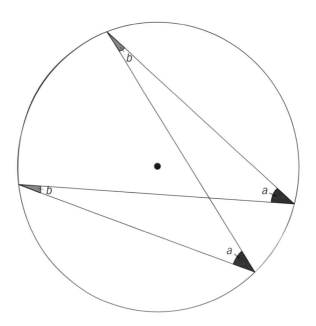

Figure 3.65   The angles at the circumference subtended by the same arc are equal

Why is this true?
We can simply use our previous proof to prove this one. By drawing in two radii from the centre of the circle to the vertices of our inscribed shape, we create the same shape we were using in our last proof, which proves that the green angles are equal (Figure 3.66).

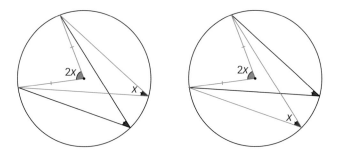

Figure 3.66   A visual proof

#5 The angle between a tangent and a radius is 90°

This can be visualised as in Figure 3.67.

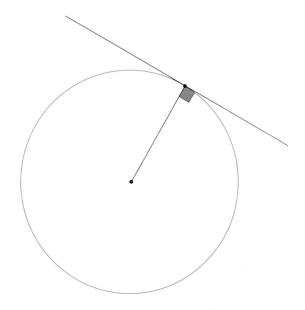

Figure 3.67   The angle between a tangent and a radius is 90°

Why is this true?

This is easiest to deduce with logic. The shortest distance between a point and a line is the perpendicular distance (you can convince yourself of this by visualising the Pythagorean Theorem – a hypotenuse can never be anything except the longest side of a right-angled triangle). As our line (the tangent) sits at a single point on the circle, but does not pass through it, then logically the radius must be the shortest distance to the tangent from the point in the centre. A shorter distance would mean the tangent passed through the circle. A longer distance would go outside of the circle.

#6 Tangents to a circle from a single point are equidistant

This can be visualised as in Figure 3.68.

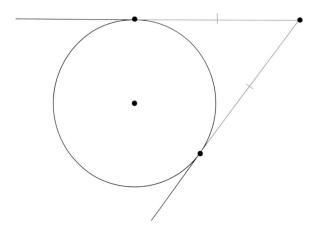

Figure 3.68 Tangents to a circle from a single point are equidistant

Why is this true?
By drawing in two radii that meet the tangential points (at right angles, which we demonstrated earlier – see #5), you can see we have two similar triangles (they share

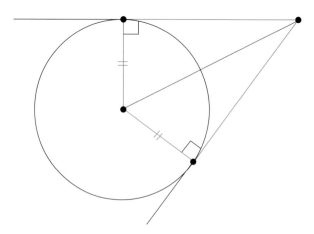

Figure 3.69 Proof that tangents to a circle from a single point are equidistant

Yes, But Why? Teaching for Understanding in Mathematics

a hypotenuse, shown in blue, and they have an equal base) (Figure 3.69). You could also use the Pythagorean Theorem to show that the tangential lines must be equal.

#7 Alternate segment theorem

The angle between the tangent and chord at the point of contact is equal to the angle in the alternate segment (Figure 3.70).

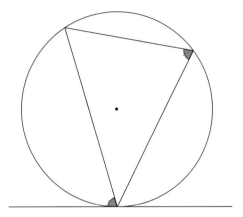

Figure 3.70   The alternate segment theorem

Why is this true?

This one is a little trickier to imagine. First, ignore two sides of the original inscribed triangle, and draw in two radii and a perpendicular bisector for the

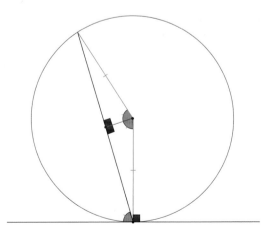

Figure 3.71   Proving the alternate segment theorem

remaining triangle side (all shown in red in Figure 3.71). Using the fact that a tangent and a radius are perpendicular to each other (from #5), we can deduce that the angles at the centre of the circle are equal to the one at the tangent (the red angles).

Now draw the other two sides of the triangle back in, and again we have our theorem #3 from earlier (Figure 3.72).

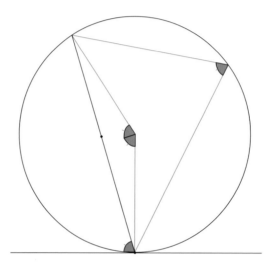

Figure 3.72 Proving the alternate segment theorem

Some rather unusual shapes

The vesica piscis

Literally meaning 'the bladder of a fish', this shape is created by two intersecting circles (Figure 3.73).

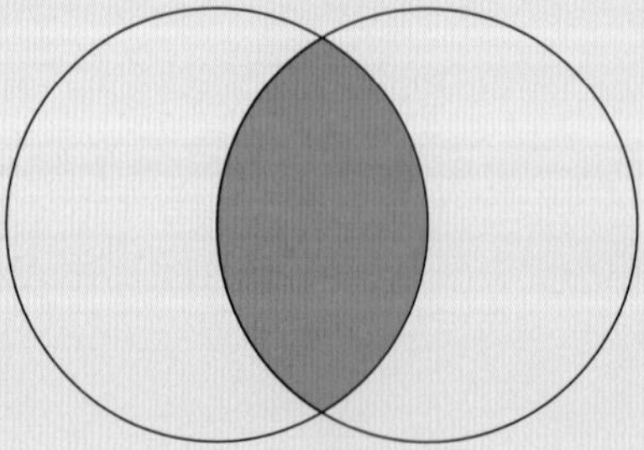

Figure 3.73 A vesica piscis

The ditrigon

A special type of hexagon with alternating edge lengths and equal interior angles (Figure 3.74).

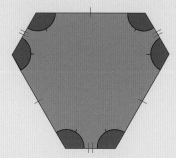

Figure 3.74   A ditrigon

The tomoe

A Japanese shape which looks similar to a comma (Figure 3.75).

Figure 3.75   A tomoe

The stadium

A shape comprising a rectangle and two semi-circles (Figure 3.76).

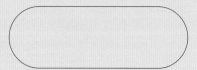

Figure 3.76   A stadium

(Continued)

(Continued)

The squircle

A contender for the best shape name of all time. The squircle is a rounded square (Figure 3.77).

Figure 3.77 A squircle

The gnomon

A shape made by removing a similar parallelogram from a larger one (Figure 3.78).

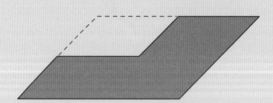

Figure 3.78 A gnomon

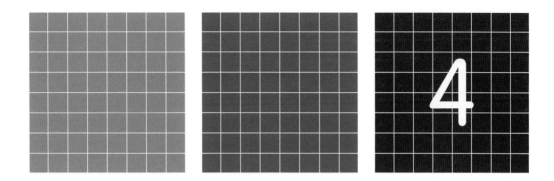

Types of Numbers (Part 2)

Now that we have dipped our feet into the basics of mathematics, I think we're ready to visit some different types of numbers, their properties and where they come from. There is a vast categorisation system in mathematics, and to this day mathematicians are finding different patterns of numbers and giving them new collective names. Only a few of these make it into the curriculum in schools, but that doesn't mean others are any less fascinating. There are vampire numbers, narcissistic numbers, cake numbers, happy numbers, evil numbers, pronic numbers, repunit numbers ... the list goes on. We'll have a look at a few of them just out of curiosity later, but for now we'll focus on one of the most intriguing things in mathematics: prime numbers.

Prime numbers

Usually a maths teacher will teach for clarity rather than mystery when explaining concepts to students. Making things seem simple is part of the art and skill of the profession. However, when it comes to prime numbers, the mystery is very much part of the package. We simply *don't know* everything about them. And that's what makes them so fantastic. It's an area of the curriculum where there is a genuine hole in our knowledge. A hole that exposes students to the fact that mathematics is not a finished product. There are many things we're still discovering, still questioning and still confused by. Prime numbers sit right at the top of that pile, as they continue to draw mathematicians towards them to try and better understand where and when they arise.

At the very least, we can define them. You may be saying to yourself 'a prime number is divisible only by itself and 1'. Well, yes and no. I can divide any number by anything to be honest. 3 is a prime number, but I can divide it by 70 if I'm inclined to do so. So let's try again:

A prime number is a positive integer greater than 1, that has no positive integer divisors other than itself and 1.

That seems a bit more rigid. A bit wordy perhaps though. The 'greater than 1' bit is a tad irritating. How about …

A prime number is a positive integer with only one positive divisor other than 1.

Short and accurate.

Well, no doubt the first response from many students will be '… so?'. Maybe they have a point. So what? Who cares? I could easily define something else and give it a fancy name. 'Monkey numbers are numbers that end in a 3' (just to clarify, that's *not* a thing … yet). By giving so little context and exploration of prime numbers, they will appear lifeless to students. They're just another *thing* with no relevance or interest. Their definition alone won't generate much enthusiasm. Let's look at how to find them, and how we use them …

Teacher tip

Allow students to create their own type of number. They must come up with a set of properties for what defines the numbers, and give them a collective name. This kind of activity exposes them to the excitement of having a newly defined number type.

Break out section

A brief history of prime numbers

- Prime numbers have been studied for a long time. Evidence exists that they were known and studied in Ancient Greece as far back as around 300 BC. At that time, the Greek mathematician Euclid produced a proof that there are infinite prime numbers.
- He also proved the Fundamental Theorem of Arithmetic, which states that every integer greater than 1 is either a prime number or a unique product of prime numbers. The latter are referred to as **composite numbers**.

- In around 200 BC the mathematician Eratosthenes created a method for finding prime numbers known as the **Sieve of Eratosthenes**.
- In the 17th Century, the mathematician Pierre de Fermat proved that prime numbers of the form **4n + 1** can be written as the sum of two squares (e.g. $17 = 4(4) + 1 = 1^2 + 4^2$).
- In the 19th Century, the **prime number theorem** was proved by Jacques Hadamard and Charles Jean de la Vallée-Poussin, which indicated that prime numbers become less common as they get bigger.
- Also in the 19th Century, the Riemann Hypothesis was stated: a conjecture that outlined a pattern for the distribution of prime numbers. It is still unproven despite a lot of evidence seemingly supporting it.
- In the 20th Century, with the advent of computers, the discovery of new prime numbers became much more frequent. Most recently, several distributed computing projects have helped find prime numbers with millions of digits.
- In 2013, a relatively unknown mathematician called Yitang Zhang proved that there are infinitely many pairs of prime numbers that differ by 70 million or less.

One of the earliest formal methods to uncover prime numbers was proposed by a mathematician called Eratosthenes. His method worked, but was very laborious. He rather modestly named it the Sieve of Eratosthenes. It works by eliminating numbers on a number line methodically. Starting at 2, eliminate all the numbers that are multiples of 2. Then move to the number 3, and eliminate all the numbers that are multiples of 3 (many of which you just eliminated when working with 2). Then move to the number 5 (4 gets covered by 2), and so on.

Eventually you'll have something that looks like Figure 4.1.

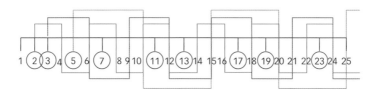

Figure 4.1   An application of the Sieve of Eratosthenes

Teacher tip

Getting students to create a version of the Sieve of Eratosthenes is a nice visual way of introducing prime numbers. It works best if you use straight lines as shown in Figure 4.1 rather than curvy lines that you'll see in most examples. Students find it a lot more difficult to trace the path of curvy lines as they start to intersect each other.

You'll notice that the numbers that have nothing passing through them are in fact prime numbers.

It's a nice iterative algorithm for identifying low prime numbers, but surely a total nightmare once you get past, say, 200. More efficient sieves have been created more recently, such as the Sieve of Sundaram (which ignores all even numbers) and the Sieve of Atkin. Both of which owe a lot to Eratosthenes.

You can even show that there is some kind of pattern around the distribution of prime numbers using a number grid with width 6 (Figure 4.2).

1	2	3	4	5	6
7	8	9	10	11	12
13	14	15	16	17	18
19	20	21	22	23	24
25	26	27	28	29	30
31	32	33	34	35	36
37	38	39	40	41	42
43	44	45	46	47	48
49	50	51	52	53	54
55	56	57	58	59	60
61	62	63	64	65	66
67	68	69	70	71	72
73	74	75	76	77	78
79	80	81	82	83	84
85	86	87	88	89	90
91	92	93	94	95	96
97	98	99	100	101	102
103	104	105	106	107	108

Figure 4.2 In a number grid 6 wide, prime numbers appear to take on a pattern

Yes, But Why? Teaching for Understanding in Mathematics

If you think about it, it becomes obvious that all prime numbers must be either $6n + 1$ or $6n - 1$ where n is a natural number ($6n$ is therefore just the 6 times table in essence). That's because primes cannot be even (except 2), nor can they be in the 3 times table (except 3). That only leaves the first and penultimate column in our grid above. Sadly, not all of the numbers in these columns are prime, otherwise the entire mystery of prime numbers would have been solved long ago.

Teacher tip

Many famous mathematicians have tried and failed to crack the puzzle of prime numbers. This makes for a positive discussion about failure and making errors. For example, Marin Mersenne was a famous mathematician who erroneously published a large quantity of prime numbers he thought he had discovered. Years later many of those numbers were found to be in fact, not prime.

So obsessed are some of us with the magic of prime numbers, that sub-categories have been spawned in recent years – all of which are fascinating in their own right:

$(p, p + 2)$	Twin primes (have a difference of 2)
$(p, p + 4)$	Cousin primes (have a difference of 4)
$(p, p + 6)$	Sexy primes (have a difference of 6)
$(p, p + 2, p + 6)$ or $(p, p + 4, p + 6)$	Prime triplets
$(p, p + 6, p + 12)$	Sexy prime triplets

Yes, those are the genuine names for each group, 'sexy' stemming from the Latin root 'sex' meaning 'six', which is obviously everyone's first thought when they read it.

There are also numbers called **semi-primes** which are not primes, but are the product of two prime numbers. For very large semi-primes, factorisation can feel like an impossible task. In fact, it takes dedicated computers an enormous amount of time. It is unexpectedly advantageous however, as enormous semi-primes are used in secure encryption techniques – whereby the semi-prime is a kind of 'lock' and its prime factors are the key.

1,127,451,830,576,035,879 is semi-prime, and its factors are 486,100,619 and 2,319,379,541. Imagine if you had a semi-prime that was thousands of digits long!

Why are prime numbers special?

Put simply, prime numbers are considered to be the mathematical DNA of all the other natural numbers. By breaking a number down into its core components, we always end up with a product of primes (unless the number we began with was itself a prime). Take 20 for example. It can be broken down using addition, but we'll end up with $1 + 1 + 1 + 1 + \ldots = 20$. That doesn't really tell us anything interesting. But by breaking it down using multiplication, we get far more interesting results.

$$20 = 10 \times 2$$

Can we break that down any further? It turns out we can. 10 can be broken down into 5×2, so:

$$20 = 5 \times 2 \times 2$$

Can we break *that* down any further? Sort of. We could say 2 is in fact 2×1, or $2 \times 1 \times 1$ but where will that get me? We'd end up with an infinite number of 1's in there and it just looks a bit stupid and starts to feel inefficient. Mathematicians are all about efficiency, so we'll stop.

What we're left with is the **prime factorisation** of the number 20. In other words, we have broken down the number 20 into its unique mathematical DNA: $5 \times 2 \times 2$. Each number is prime (hence the reason why we can't break them down any further). We know multiplication is commutative, so we can reorder it if need be, but it will always contain a single 5, and two 2's all multiplied together. There is *no other number* that has this prime multiplication sequence. Furthermore, there is *no other set of prime numbers* to multiply and arrive at an answer of 20. The second point may seem obvious with a number as low as 20, but if we consider a larger number like, say, 405205101228 it starts to feel pretty weird that there is only one set of prime numbers that will multiply to equal that number. This is known in the world of mathematics as the **Fundamental Theorem of Arithmetic**, which we referred to earlier.

Prime factors can tell us all sorts of things too. We can find all the factors of a number (composite as well as prime), or the common factors of a pair of numbers (or larger group of numbers), or even whether a number has an integer square root. You are no doubt familiar with the use of a factor tree and Venn diagram to determine both the highest common factor and lowest common multiple, but it's quite a long-winded and, at first glance, bizarre way of working them out. Figures 4.3 and 4.4 are an example to remind ourselves.

Let's take a closer look at that final stage. The factor tree is perhaps quite self-explanatory, but why does that Venn diagram produce the highest common factor and lowest common multiple of our two original numbers?

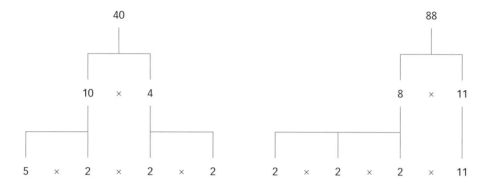

Figure 4.3 An example of two factor trees to determine the prime factors of 40 and 88

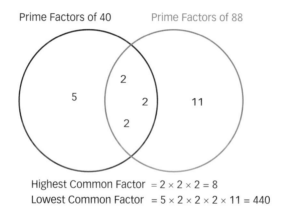

Prime Factors of 40   Prime Factors of 88

Highest Common Factor $= 2 \times 2 \times 2 = 8$
Lowest Common Factor $= 5 \times 2 \times 2 \times 2 \times 11 = 440$

Figure 4.4 A Venn diagram to determine the lowest common multiple and highest common factor of 40 and 88

Why does the Venn diagram method produce the highest common factor and lowest common multiple of two numbers?

Let's start with a different question: how can we use our factor tree to find *any* factor of our starting number? Well, we have its prime factorisation, so any *prime* factor is already on display. Any *composite* factor must therefore be a combination of two or more of our prime factors multiplied together. So if we start with the number 40 we obtain the factor tree in Figure 4.5.

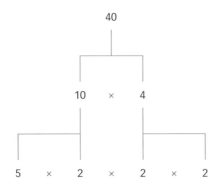

Figure 4.5 A factor tree to determine the prime factors of 40

Any combination of 2, 2, 2 and/or 5 multiplied together will produce a factor of 40. That's because the prime factors of those numbers are embedded within the prime factors of 40.

Factor of 40:	40	4	10	2	20	5	8
Prime factorisation of that factor:	$2 \times 2 \times 2 \times 5$	2×2	2×5	2	$2 \times 2 \times 5$	5	$2 \times 2 \times 2$

Now we can extend this notion, such that any *common* prime factors across two (or more) numbers, must also create a number that is a factor of *both* our original numbers.

If we look at the common prime factors of 40 and 88:

$$40 = 2 \times 2 \times 2 \times 5$$

$$88 = 2 \times 2 \times 2 \times 11$$

The common prime factors are $2 \times 2 \times 2$

And so any combination of these (i.e. 2, $2 \times 2 = 4$ and $2 \times 2 \times 2 = 8$) will produce a factor of both 40 *and* 88:

$$2 \times 20 = 40 \text{ and } 2 \times 44 = 88$$

$$(2 \times 2) \times 10 = 40 \text{ and } (2 \times 2) \times 22 = 88$$

$$(2 \times 2 \times 2) \times 5 = 40 \text{ and } (2 \times 2 \times 2) \times 11 = 88$$

We can extend further still, and look to multiples as well. A multiple of a number n must share n's prime factors (it will have at least one more, or else it would just be the same number!). In other words, the number we start with is going to become a factor of the new multiple, and so its *prime* factors must be *within* the new number's own prime factors.

For example, 60 is a multiple of 30. So we can deduce that the prime factors of 30 must be *within* the prime factors of 60 (Figure 4.6).

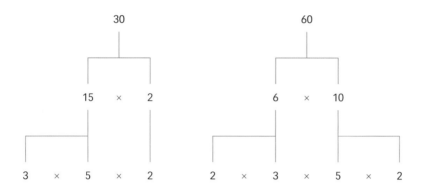

Figure 4.6 If one number is a multiple of another, then it shares their prime factors within its own

A **common multiple** of two (or more) numbers must therefore have the prime factors of both original numbers within it, as both original numbers are going to become factors of the new number. For example, the prime factors of 20 and 30 *must* be within the prime factors of 60 (Figure 4.7).

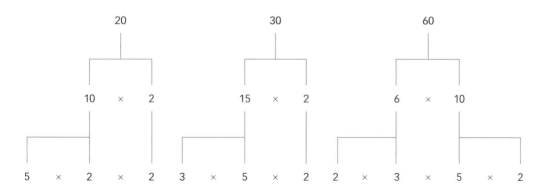

Figure 4.7 A common multiple of two numbers will share the prime factors of each of them within its own

If we want the *lowest* common multiple, then we need to be super-efficient with how we duplicate the prime factors of our original numbers. For example, for 40 and 88:

$$2 \times 2 \times 2 \times 5 = 40$$

$$2 \times 2 \times 2 \times 11 = 88$$

I can get a common multiple by using:

$$2 \times 2 \times 2 \times 5 \times 2 \times 2 \times 2 \times 11 = 3520$$

It has all the prime factors of both numbers in it, so it *must* be a multiple, but to get the *lowest* multiple I don't need to duplicate *common* prime factors:

$$2 \times 2 \times 2 \times 5 \times 11 = 440$$

440 still has all the prime factors in 40, and all the prime factors in 88, but it has no extras. It's therefore the lowest possible common multiple of 40 and 88. A Venn diagram therefore is just a nice way to organise our prime factors to remove any unnecessary duplicates. So if you wanted, rather than multiplying everything in the Venn diagram together for the lowest common multiple, you could just multiply one of your original numbers by the other's *uncommon* prime factors. You're essentially just doing the same thing in a different way (Figure 4.8).

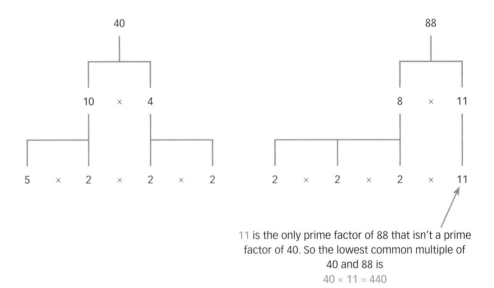

11 is the only prime factor of 88 that isn't a prime factor of 40. So the lowest common multiple of 40 and 88 is
40 × 11 = 440

Figure 4.8   You can shortcut to the lowest common multiple of two numbers without the use of a Venn diagram

Yes, But Why? Teaching for Understanding in Mathematics

At this point it seems like a good time to address one of the most common questions students have about prime numbers …

Why isn't 1 a prime number?

Well, in truth, it used to be. It has been in and out of the prime number club a few times over the centuries, but one of the main reasons it has been seemingly permanently booted out is because of the Fundamental Theorem of Arithmetic. All of our lovely neat unique prime factorisations of numbers would be utterly ruined by the number 1 getting in the way.

6 would no longer be just 3×2, it could also be $3 \times 2 \times 1$ or worse, $3 \times 2 \times 1 \times 1 \times 1$. Ugh. 1 is a ruiner. It created a bit of a loose end, and so eventually found itself in the ex prime number bin.

Incidentally, whilst we're on the topic of factors, have you ever wondered why negative numbers aren't factors? Or decimals for that matter? It seems unfair that despite the fact that $-2 \times -2 = 4$, it doesn't get into the factor club. Similarly $0.2 \times 20 = 4$ but 0.2 doesn't get a look-in.

Why don't we include negatives and decimals as factors of numbers?

Let's start with the decimals, as it's a quick answer. If we allow (for example) 0.2 into the factor club, then we've got to let in 0.02, and 0.002, and 0.0002, and so on. We'd soon have quite a few (infinite in fact) factors to choose from, and the whole factorisation process becomes quite meaningless. So they're out. Negatives on the other hand, would simply double our quantity of factors, so in theory they could go in … in fact some mathematicians argue that they *should* be considered factors. The vast majority however, prefer to exclude them for convention.

Calculating square roots with prime factors

If we take a look at a number we know has an integer square root, such as 324, look at the prime factorisation:

$$2 \times 2 \times 3 \times 3 \times 3 \times 3$$

Take another look with some brackets:

$$(2 \times 2) \times (3 \times 3) \times (3 \times 3)$$

One last time:

$$2^2 \times 3^2 \times 3^2 = (2 \times 3 \times 3)^2$$

Well, taking the square root would simply remove the 'squared' bit from above, leaving $2 \times 3 \times 3 = 18$ (Figure 4.9).

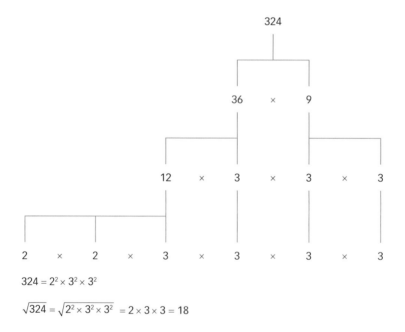

$$324 = 2^2 \times 3^2 \times 3^2$$

$$\sqrt{324} = \sqrt{2^2 \times 3^2 \times 3^2} = 2 \times 3 \times 3 = 18$$

Figure 4.9   You can determine whether a number has an integer square root by inspecting its factor tree

Thus, as long as we can pair off identical prime factors, without anything left over, we know that a number has an integer square root and can calculate it fairly easily.

Similarly if we can group prime factors into identical sets of 3, with nothing left over, then we know a number has an integer **cube** root.

Indices (exponents)

You'll notice we sneaked in a couple of indices just a paragraph ago ($2^2 \times 2^2 \times 3^2 = (2 \times 2 \times 3)^2$ if you've forgotten). They should probably get a mention now.

Indices are a neat and efficient way to raise a number (we're going to call it *base* for this section) to a given power. They're also referred to as powers (as in 'to the power of ...'), and perhaps most commonly, **exponents**.

Here are some examples of what happens when raising a base to a power (which is known as **exponentiation**) of differing quantities

$$7^3 = 7 \times 7 \times 7 \text{ (Figure 4.10)}$$

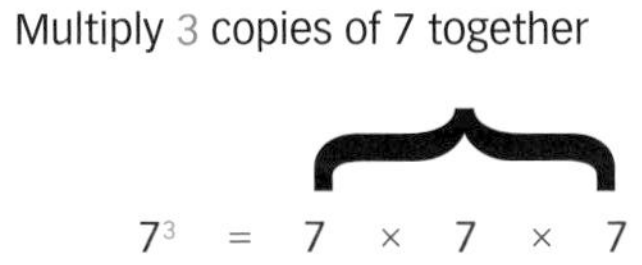

Multiply 3 copies of 7 together

$$7^3 \quad = \quad 7 \quad \times \quad 7 \quad \times \quad 7$$

Figure 4.10 7 to the power of 3

$$3^3 = 3 \times 3 \times 3 = 27$$

$$7^2 = 7 \times 7 = 49$$

$$7^1 = 7$$

$$7^0 = 1$$

Anyone confused by that last one? Don't worry, it's expected.

Why does $a^0 = 1$?

It's perfectly reasonable to question this result, it doesn't follow the pattern very well at first glance. Logic tells you it's going to give you an answer of zero but ... alas. To understand what's going on here, we need to take a look at the **laws of indices**:

Law 1: $a^x \times a^y = a^{x+y}$

This one's easy when you work through it. If we rewrite the multiplication without indices, then all becomes clear:

$$2^3 \times 2^4 = (2 \times 2 \times 2) \times (2 \times 2 \times 2 \times 2) = 2 \times 2 \times 2 \times 2 \times 2 \times 2 \times 2 \times = 2^7$$

Law 2: $a^x \div a^y = a^{x-y}$

Again, looking at a simple example this makes sense:

$$3^4 \div 3^2 = (3 \times 3 \times 3 \times 3) \div (3 \times 3) = 3 \times 3 \times (3 \times 3) \div (3 \times 3) = 3 \times 3 \times 1 = 3^2$$

Law 3: $(ab)^c = a^c \times b^c$

This is a sneaky application of the commutative law of multiplication. Using a simple example:

$$(12)^2 = (3 \times 4)^2 = (3 \times 4) \times (3 \times 4) = 3 \times 4 \times 3 \times 4 = 3 \times 3 \times 4 \times 4 = 3^2 \times 4^2$$

Law 4: $(a^x)^y = a^{xy}$

Looking at $(4^3)^2$

$$(4^3)^2 = (4^3) \times (4^3) = (4 \times 4 \times 4) \times (4 \times 4 \times 4) = 4 \times 4 \times 4 \times 4 \times 4 \times 4 = 4^6$$

Right, that was a quick introduction, but let's go back to the weird example of $3^0 = 1$

Look again at Law 2: $a^x \div a^y = a^{x-y}$

Well if we work backwards, then $3^1 \div 3^1 = 3^0$ (because $1 - 1 = 0$). We were happy enough with $3^1 = 3$ so what we have is this:

$$3^1 \div 3^1 = 3 \div 3 = 1$$

and we know that $3^1 \div 3^1 = 3^0$ so therefore $3^0 = 1$.

Easy!

That leads us nicely into another explanation:

Why does $a^{-1} = \dfrac{1}{a}$?

We can just continue from where we left off to see how this works:

$$a^0 \div a^1 = a^{0-1} = a^{-1}$$

We know $a^0 = 1$ so we're really just saying:

$$a^{-1} = a^0 \div a^1 = 1 \div a = \frac{1}{a}$$

Similarly
$$a^{-2} = a^{-1} \div a^1 = \frac{1}{a} \div a = \frac{1}{a^2}$$

And so on …

You can see this pattern perhaps more visually in Figure 4.11.

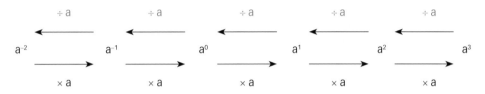

Figure 4.11 The relationships between indices with the same base

Okay, now we're ready for a little challenge. What would the answer to this be:

$$3^{2^0} = ?$$

It could conceivably be this:

$$3^1 = 3$$

or this:

$$9^0 = 1$$

Well, again, counter-intuitively some might say, when we stack exponents, we work right to left, so the answer to the above is 3. If we performed it left to right, we are essentially replicating $(a^b)^c$ rather than creating something new. Hence, convention has dictated we make it do a new thing, rather than repeat something we can do just by writing $(a^b)^c$.

Surds and square roots

A surd (or *radical* if you're American) is indicated by the following symbols:

$$\sqrt[a]{b}$$

where *a* is the *index*, *b* is the *radicand*, the horizontal part of the line is called the *vinculum* and the bit that looks like a tick is the *radix* (Figure 4.12).

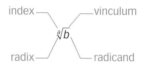

Figure 4.12   A labelled surd

If there isn't an index shown, it can be assumed that it is a 2. There are two possible answers to a square root – one positive and one negative. For example, $(2)^2 = (-2)^2 = 4$.

However, we must be careful with our notation, as a square root operation technically only has a single answer, despite it being two possibilities. We should therefore write it as follows:

$$\pm\sqrt{4} = \pm 2$$

The 'square root' is generally assumed to be the positive solution – known as the *principal* solution, unless otherwise stated.

The word 'surd' is usually used to describe an *irrational* root of an integer (although some definitions class a surd simply as an *unresolved* root). For example, $\sqrt{4}$ would normally be written as 2. However, $\sqrt{3}$ cannot be written as a rational number. The decimal equivalent of $\sqrt{3}$ is an infinite non-repeating decimal. Hence, we would describe $\sqrt{3}$ as a surd.

Leaving $\sqrt{3}$ in surd form preserves its accuracy, and makes it easier to manipulate, as we'll see shortly.

But where does the word 'surd' come from?

Strangely, surd comes from the Latin word *surdus* meaning 'deaf'. That doesn't seem very logical, however. That's because it isn't. Surd was an Arabic mistranslation of a Greek word *alogos* meaning 'irrational' – but the word *logos* has two meanings, the second being 'discourse'. They chose 'discourse', which was translated into Latin by Europeans to *surdus* (someone without discourse – *alogos* – can be interpreted as deaf). So we really shouldn't have 'surd' at all. If Europeans were adamant that surds (as we now know them) came from Latin origins, and were translated correctly, then we'd be calling them *alogum*.

Surd laws

Surds behave in certain ways. Their behaviour is logical, but sometimes requires a little thought to figure out why.

Yes, But Why? Teaching for Understanding in Mathematics

Law 1: $\sqrt{a} \times \sqrt{a} = a$

This one is probably the most straightforward. If we consider a square number, say, 36, we know the square root is 6:

$$6 \times 6 = \sqrt{36} \times \sqrt{36} = 36$$

No issues there.

Law 2: $x^{\frac{a}{b}} = \sqrt[b]{(x^a)}$

This perhaps should have gone into our 'laws of indices' section, but it requires us to talk about square roots and surds so it's going here. We're going to use Law 1 of our laws of indices here:

$$x^{\frac{1}{2}} \times x^{\frac{1}{2}} = x^1$$

$$\therefore x^{\frac{1}{2}} = \sqrt{x}$$

$$x^{\frac{1}{4}} \times x^{\frac{1}{4}} \times x^{\frac{1}{4}} \times x^{\frac{1}{4}} = x^1$$

$$\therefore x^{\frac{1}{4}} = \sqrt[4]{x}$$

$$\text{generalising: } x^{\frac{1}{b}} = \sqrt[b]{x}$$

That's the first part taken care of, now we need Law 4 of our laws of indices:

$$x^{\frac{2}{3}} = \left(x^2\right)^{\frac{1}{3}} = \sqrt[3]{x^2}$$

Job done!

Law 3: $\sqrt{ab} = \sqrt{a} \times \sqrt{b}$

This one is perhaps a little less intuitive. But we can call upon our laws of indices from earlier to help us (Law 3 specifically):

$$\sqrt{ab} = (ab)^{\frac{1}{2}} = a^{\frac{1}{2}} \times b^{\frac{1}{2}} = \sqrt{a} \times \sqrt{b}$$

Law 4: $\sqrt{\dfrac{a}{b}} = \dfrac{\sqrt{a}}{\sqrt{b}}$

Again, we're going to fall back on our laws of indices from earlier:

$$\sqrt{\frac{a}{b}} = (a \div b)^{\frac{1}{2}} = a^{\frac{1}{2}} \div b^{\frac{1}{2}} = \sqrt{a} \div \sqrt{b} = \frac{\sqrt{a}}{\sqrt{b}}$$

Polygonal numbers

We've managed to talk relatively little about 'squared' and 'cubed' throughout our trip through the world of exponents. Now's the time to discuss these ideas with a little more focus. The term 'squared' refers to multiplying a number by itself, which we write as an exponent of 2:

'3 squared' means $3^2 = 3 \times 3 = 9$.

And similarly '3 cubed' means $3^3 = 3 \times 3 \times 3 = 27$.

But where do those names come from?

Why is an exponent of 2 referred to as 'squared', and an exponent of 3 referred to as 'cubed'?

These are not names that are randomly assigned. If we consider a square (Figure 4.13).

Figure 4.13 Each side of a square is the same

It has equal side lengths, and perpendicular sides. The area of a square can be calculated by multiplying the length by the height. This can be written more succinctly as (side)^2 because each side is the same. We therefore only need one side, and we multiply it by itself, or *square* it. Thus, the process of 'squaring' a number draws upon the idea of finding the area of a square.

Similarly we only need one side length of a cube to find its volume, then we multiply it by itself twice, which can be written as (side) $\times$ (side) $\times$ (side) = (side)^3.

Again, the process of 'cubing' a number draws upon the idea of finding the volume of a cube.

This explains why we stop at 'cubed'. Exponents of 4 have no such special name, probably because we don't have a 4th dimension.

Square numbers are slightly different to 'squared'. A square number is the product of an integer multiplied by itself.

For clarity, that means that even though we are 'squaring' 3.5 below, it does not produce a *square number* because we didn't start with an integer:

$$(3.5)^2 = 3.5 \times 3.5 = 12.25 \text{ (12.25 is } not \text{ a square number)}$$

$$4^2 = 4 \times 4 = 16 \text{ (16 is a square number)}$$

Hence, the formula for a square number is n^2 for any integer n.

Square numbers can also be written as a series of dots that will create a square (Figure 4.14).

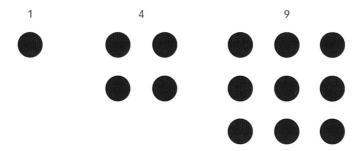

Figure 4.14   A visual representation of square numbers

Of course this is no coincidence! We can use square numbers to find the sum of consecutive odd numbers too, which is pretty amazing (Figure 4.15).

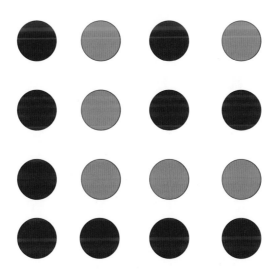

Figure 4.15   The sum of n consecutive odd numbers (starting at 1) is n^2

Similarly, **triangle numbers** can be written as a series of dots that make a triangle (Figure 4.16).

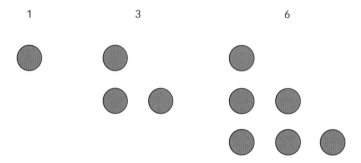

Figure 4.16   A visual representation of triangle numbers

By looking at each row, you can see that triangle numbers are calculated as a sequence: 1, 1 + 2, 1 + 2 + 3, ...

The general (nth term) formula for a triangle number is: $\dfrac{n(n+1)}{2}$, which is derived algebraically in Chapter 7 if you want to jump ahead, but I prefer the visual proof in Figure 4.17.

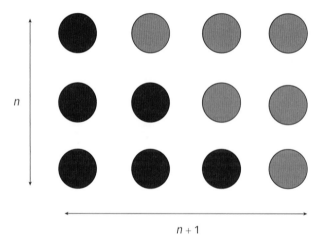

Figure 4.17   A visual proof that the nth term of triangular numbers is $\dfrac{n(n+1)}{2}$

You may have just noticed that triangle numbers are the sum of consecutive numbers. So if anyone asks you what the sum of the numbers 1–50 is, you can just use $n = 50$, and ...

$$\frac{50(50+1)}{2} = 1275$$

There is an age-old tale of Carl Friedrich Gauss, one of the most famous mathematicians who ever lived, who when challenged by his (presumably smug) teacher to add together the numbers 1–100, did so surprisingly quickly by deducing a version of this method. He was eight.

Triangle and square numbers are closely linked. For example, you can show quite simply that the sum of two consecutive triangle numbers is always a square number (Figure 4.18).

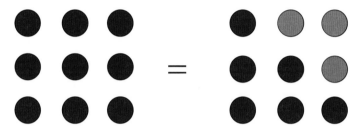

Figure 4.18   A visual proof that two consecutive triangular numbers make a square number

Teacher tip

When showing a triangle number in 'dot' format, it's often more helpful and clear to show it as a right-angled triangle rather than an isosceles. The visual proof above is a good reason why!

Some numbers even have a weird kind of duality, in that they are both triangle **and** square numbers. 36 for example is 6^2 and $1 + 2 + 3 + 4 + 5 + 6 + 7 + 8$.

Some are both square numbers and cube numbers, like 64 (4^3 and 8^2), sometimes referred to as sqube numbers!

Other types of number

Apocalyptic numbers have three consecutive 6's in 2^n where n is the original number.

Cake numbers follow a sequence based on the maximum number of slices a cylindrical cake can be cut into using n straight edge-to-edge cuts.

(Continued)

(Continued)

Evil numbers have an even number of 1's when written in binary (e.g. 3 is '11' in binary).

Happy numbers are defined as numbers that, when squaring and summing each digit (and repeating ad infinitum) eventually equal 1 (e.g. $13 \rightarrow 1^2 + 3^2 = 10 \rightarrow 1^2 + 0^2 = 1$).

Harshad numbers are divisible by the sum of their digits (e.g. 24, divisible by 2 + 4).

Narcissistic numbers are numbers whose digits can be raised to an exponent equal to the quantity of digits, and summed to equal the original number (e.g. $407 = 4^3 + 0^3 + 7^3$).

Perfect numbers are equal to the sum of their divisors (e.g. $28 = 1 + 2 + 14 + 7 + 4$).

Pronic numbers are the product of two consecutive numbers (e.g. $42 = 6 \times 7$).

Repunit numbers are made entirely of 1's (e.g. 1111).

Undulating numbers are of the form *aba*, or *abababa* … etc. (e.g. 161 or 1313).

Vampire numbers are numbers with an even quantity of digits that can be written as a factor pair using a combination of all the digits of the original number (e.g. $2187 = 27 \times 81$). The factor pair must both contain an equal number of digits.

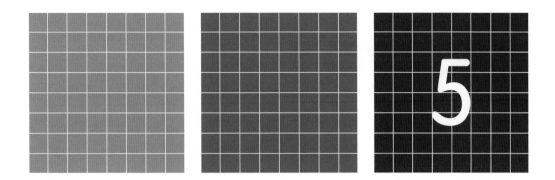

5

Fractions and Proportionality

What is a fraction?

Fractions are a deceptively tricky concept to teach to students. Whilst they are used almost daily by most of us in real life, the interchangeable meaning of what a fraction actually is, and the seemingly mysterious rules to manipulate them, make the whole concept rather complicated for students. The term *fraction* literally means 'a piece broken off something', and shares its origins with other words such as *fragile* and *fragment*. Here we will look at the different uses of fraction notation, and look closer at why the algorithms for fractional addition, subtraction, multiplication and division work.

Fraction incarnation #1: Proportions of a whole

Before we begin here, notice that the term 'whole' can be somewhat problematic from the outset, because it doesn't really refer to a fixed 'amount' from one case to another. For example, 'half of a chocolate bar' and 'half of three chocolate bars' each have a different 'whole', respectively. Often the 'whole' is intended to be 1, but again this can cause issues. Whilst 3/8 can, in isolation, be assumed to be 3 of 8 equal parts of 1, it can also be 3 of 8 equal parts of *anything* contextually.

It is important for students to conceptualise the idea of fractions being applicable to anything, not just a particular shape or object (pizzas and chocolate bars are frequently used due to their familiarity, for example). Try to use a variety of shapes, and a variety of sizes, when discussing examples of fractions – not just circles and rectangles. This will help detach the notion of a literal size of a fraction, and emphasise the concept of a proportion of a *total* or *set* instead.

It's understandable how difficult this concept can be. Whilst cutting physical objects like chocolate bars into halves or quarters can feel intuitive to begin with, appreciating that a half doesn't have a specified appearance can be confusing (Figure 5.1).

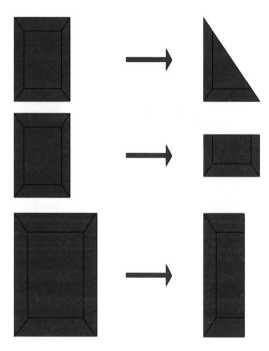

Figure 5.1   A half does not have a specific appearance

How can they be equal, when they look different? Halves can be different sizes and different shapes. Perhaps some confusion is partially to do with student understanding of what *equal* means, and that it is subtly different to 'identical to'.

When starting work with fractions, ask students to find a half or a quarter of a shape in *different* ways. For example, giving students four identical rectangles, you might expect results like Figure 5.2.

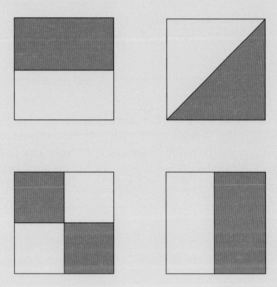

Figure 5.2   Different ways of showing a half

This can in turn inform a deeper conversation about what that fraction represents, and move further away from any association between a half and a particular shape.

To extend this task, you could ask students to shade a half of the rectangle but with two separate strips. Again, this will help remove misconceptions about what the term 'half' means in this context.

Fraction incarnation #2: Fractions as division

Fractions take on a seemingly different meaning later on at school. They become the full time replacement of the ÷ symbol and long division symbol. Sadly this is initially often to the detriment of the learner, as many students fail to recognise that 3/4 means '3 divided by 4', and hold onto the idea that it means '3 out of 4', causing trouble when examiners seize the opportunity to ask students to 'calculate 2/9', for example.

Although fractions as division may seem far removed from proportions of a whole, they are not entirely separate interpretations of what a fraction is. For example, by shading 1/4 of a rectangle, we are implicitly dividing the rectangle by 4. By shading 3/4 of a rectangle, we are implicitly dividing the rectangle by 4 and multiplying the 'answer' by 3.

Fractions as division allow us to represent many numbers as fractions:

$$1 = \frac{1}{1}$$

$$2 = \frac{2}{1}$$

$$0.5 = \frac{1}{2}$$

In fact, as we saw in Chapter 1, these numbers are collectively referred to as **rational** numbers, which are represented with a $\mathbb{Q}$ that stands for **quotient** (meaning the division of one quantity by another, derived from the Latin *quotiens* meaning 'how many times'). They handily help us fill in the gaps on a number line too (Figure 5.3).

Figure 5.3 Fractions on a number line

Of course, we could use decimals instead, but we'd quite often find that some rational numbers aren't easy to write as decimals. 1/3 is a familiar example, which as a decimal is 0.3 recurring (the 3's go on forever). Decimal notation is generally considered to be less accurate than fractional equivalents (at least in pure mathematics. In a real world situation involving measuring physical objects however, you would probably prefer to measure in decimal format). Whilst some decimal equivalents are quite simple, such as 1/2 and 0.5, most are hard to write accurately. 1/107 for example, has an equivalent 53-digit recurring decimal! Numbers like that will not be accurately portrayed on a calculator, as the digits simply don't fit on the screen. This may seem harmless, but if you were to make a series of calculations, the accuracy of your answer could potentially diminish significantly.

Yes, But Why? Teaching for Understanding in Mathematics

Fraction incarnation #3: Ratios

Just to confuse matters further, ratios are sometimes written *in the style of* fractions. The ratio 1:2 for example, could sometimes be written as 'the ratio 1/2', which is a dangerous thing without context, as the ratio 1:2 is strictly $\frac{1}{3}:\frac{2}{3}$ if they were written literally as fractions (one portion to two portions), whereas writing it as 1/2 implies a 1:1 relationship to the uninitiated (half each)! It's not often that you'll see ratios written in this way (especially in a school text book), which is good, because they're counter-intuitive. However, outside of school they are fairly common. Most betting odds for example, are written in the form x/y where you place your bet with winning odds of $y:x$. This is even more confusing, as the odds are written back to front! It's probably a good idea not to talk about betting shops anyway. Let's move on.

Types of fraction

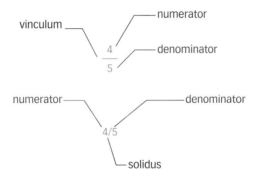

Figure 5.4   The language of fractions

There are lots of peculiar words in Figure 5.4.

Numerator: This tells us how many equal parts of a whole we have. Numerator stems from the Latin *numerare* meaning 'to count'.

Denominator: This tells us how many equal parts our whole set is divided into. Denominator stems from the Latin *denominare* meaning 'to name'. In other words, we are *naming* (identifying) what we are dividing by.

Vinculum: This stems from the Latin *vincire* meaning 'binding'. It's also used when writing a square root.

Solidus: This is Latin for *compact*. The symbol is sometimes used in fractions largely because in the early days of computers, there was no way to write a fraction. Hence, the solidus compensated for the vinculum.

Proper fraction

A 'proper' fraction is a fraction where the numerator is less than, or equal to the denominator such as:

$$\frac{2}{3}, \frac{4}{5}, \frac{1}{1}$$

Improper fraction

An *improper* fraction is a fraction where the numerator is greater than the denominator, and hence the fraction has a numerical value of more than 1:

$$\frac{4}{3}, \frac{5}{2}, \frac{9}{3}$$

Mixed number

A *mixed number* is a whole number alongside a fraction:

$$4\frac{1}{3} \quad 5\frac{9}{10} \quad 9\frac{4}{5}$$

Most mathematicians would avoid writing a mixed number, and would opt to use an improper fraction instead, as there is no room for ambiguity. A mixed number could conceivably be misinterpreted as the multiplication of a whole number by a fraction.

Common fraction

A *common fraction* has a numerator and denominator that are both integers.

$$\frac{3}{4}, \frac{5}{6}, \frac{7}{8},$$

Complex fraction

A *complex fraction* has a fraction as either or both the numerator and denominator.

$$\frac{\frac{2}{3}}{\frac{4}{5}}, \frac{\frac{4}{5}}{\frac{3}{4}}, \frac{7}{\frac{3}{4}}$$

These are not explicitly taught at primary or secondary school, although they often come up when GCSE students are working with complicated algebraic expressions. Despite being ugly to look at, we'll find these useful later when exploring why fraction operations work.

Equivalent fraction

Fractions are said to be *equivalent* if they are equal. For example:

$$\frac{1}{2} = \frac{2}{4} = \frac{3}{6}$$

Understanding *why* some fractions are equivalent is perhaps best seen visually (Figure 5.5).

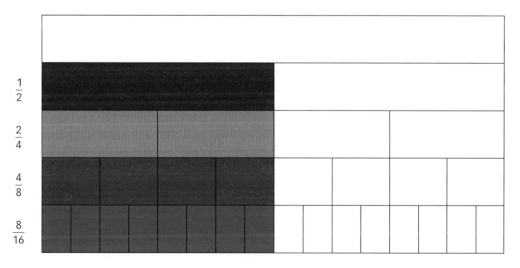

Figure 5.5 Equivalent fractions

We can also use a little algebra to show a generalisation:

$$\frac{a}{b} = \frac{ac}{bc} = \frac{a}{b} \times \frac{c}{c} = \frac{a}{b} \times 1$$

Teacher tip

To aid understanding of equivalent fractions, ask students which of the portions of white chocolate in Figure 5.6 would fill them up the most.

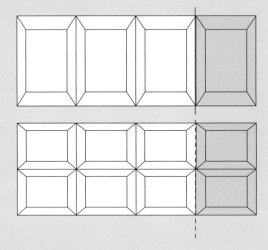

Figure 5.6   Equivalent chocolate

It will prompt an interesting discussion about equivalency. What questions might they have? Are we assuming equal volume? Can they be equal if they look different?

Reduced fraction

A *reduced* (or irreducible) fraction is one which is written in its lowest terms. In other words, the numerator and denominator have been divided by their highest common factor:

$$\frac{2}{3}, \frac{5}{6}, \frac{9}{10}$$

The following fractions are *not* reduced:

$$\frac{5}{10}, \frac{8}{12}, \frac{7}{21}$$

This is because each fraction has a numerator and denominator with a common factor greater than 1. If we look at the first fraction:

$$\frac{5}{10} = \frac{1 \times 5}{2 \times 5} = \frac{1}{2} \times \frac{5}{5} = \frac{1}{2} \times 1 = \frac{1}{2}$$

Similarly:

$$\frac{8}{12} = \frac{2 \times 4}{3 \times 4} = \frac{2}{3}$$

$$\frac{7}{21} = \frac{1 \times 7}{3 \times 7} = \frac{1}{3}$$

Often maths teachers will reduce fractions in the middle of a calculation, so that the numbers being handled are smaller and therefore easier to use in mental calculations. For example, reducing a fraction may look like either of those in Figure 5.7.

$$\frac{2\cancel{0}}{3\cancel{0}} \qquad \frac{\cancel{12}^{4}}{\cancel{15}_{5}}$$

Figure 5.7 Reducing fractions

In the example on the left, $\frac{20}{30}$ has been reduced to $\frac{2}{3}$ by dividing both the numerator and denominator by a common factor of 10. In the second example, $\frac{12}{15}$ has been reduced to $\frac{4}{5}$ by dividing both the numerator and denominator by a common factor of 3.

Whilst it may be tempting to reduce fractions in this way, be mindful that students may not be able to follow what has been done without explicit reference to it.

Fraction operations: addition and subtraction

Note, whilst the following is written exclusively about the addition of fractions, it should be noted that everything mentioned applies to subtraction as well, and as such, subtraction will not be explicitly mentioned in a separate section.

It is perhaps clearest to demonstrate operations with fractions pictorially in the first instance. There are four tiers of difficulty when adding two fractions together.

1. Addition with the same denominators

Adding two fractions together with identical denominators is quite straightforward, but only because it's intuitive. Consider Figure 5.8.

Figure 5.8   A visual representation of 1/3

The bar is clearly split equally into three, and we have one third shaded. If we were to add another third, we simply shade a second segment of the diagram, as they're all equal (Figure 5.9).

Figure 5.9   A visual representation of 2/3

Hence:

$$\frac{1}{3} + \frac{1}{3} = \frac{2}{3}$$

This is a nice introduction to the world of adding fractions for two reasons: first, it is very intuitive as to how to add a third to a third, and second, it gives us an irreducible fraction for our answer. Whilst it may be tempting to start with the addition of two quarters, we immediately are faced with a second tier to the problem, that of reducing fractions. In this example there is no second part – we can focus solely on the initial stage of addition.

2. Addition with the same denominators, with reduction or an answer greater than 1

This is really an extension of 'Addition with the same denominators', above, the difference being that the sum of two fractions may well be greater than 1, which will

Yes, But Why? Teaching for Understanding in Mathematics

inevitably need to be a teaching point, and will require a little additional knowledge and skill. Note the explicit use of 1 rather than 'a whole'. Whilst there is nothing wrong with using language like 'three quarters of a whole', the term 'whole' is later discarded in mathematics, and arguably doesn't contribute to understanding. 'Half of a whole' may well refer to a familiar shape (e.g. rectangle), or a familiar item (e.g. pizza), in any case it should be 'half of a whole *pizza*', not just 'half of a whole'. At which point, 'half of one pizza' will benefit students in the long run when they begin to work with fractions of a set.

When dealing with addition of fractions with common denominators in general, you can see that we are simply adding the numerators, and leaving the denominators as they were:

$$\frac{3}{5} + \frac{1}{5} = \frac{3+1}{5} = \frac{4}{5}$$

We've seen why this works pictorially, but it's also clear simply by writing it without fraction notation:

$$(3 \div 5) + (1 \div 5) = (3 + 1) \div 5$$

3. Addition of fractions where one denominator is a factor of the other

Now things start to get less intuitive, especially without visual representation.

If we add $\frac{1}{3}$ and $\frac{1}{6}$ we are presented with a new conundrum. What do we do with the denominators? Can we still just add the numerators? Curiously, students often opt to add the numerators, which whilst incorrect is at least understandable, as we did it before – but they often also add the denominators, despite not doing that at all in the more intuitive cases. It seems as though when presented with this conundrum, the default approach is to just 'add everything'. Some well thought out examples can at least help students see why this won't work.

$$\text{True or false? } \frac{1}{2} + \frac{2}{4} = \frac{3}{6} \text{ Explain your answer.}$$

The above is a nice example. Discouraging students from converting the second fraction into 1/2 yields an erroneous answer of 3/6 if students just add everything up. So essentially students are saying that $\frac{1}{2} + \frac{1}{2} = \frac{1}{2}$. Clearly that's not right!

So we need to get identical denominators – but why?

Again, a visual explanation perhaps works best here. Let us consider some fraction strips (Figure 5.10).

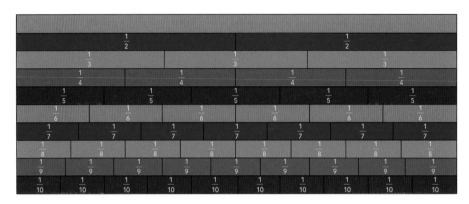

Figure 5.10 A set of unit fractions as 'fraction strips'

Lined up, we can see that two halves are equal to 1, as are three thirds, etc.

What's also nice is that we can see the relative sizes of each fraction compared to one another. An eighth is clearly much smaller than a half for example. Whilst these relative sizes are intuitively obvious to us as teachers, for a student who is beginning their exciting fraction adventure, they may have overlooked the relative sizes of each fraction until this point.

Using fraction strips, we can place two fractions with different denominators alongside each other. In Figure 5.11, the top row is the addition of $\frac{1}{3} + \frac{1}{6}$.

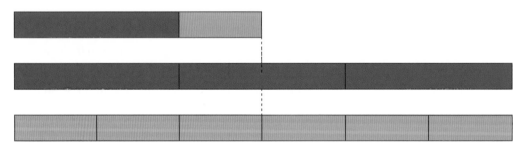

Figure 5.11 1/3 + 1/6 is equivalent to 3/6

If we were to attempt to explain our answer as thirds, we can see that our answer would not be in terms of whole thirds (our numerator would not be an integer). We'd have fractions of fractions, which are those **complex fractions** we looked at earlier: $\frac{\frac{3}{2}}{3}$. This is not technically wrong, it's perfectly acceptable. It's just ugly and confusing. We're much better off making sure our fractions have common denominators, so that we have an integer as our numerator, and an integer as our denominator, in other words, we want a **common fraction** as our answer to ensure clarity and prettiness.

For our example, $\frac{1}{3}+\frac{1}{6}$, we need to find the lowest common multiple of 3 and 6. It's quite easy in this example, as 6 is both a multiple of 3 and 6 – hence only one fraction will need altering (whereas in the fourth tier of difficulty both fractions will need altering).

$$\frac{1}{3}+\frac{1}{6}=\frac{2}{6}+\frac{1}{6}$$

Now our addition problem is in the form we looked at earlier, and so we can add the numerators as before:

$$\frac{2}{6}+\frac{1}{6}=\frac{3}{6}=\frac{1}{2}$$

4. Adding fractions with different denominators

We are simply extending the basic notion of adding fractions to the most compli-cated cases now. In the previous case, we needed to alter one of the fractions to create a sum with two identical denominators. Here, both fractions will require alterations.

A visualisation of the issue can be seen in Figure 5.12.

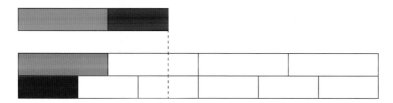

Figure 5.12   1/4 + 1/6 requires a new denominator

You can see that $\frac{1}{4}+\frac{1}{6}$ does not line up with quarters or sixths. We therefore need a new common denominator for *both* fractions to enable us to have an answer in the form of a common fraction.

To do this, we need to find a common multiple for each denominator, which in turn will become our new denominator for both fractions. We then need to find **equivalent** fractions of our originals, using this new denominator:

$$\frac{1}{2}+\frac{1}{3}=\frac{3}{6}+\frac{2}{6}=\frac{5}{6}$$

Again, we can show why this needs to happen just using the order of operations too. If we do not find a common denominator:

$$\frac{1}{2} + \frac{1}{3} = 1 \div 2 + 1 \div 3$$

Clearly in the example above, I need to divide 1 by 2, then divide 1 by 3, and add the two answers together.

However, converting the fractions to have common denominators allows for a clever rearrangement so that brackets 'trump' division as the first thing we do:

$$\frac{3}{6} + \frac{2}{6} = 3 \div 6 + 2 \div 6 = (3 + 2) \div 6$$

The bar modelling method of adding fractions

The bar modelling method of adding fractions is very similar to using fraction strips. Figure 5.13 gives a bar modelling approach for

$$\frac{1}{3} + \frac{1}{3}$$

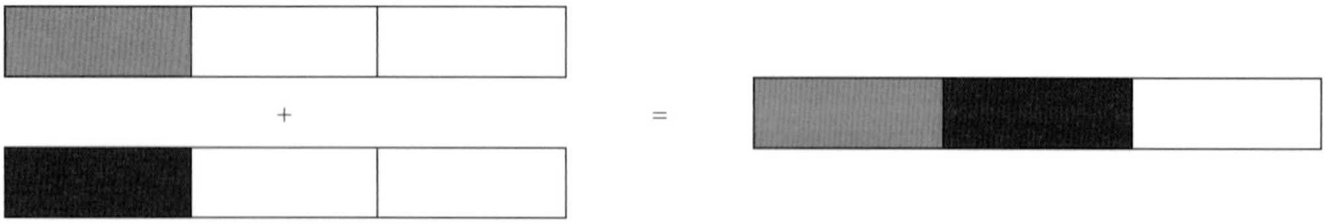

Figure 5.13 Using bar modelling to represent 1/3 + 1/3

Each equally sized bar is split equally into three, to represent thirds. As we are adding a third to a third, we shade each bar accordingly. Our answer uses the same denominator, so again we split our bar into three equal parts, and add together the two shaded segments.

By perfectly aligning the two bars in the sum, it is arguably more intuitive to see how to subdivide a fraction if we need to alter one of the denominators (Figure 5.14).

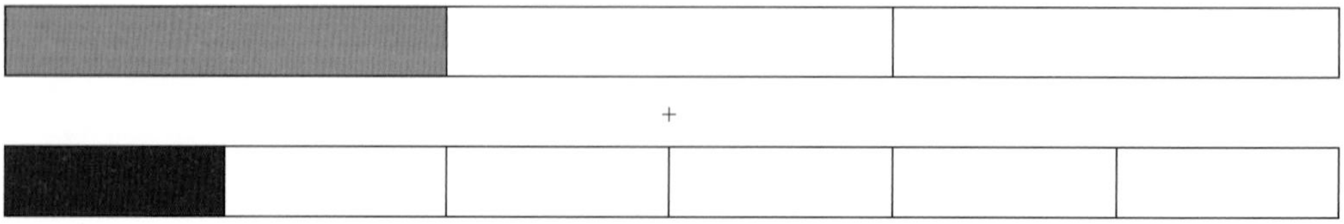

Figure 5.14 Using bar modelling to show 1/3 + 1/6

Here we are adding $\frac{1}{3} + \frac{1}{6}$ and we therefore need to represent a third as two sixths. We can see that this will work visually, as a third lines up perfectly with two sixths, so they are equal (Figure 5.15).

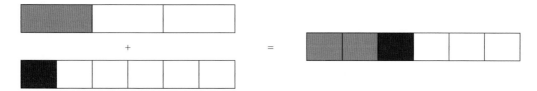

Figure 5.15 A bar modelling solution to 1/3 + 1/6

Finally, when we need to alter both denominators, each needs to be equally partitioned into what will become the common denominator (Figure 5.16).

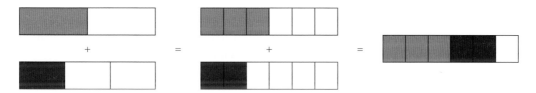

Figure 5.16 A bar modelling solution to 1/2 + 1/3

In the figure, we can see that $\frac{1}{2} + \frac{1}{3} = \frac{3}{6} + \frac{2}{6} = \frac{5}{6}$.

Multiplication of fractions by fractions

First, we should clarify what is being asked of us when we're multiplying two fractions together.

Consider:

$$\frac{1}{3} \times \frac{1}{4}$$

You may think this is simply a third multiplied by a quarter, but we can be clearer in our explanation with a simple change of phrase. What we're being asked here is to find a third *of* a quarter (or a quarter *of* a third, thanks to the commutative law – both yield the same result).

A *third of a quarter* is arguably easier to visualise than $\frac{1}{3} \times \frac{1}{4}$, especially with a nice diagram.

To find the answer we need to divide the shaded section into thirds, but to *interpret* the answer correctly, we need to divide *all* parts into thirds (Figure 5.17).

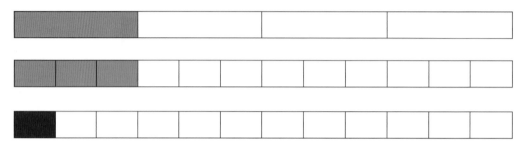

Figure 5.17   A bar modelling solution to finding a third of a quarter

What we are left with, is $\frac{1}{12}$ (shown in blue).

We often rely on teaching the algorithm 'times the tops, times the bottoms' as a short and easy way to multiply two fractions, but a visual model helps explain why that works.

Multiplying fractions using bar modelling

Again, this is an extension of the diagrams we used in the previous section. Below is an illustration for $\frac{1}{3} \times \frac{1}{4}$.

First we create a block such that it has a number of columns equal to the first denominator, and a number of rows equal to the second denominator. In our example, that's 3 columns and 4 rows, making a 3 × 4 grid (Figure 5.18).

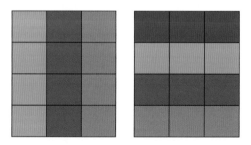

Figure 5.18   Bar models highlighting thirds and quarters on a grid

This has created our common denominator for us, which is 12 (there are 12 squares in the grid).

We now shade in one quarter and one third such that they cross over.

The part which is shaded twice is our answer (Figure 5.19).

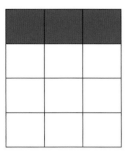 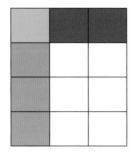 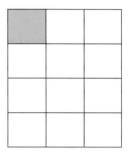

Figure 5.19   A bar modelling solution to 1/3 × 1/4

If you study the figure carefully, you'll realise we have been subdividing a shape, and have ended up shading in *a quarter of a third* (or a third of a quarter).

Similarly, we can show why this works just using the properties of multiplication. Below is an expansion of the sum $\frac{2}{3} \times \frac{4}{5}$

$$\frac{2}{3} \times \frac{4}{5} = (2 \div 3) \times (4 \div 5) = 2 \times \frac{1}{3} \times 4 \times \frac{1}{5} = 2 \times 4 \times \frac{1}{3} \times \frac{1}{5} = (2 \times 4) \div 3 \div 5$$
$$= (2 \times 4) \div (3 \times 5)$$

We can generalise using algebra if we're feeling confident:

$$\frac{a}{b} \times \frac{c}{d} = a \times \frac{1}{b} \times c \times \frac{1}{d} = ac \times (1 \div (b \times d)) = ac \times (bd)^{-1} = \frac{ac}{bd}$$

It is sometimes possible to simplify fractional multiplication before you begin. This is sometimes referred to as 'cross cancelling' (Figure 5.20).

$$\frac{7}{\cancel{6}_2} \times \frac{\cancel{3}^1}{9} = \frac{7}{18}$$

Figure 5.20   Cross cancelling

It's a clever way to make the maths easier – but can you explain it?

It's an application of breaking down multiplication and the commutative properties of multiplication:

$$\frac{7}{6} \times \frac{3}{9} = \frac{7 \times 3}{6 \times 9} = \frac{3 \times 7}{3 \times 2 \times 9} = \frac{3}{3} \times \frac{7}{2 \times 9} = \frac{7}{18}$$

Reciprocals

Now that we're a little clearer on the process for multiplying two fractions together, it's time to explore the concept of **reciprocals** – which are fundamental in understanding fraction manipulation.

A reciprocal is the **multiplicative inverse** of a number. In other words:

The reciprocal of $\dfrac{a}{b}$ is $\dfrac{b}{a}$

Whilst it is simple to write the reciprocal of a common fraction, it is not immediately clear how to write the reciprocal of an integer. The reciprocal of 4 for example, is $\dfrac{1}{4}$. We need here to appreciate that 4 is in fact just $\dfrac{4}{1}$.

We can write the reciprocal of a number, a as a^{-1}

For example:

$$\left(\frac{2}{3}\right)^{-1} = \frac{3}{2}$$

The key property of reciprocals, which makes them important (and, thankfully, interesting) is that when we multiply something by its reciprocal, we always get an answer of 1. It makes intuitive sense for integers. A quarter of 4 is 1, a third of three is 1, etc. But it works for fractions too:

$$\frac{1}{3} \times \frac{3}{1} = 1$$

$$\frac{2}{5} \times \frac{5}{2} = 1$$

Generalising:

$$\frac{a}{b} \times \frac{b}{a} = \frac{ab}{ab} = \frac{a}{a} \times \frac{b}{b} = 1 \times 1 = 1$$

This is particularly important when we look at why the division algorithm for fractions works.

Division of fractions by fractions

Understanding what is being asked of us is again critical here. For example, what does $\frac{2}{3} \div \frac{4}{5}$ actually mean? Is there a metaphor we can fall back onto to help students grasp the concept? Before you read on, try and think of one yourself. Would it involve our delicious pizzas or chocolate bars? Will that work here?

Once you have a metaphor in your mind that you think might work, ask yourself if what you've come up with is division by fractions, or in fact, multiplication by fractions? The two become easily confused in metaphor.

$\frac{2}{3} \div \frac{1}{2}$ means 'how many $\frac{1}{2}$'s are contained in $\frac{2}{3}$?' – which does *not* mean 'what is half of $\frac{2}{3}$?'.

As such, metaphors need careful consideration if we're going to stick with food. 'I find some pizza in the fridge. If 1/2 of what I have is 2/3 of a full pizza, how much pizza did I find in the fridge?'. It's tricky just to get your head around what is being asked, let alone how to solve it.

A better, clearer example is given below:

The area of a field is 2/3 km², and we know one side is 4/5 km long. What is the length of the other side (Figure 5.21)?

Figure 5.21   What is the length of the other side?

This presents us with a clear need to divide a fraction by a fraction. And so we would need to calculate:

$$\frac{2}{3} \div \frac{4}{5}$$

The fractional division algorithm

We often show that we 'flip and multiply' when dividing fractions, like this:

$$\frac{2}{3} \div \frac{4}{5} = \frac{2}{3} \times \frac{5}{4} = \frac{2 \times 5}{3 \times 4} = \frac{10}{12}$$

It's another classic case of creating unnecessary mystery instead of promoting genuine understanding of what is happening mathematically. A student seeing this for the first time is likely to be somewhat bewildered. It doesn't seem to make any sense, especially if there is no explanation about why this works.

So why does it work?

We need to pull together both complex fractions *and* the properties of reciprocals:

$$\frac{2}{3} \div \frac{4}{5} = \frac{\frac{2}{3}}{\frac{4}{5}}$$

Now, if we multiply by 1, nothing changes. And if we multiply by:

$$\frac{\frac{5}{4}}{\frac{5}{4}}$$

we're still multiplying by 1 (because $\frac{a}{a} = 1$), but this is a clever way of converting the denominator into 1:

$$\frac{\frac{2}{3}}{\frac{4}{5}} \times \frac{\frac{5}{4}}{\frac{5}{4}} = \frac{\frac{2}{3} \times \frac{5}{4}}{\frac{4}{5} \times \frac{5}{4}} = \frac{\frac{2}{3} \times \frac{5}{4}}{1} = \frac{2}{3} \times \frac{5}{4}$$

Division of fractions using bar modelling

Demonstrating the division of fractions using bar modelling is a little complicated, but it emphasises the concept very well. There are a few variations of an over-arching method. The first is the most intuitive, but also limited to only a handful of fractional division problems like:

$$\frac{2}{3} \div \frac{1}{6}$$

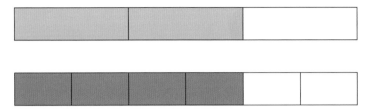

Figure 5.22 A simplistic bar modelling approach to 2/3 ÷ 1/6 shows that 1/6 fits into 2/3 **four** times

In Figure 5.22 we are showing how many 1/6's fit into 2/3, and the answer is 4. That was easy! It's intuitive and aids understanding. Like in previous bar modelling examples, we simply create two identically sized bars, and divide each into the respective denominators of our fractions, then shade them in appropriately.

We then count up how many of our second fractions line up perfectly with our first fraction.

However, you may have already seen the shortfall of this method.

Let's try:

$$\frac{2}{3} \div \frac{1}{5}$$

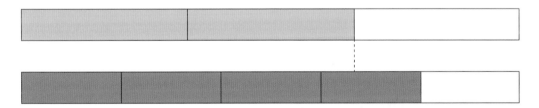

Figure 5.23 This bar modelling approach to 2/3 ÷ 1/5 needs adapting. 1/5 fits into 2/3 three times, but there is a partial fraction left over

Now the answer is less clear, because it's not a whole number (Figure 5.23). We can see it's 3 and ... a bit. Oh dear. We're into the realms of complex fractions again. Whilst this may serve as a nice entry point to understanding what is being asked, the method is not reliable to solve fractional division problems where one denominator is not a factor of the other. However, this can be overcome by converting the fractions so that they have common denominators, much like when we added fractions together earlier.

Whilst bar modelling can be a useful tool to help students visualise fractions and more general proportion problems, be mindful that there are many ways to show students visual representations of mathematics. The use of bar modelling to demonstrate fraction division is possible, but complicated. The aim is to make things make sense – which doesn't necessarily mean you need bar modelling. For example, you may have noticed that once our fractions have the same denominator, we can effectively ignore the denominators altogether:

$$\frac{12}{15} \div \frac{10}{15} = 12 \div 10 = \frac{12}{10}$$

Here's another example:

$$\frac{6}{7} \div \frac{2}{3} = \frac{18}{21} \div \frac{14}{21} = 18 \div 14 = \frac{18}{14}$$

If you're wondering why:

$$\frac{18}{21} \div \frac{14}{21} = ax \div bx = \frac{ax}{bx} = \frac{a}{b} = \frac{18}{14}$$

Having a range of strategies so that you are able to explain things in different ways is the key to good teaching.

Converting between fractions, decimals and percentages

As we have seen, fractions can be plotted on a number line as divisions, for example:

$$\frac{2}{5} = 2 \div 5$$

By extension, we can convert a fraction to a decimal value, based on this division:

$$\frac{2}{5} = 2 \div 5 = 0.4$$

Similarly:

$$\frac{3}{8} = 3 \div 8 = 0.375$$

We can also work backwards from a decimal to find its fractional equivalent, using our knowledge of place value:

$$0.62 = 62 \text{ hundredths} = \frac{62}{100}$$

Then we can simplify our fraction:

$$\frac{62}{100} = \frac{31}{50}$$

Recurring decimals are a little trickier, and we need to resort to algebra to find a solution:

$$0.41414141\ldots$$

$$\text{Let } b = 0.\dot{4}\dot{1}$$

$$100b = 41.\dot{4}\dot{1}$$

$$99b = 41$$

$$b = \frac{41}{99}$$

We often interchange the use of fractions, decimals and percentages to refer to proportionality. For example, we might want to find 1/2 of an amount, or we may want to find 50% of an amount (they mean the same thing proportionately). Similarly, we may find that the probability of an event is 0.5, which again means (in this context) 1/2, or 50%.

We can use decimals as multipliers to find percentages.

For example, if I wanted to find 30% of 60:

$$30\% \text{ of } 60 = (30 \div 100) \times 60 = 0.3 \times 60 = 18$$

The per cent symbol % evolved from various incarnations of shorthand for the words *per cento*, such as *p/c°*.

Proportionality

General proportionality

The concept of proportionality extends across many areas of mathematics. Proportionality is where two measures a and b, are related such that:

$$a = kb$$

Or, rearranged:

$$\frac{a}{b} = k$$

This relationship is known as *direct* proportion, and is often denoted by the symbol $\propto$, which disappointingly has no name other than 'the proportionality symbol'.

$$a \propto b$$

Proportionality underpins a lot of concepts in mathematics, although it isn't necessarily obvious at first glance. Here we will look at some of the elements of mathematics whose foundations are in proportionality.

Proportionality in percentages

Percentages are an area of mathematics that students instantly recognise from their daily lives. Sales, loans, interest rates, battery life and so on.

It's simple enough to be able to work out say, 20% of something. We divide by 5, or alternatively, multiply by 0.2. But why does that work exactly?

The term per cent literally means 'per one hundred', and is a typical example of proportionality. 20% for example, is proportional to 100% in the following way:

$$20\% = 0.2 \times 100\%$$

Or, we could say 100% is proportional to 20%:

$$100\% = 5 \times 20\%$$

We can extend this idea to percentages *of an amount*. For example, 20% of £50 (Figure 5.24).

Figure 5.24 20% of £50 is?

Above, we multiplied 100% by 0.2 to get 20% (or if you prefer, divided by 5). As such, we apply the same operation to £50, and find the answer, £10.

Proportion questions in mathematics can almost always be written as in Figure 5.25.

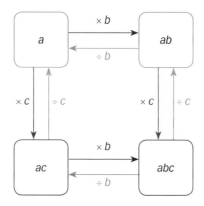

Figure 5.25 A handy diagram for proportion-style questions

Let's take a look at how handy this diagram can be in all proportion-style questions:

A T-shirt is on sale for £30 at 25% off, what is its original cost?

First, no-one cares, it's on sale so that's what we're going to pay. However, since we need the marks, we'll use Figure 5.26.

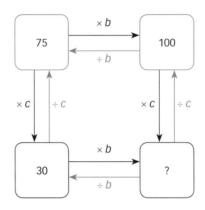

Figure 5.26 What is the original cost of the T-shirt?

Pick a route! We'll go left to right here.

$$75 \times \frac{4}{3} = 100$$

$$30 \times \frac{4}{3} = 40$$

So the answer is £40.

Equally, we could have worked top to bottom:

$$75 \times 0.4 = 30$$

$$100 \times 0.4 = 40$$

Let's try a harder one:

A man invests money at an interest rate of 2.5% per annum, and has £512.50 after one year. How much did he invest? (Figure 5.27)
We can find b easily enough:

$$b = \frac{102.5}{100} = 1.025$$

Hence, our missing amount is:

$$\frac{512.50}{1.025} = £500$$

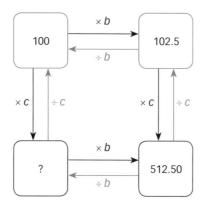

Figure 5.27   How much did the man invest?

Again, we could work this out going top to bottom instead:

$$102.5 \times 5 = 512.50$$

Hence, for our missing amount:

$$100 \times 5 = 500$$

Proportionality in ratios

Divide £250 into the ratio 1:4 (Figure 5.28).

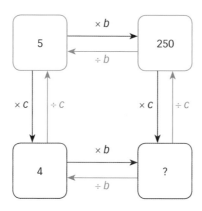

Figure 5.28   Divide £250 into the ratio 1:4, approach 1

Here, $c = \dfrac{4}{5}$ and $b = 50$. Therefore, 4 equal parts of £250 = 200. We can then deduce the remaining amount is 50, hence £250 into the ratio 1:4 is 50:200.

Alternatively we can do it the other way around, and we arrive at the same answer (Figure 5.29).

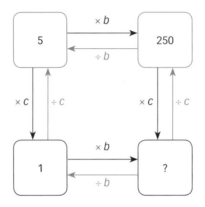

Figure 5.29   Divide £250 into the ratio 1:4, approach 2

Here, $c = \dfrac{1}{5}$ and $b = 50$. Therefore, 1/5 of £250 = 50. We can then deduce the remaining amount is 200, hence £250 into the ratio 1:4 is 50:200.

Proportionality in worded questions

If 12 equally priced posters cost £4.80, how much will 7 of them cost? (Figure 5.30)

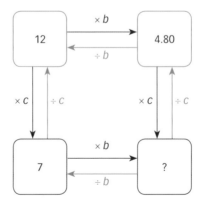

Figure 5.30   How much will 7 posters cost?

Here, $c = \dfrac{7}{12}$ and $b = 0.4$. Therefore, 7 posters will cost:

$$7 \times 0.4 = \pounds 2.80$$

$$\text{or } \dfrac{7}{12} \times \pounds 4.80 = \pounds 2.80$$

Proportionality in shapes

Similar shapes and enlargements of shapes (which are ... still similar shapes!) are proportionally the same. As always, our handy four-square tool is perfectly useable here too.

Find the missing side length for this pair of similar triangles (Figure 5.31).

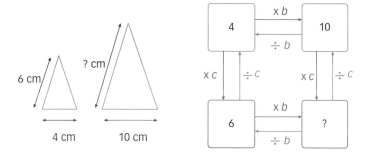

Figure 5.31   Find the missing side length for this pair of triangles

$$b = \dfrac{10}{4}$$

$$4 \times \dfrac{10}{4} = 10$$

$$6 \times \dfrac{10}{4} = 15$$

The missing side length is 15 cm.

Proportionality in trigonometry

As we will see in Chapter 10, trigonometry is also built upon proportionality (Figure 5.32).

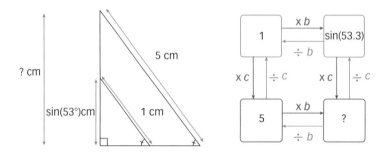

Figure 5.32 Find the queried side length

Hence, the missing side length is $5 \times \sin(53°) = 3.99$ cm (2dp)

A history of fractions

The first known use of fractions was in Ancient Egypt. Hieroglyphics indicated that Ancient Egyptians were knowledgeable about the concept of the reciprocals of natural numbers. These were written with a distinctive oval above the number.

For example, the number ten would be written as ⌒ and the reciprocal of ten $\left(\frac{1}{10}\right)$ would be written as ⌒̊.

Extending the use of reciprocals, the Ancient Egyptians would write other fractions as a sum of the reciprocals of natural numbers. In other words, they would only write fractions in the form of $\frac{1}{n}$ (fractions in this form are commonly known as unit fractions), or the sum of several fractions of the form 1/a + 1/b, etc.

In cases where we might today write a fraction as, say, $\frac{2}{n}$, our Egyptian counterparts would write that same fraction as a sum of several different fractions with a numerator of 1.

For example, where we might write 2/5, Ancient Egyptians would write (using their own symbols):

$$\frac{1}{3} + \frac{1}{15}$$

Modern fractions use a dividing line called a *vinculum*, which is Latin for *bond*. This symbol has been used in a variety of ways over time. It started life as a way of grouping numbers together in long expressions, but that use was replaced by the use of brackets, largely because of the difficulty of *printing* the vinculum:

$$2 \times (3+4) = 2 \times \overline{3+4}$$

However, it still gets used in this way for finding roots:

$$\sqrt{3+6}$$

In recurring decimals:

$$0.345345345 \ldots = 0.\dot{3}4\dot{5} = 0.\overline{345}$$

and geometry:

$$\overline{AB} = \text{the line joining points A and B}$$

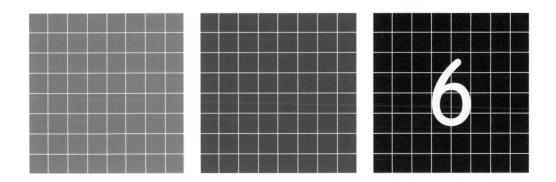

Measurement

Measuring seems like a simple concept: we are calculating the size of something, be it the space inside a shape (area), the border of a shape (perimeter), the temperature of a liquid, a time, a distance, mass, etc. Each of these is relatively simple to do in modern times. However, standard units of measurement have not always existed. Here, we will explore where these units came from, and how they were derived.

Temperature

Temperature is measured in degrees Celsius (°C), degrees Fahrenheit (°F) or Kelvins (K), but where did these units come from? And why do we have different types? Celsius, which is also referred to as Centigrade, is used by the vast majority of countries in the world as the primary temperature measurement of choice. The name Celsius refers to Anders Celsius, a Swedish astrologer in the 18th Century; however, the scale itself is not identical to the one he created, and was referred to as Centigrade before being renamed in 1948.

You may recall that the boiling point of water is 100°C, and that it freezes at 0°C. These nicely rounded numbers are no coincidence, and are in fact the beginnings of how the scale was created. Anders Celsius created a scale whereby water froze at 100°C and boiled at 0°C. Curiously, independent of Anders Celsius, French scientist, Jean-Pierre Christin also created an identically structured scale based on the boiling and freezing points of water, albeit from 0 to 100 rather than 100 to 0. Alas, his proposed scale was created slightly later than Celsius' and even though it was he who successfully proposed the reversal of Celsius' scale, his name is not directly associated with it.

SAGE would like to acknowledge that most figures in this chapter were created with GeoGebra (www.geogebra.org).

Meanwhile in Germany, a separate scale was developed, now known as Fahrenheit, named after its creator, German scientist Daniel Gabriel Fahrenheit. His scale was based on three key temperature indicators: the temperature of a brine solution, the (estimated) temperature of the human body, and the melting point of ice. The brine solution part might seem a bit bizarre, but the solution itself is known as a *frigorific* mixture, which stabilises its own temperature independent of its component parts. Since he did not base his scale on water, the freezing and boiling points of water are not as nice as they are in Celsius. The freezing point of water is 32°F, and the boiling point is 212°F, a difference of 180°F.

You can freely convert between °F and °C using the formula:

$$F = 1.8C + 32$$

Interestingly, at −40° both temperatures register the same:

$$-40 = 1.8(-40) + 32$$

Kelvin units, named after Irish scientist Lord William Kelvin, measure temperature from the coldest possible temperature (known as absolute zero) upwards. Hence, the lowest possible temperature, in Kelvins, is zero. Absolute zero is equivalent to −273.15°C or −459.67°F.

There is no known 'absolute hot' or maximum possible temperature.

Distance

The most common units used to measure distance are kilometres, metres, centimetres, millimetres and miles. All of these derive from the metre (although the mile was originally 'a thousand paces'), and are simple subdivisions or multiples of that measure. So where did metres originate?

In fact, the metre has changed length a little over time. It was originally defined in two different ways. One way was to measure the length of a seconds pendulum (a pendulum with a half period of a single second). The other was taken as one ten-millionth of the distance from the equator to the North Pole. The latter method triumphed during the French Revolution. This method was unsurprisingly problematic, not only because the distance from the equator to the North Pole was a rough estimate at the time, but the international measures of a metre were based on copies of a 'metre bar' (a physical metal bar measuring the size of a metre), which varied in length across the globe primarily due to general wear and tear. Nowadays, in the interest of absolute accuracy, a metre is measured as the length of the path travelled by light in a vacuum during 1/299,792,458 of a second. So metres are in an odd way a derivative measure of time.

Mass

Whilst artefacts such as the physical metre stick have been surpassed by more accurately replicable properties of the universe, it seems somewhat primitive that our beloved kilogram is in fact, to this day, still based on a physical prototype. The International Prototype Kilogram, or IPK for short, is still in existence and is held in Sèvres, France. The kilogram was derived from the mass of a cubic decimetre of water (a litre). Mass differs from *weight*, in that it is independent of gravity. The future lifespan of the IPK is likely to be short. There are 40 copies of it in existence, and their masses deviate slightly from the IPK. The kilogram is in the process of being redefined, but it hasn't happened yet.

Time

Upon first inspection, time is a relatively straightforward thing to comprehend. 365 days in a year comprising 12 months, 7 days in a week, 24 hours in a day, 60 minutes in an hour and so forth. However, it becomes a lot more complicated when we start to question why those seemingly arbitrary numbers apply to each aspect of our time system. Have there always been 7 days in a week? Why not 10? It would make sense, since we count in a decimal system. Who decided there were 60 seconds in a minute? Who decided how long a second was exactly? Why do we have a month with only 28 days in it (most of the time)? Suddenly time doesn't seem so simple after all.

Why are days split into 24 hours?

It may seem odd to ask, but at some point in time, a decision was made to divide the length of a day into 24 parts. Days themselves are an intuitive way of measuring the passage of time, based simply on the Earth's rotation on its axis (or more simply, the time between sunrise, sunset and the next sunrise – although modern measures of time are far more accurate than that). So measuring time by days is pretty self-explanatory, but why not divide them into 10 parts? Or 100? Twenty-four seems a little odd.

Well, the earliest records of the use of a 24-hour day are Egyptian, in around 4000 BC. In fact, they *did* use 10 hours as their measure of daytime, but also allowed for an hour of twilight at sunrise and sunset. The night was measured as a full 12 hours based on the observation of different rising star constellations.

Incidentally, there *have* been calendars in existence that divided the entire day equally into 10 parts (the Chinese once used one, and the French Revolution almost created one!). It may seem surprising that different countries measured time in different ways, but this is mostly long before international travel existed. The Chinese New Year is a good example of a festival based on a time cycle that has since been universally standardised and hence replaced.

When is 12pm?

'am' stands for *ante meridiem* meaning 'before midday', and 'pm' stands for *post meridiem* meaning 'after midday'. As such, 12-hour time is often used with either am or pm to differentiate afternoon and morning times. However, 12pm and 12am are somewhat problematic. Noon is simply neither before nor after itself. As such, depending on the source, 12am and 12pm are essentially interchangeable. Sometimes 12am is intended to mean midnight, whereas other sources may state 12pm is used for the same time. It's all rather confusing and best avoided altogether by talking in 24-hour time, where 00:00 is classed as midnight, or by using 'midday' and 'midnight' instead. There simply isn't a formal agreement on what time 12pm actually is, or whether it should even exist!

Why are hours split into 60 minutes?

We can thank the Babylonians for this. The Babylonians used a number system in base-60. Why? Well, it's not entirely clear. A popular theory is that 60 was used because it has a large number of factors, and so it can be divided equally in a number of different ways. You'll notice that 60 is also the number of seconds in a minute. These examples are rooted in the Babylonian base-60 number system.

Why do we measure years?

Years, like days, are based around astronomy. The Earth completes a full orbit of the Sun in just over 365 days (about 365.256). Years were observed before this level of understanding by marking the occurrence of the equinox (when day and night are equal in length), and the summer and winter solstices.

The leap year, which includes an additional day in February, was created to realign the year with the Earth's orbits. Without the leap year, after 100 years or so our calendar would be significantly out of sync with the seasons.

Why do we have 12 months?

The Roman Calendar originally had only 10 months, beginning in March. Remnants of this ancient structure still appear confusing today. Anyone familiar with a decagon may wonder why December is in fact the twelfth month, and not the tenth. Similarly, September, October and November all have numerical prefixes which do not align with their place in the order of months. Their names are clues to their past, wherein they were in fact the seventh, eighth, ninth and tenth months. In fact, two other months originally had literal numerical meanings (Quintilis and Sextilis) but these were later renamed to honour Julius and Augustus Caesar.

Close to this time, the number of months also became 12, which completed two purposes. First, it filled in a rather bizarre winter gap that Romans observed between December and March, which was not originally counted in the same manner. Second, it aligned the year length with the solar year. And so in came January and February to complete the set.

What is the meaning behind the names of the months (Table 6.1)?

Table 6.1 The meanings behind the names of the months

Month	Meaning
January	The month of Janus, the god of transition and new beginnings
February	The month of Februa, the festival of purification. The additional day in leap years is added to February because of its purification theme
March	The month of Mars, god of war. March was originally the first month of the year, which was traditionally when wars were resumed
April	The month of Aphrodite, goddess of love
May	The month of Maia, the goddess of growth (or Spring)
June	The month of Juno, the goddess of marriage. June was traditionally a popular month for marriage
July	The month of Julius Caesar. Originally this month was called 'Quintillus', simply meaning the fifth month. After the introduction of January and February, it became the seventh month, and was renamed after Julius Caesar ... by Julius Caesar
August	The month of Augustus Caesar. Originally this month was called 'Sextilis', meaning the sixth month. Again, the month moved forward two places after the introduction of January and February. Sextilis was renamed by Augustus Caesar, presumably because if Julius Caesar could do it, then why not?
September	September simply means the 'seventh month', which is somewhat confusing without the backstory of adding January and February later. September is now the ninth month, and seemingly escaped being renamed after a Roman leader
October	October simply means the eighth month
November	November means the ninth month
December	December means the tenth month. Despite now being the twelfth month

Why are there seven days in a week?

The week itself is an amalgamation of both religious and celestial observations.

The Babylonians and Egyptians both attributed each day to a planet. At the time, the only known 'planets' were Saturn, Jupiter, Mars, Earth, the Moon, Venus, Mercury and the Sun. Earth doesn't count, so that leaves a total of seven 'planets', hence seven-day cycles were marked as important. Uranus wasn't discovered until 1781, Neptune was discovered around 1846 and Pluto was discovered in 1930 (and later reclassified as a dwarf planet in 2006).

Meanwhile, Judaism followed a different cycle, albeit identical in length. Six days of work were followed by a day of rest, known as the *Sabbath*.

Over the centuries, different cultures have adopted their own variations of either/both of these themes when adopting names for each day. Often a day named after one God was renamed after a God more meaningful to that particular nation. As a result, from one language to another, you can identify a range of day etymologies from planets, to Gods, to simple place markers.

Let's look at a comparison between the French and English names for example (Table 6.2).

Table 6.2   The meanings behind the names of the days of the week

English	Meaning	French	Meaning
Sunday	Day of the Sun	Dimanche	Day of the Lord
Monday	Day of the Moon	Lundi	Day of the Moon
Tuesday	Day of Tiw (Germanic God of War)	Mardi	Day of Mars
Wednesday	Day of Odin (Norse God)	Mercredi	Day of Mercury
Thursday	Day of Thor (Norse God)	Jeudi	Day of Jupiter
Friday	Day of Frigga (Germanic Goddess, wife of Odin)	Vendredi	Day of Venus
Saturday	Day of Saturn	Samedi	Day of the Sabbath

Area

Measurement does not sit only within the confines of time and distance. We measure a whole range of things in different ways. Whilst perimeters of shapes are indeed distances of sorts, area is not. Area is a measure of the space inside the boundary of a shape. It is a measurement of the size of a surface.

The measurement of area can use a multitude of units, but is always referred to as 'squared'. For example, centimetres squared (cm^2), metres squared (m^2) or yards squared (yd^2). But why do we use 'squared' universally?

Well, put simply, we measure area by comparing it to an equivalent measure of squares. The size of those squares is dependent upon the units we are using. For example, a rectangle with area 30 cm^2 has an area equivalent to 30 squares of size 1 cm × 1 cm. This is clearer when using phrases such as '30 square metres' rather than '30 metres squared'. In fact 'square centimetres' and 'square metres' are more appropriate ways of describing cm^2 and m^2 respectively. It is only with the passage of time that they have become synonymous with 'centimetres squared' and 'metres squared'.

The red triangle in Figure 6.1 has an area of 8 square centimetres (8 cm^2) as demonstrated (not drawn to scale).

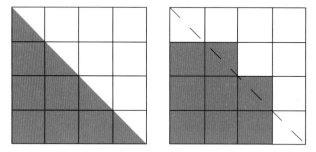

Figure 6.1 The formula for area of a triangle is half that of a rectangle

The area formula for a triangle can be calculated using the formula:

$$\text{Area} = \frac{1}{2} \times \text{base} \times \text{height}$$

There are specific formulae for a variety of shapes. But where do they all come from?

The square

Although this one is probably the most straightforward area formula, it is often written as:

$$\text{Area} = \text{length} \times \text{width}$$

which is unhelpful for several reasons. First, length is defined as the longest dimension of an object, and width is considered the distance from side to side. Well, there is no 'longest dimension' in a square, they're all the same (Figure 6.2). So why are we referring to two different things at all?

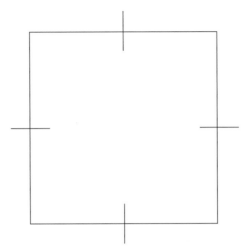

Figure 6.2 We need only one side to calculate the area of a square

A much simpler formula eradicates the unhelpful use of two different names for the same thing. We can simply use:

$$\text{Area} = s^2$$

Where s is the length of the side of the square. Not only is this more helpful, it also helps identify the link between the word 'squared' and the square itself. Furthermore, it introduces indices quite early on in a student's mathematical journey.

The reason this formula works is quite simple (Figure 6.3).

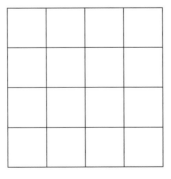

Figure 6.3 Rows and columns of unit squares are equal in a square

You can see that with any square, the area is s rows of s squares, hence $s \times s = s^2$.

The rectangle (Figure 6.4)

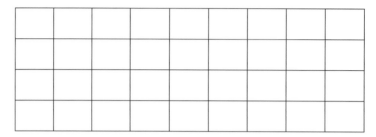

Figure 6.4   Rows and columns of unit squares are not equal in a rectangle

Again, it's simple enough to see that the formula for a rectangle is:

$$\text{Area} = \text{length} \times \text{width} = lw$$

Two terms are clearly relevant here, as we have two different lengths for rectangles (apart from the degenerate rectangle, which is a square). As a centimetre square grid (or whatever other unit you're using) this can be thought of simply as the number of rows multiplied by the number of columns.

The triangle

Here's where things get a little more interesting. The formula we generally use for the area of a triangle is:

$$\text{Area} = \frac{1}{2} \times \text{base} \times \text{height}$$

In other words, half of the area of a rectangle. Albeit that we have now replaced the terms width and length with base and height. It would probably be best if we just

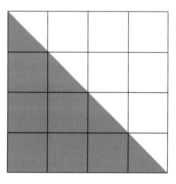

Figure 6.5   The area of a right-angled triangle is intuitive if it is half a square

used base and height for both, but textbooks are seemingly determined to confuse things. Never mind, with a right-angled triangle, this formula seems quite straightforward (Figure 6.5).

You can see how the area of the triangle is exactly half of the area of the square above. And it doesn't take too much imagination to picture this working with an ordinary rectangle either (Figure 6.6).

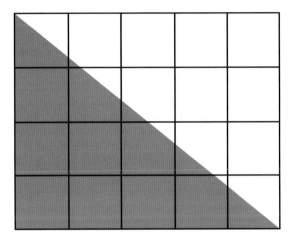

Figure 6.6   The area of a right-angled triangle is intuitive if it is half of a rectangle

However, it's perhaps less intuitive when we consider different types of triangle; for example, Figure 6.7.

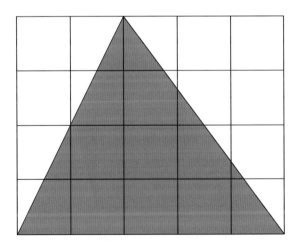

Figure 6.7   The area of a non-right-angled triangle is less intuitive

It's harder to spot, particularly without the grid behind it, that this triangle is still half the area of the rectangle.

However, by drawing in a straight line, and looking at the resulting two smaller rectangles, everything becomes clear (Figure 6.8).

We will use the handy triangle to show how other formulae for areas of common shapes can be derived.

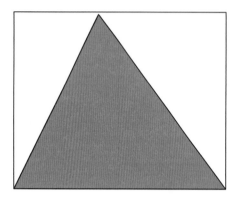 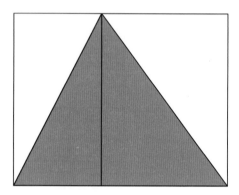

Figure 6.8 The area of a non-right-angled triangle becomes more obvious with the addition of a perpendicular line

The parallelogram

The formula for the area of a parallelogram is:

$$\text{Area} = \text{base} \times \text{height}$$

Which you could use as the same formula as we had for a rectangle (and a square!) (Figure 6.9).

Figure 6.9 By slicing a section from a parallelogram, it becomes clear that the area formula will be the same as for a rectangle

Yes, But Why? Teaching for Understanding in Mathematics

Or as twice the formula we had for a triangle (Figure 6.10).

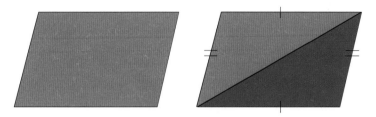

Figure 6.10 By drawing a diagonal line across the vertices it becomes clear that the area of the parallelogram is twice that of a triangle

The trapezium

The formula for the area of a trapezium is a little more complicated than those we have covered so far (Figure 6.11):

$$\text{Area} = \frac{(a+b)}{2} h$$

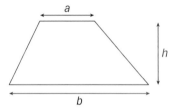

Figure 6.11 The area formula for a trapezium is less obvious on first inspection

By splitting a trapezium into two triangles, as shown in Figure 6.12, you can see that the area of the red triangle is $\frac{1}{2} \times b \times h$.

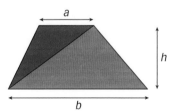

Figure 6.12 By drawing a diagonal line across the vertices, the area formula for a trapezium becomes clearer

And with a simple rotation, it becomes clear that the area of the blue triangle is $\frac{1}{2} \times a \times h$ (Figure 6.13).

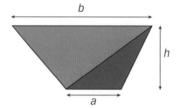

Figure 6.13   By rotating a trapezium we can see it is made up of two triangles with different bases and the same height

And so the combined area of the whole shape (i.e. the trapezium) is:

$$\frac{1}{2} \times a \times h + \frac{1}{2} \times b \times h$$

$$= \frac{1}{2}(ah + bh) = \frac{(a + b)}{2}h$$

The circle

The formula for the area of a circle is well known:

$$\text{Area} = \pi r^2$$

But where does that come from?

Again, we can rely on the trusty triangle to see us through.

If we split the circle into sectors (Figure 6.14),

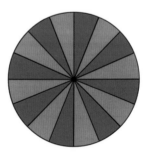

Figure 6.14   Slicing a circle into equal sized sectors

we can in fact slot each sector together to form an 'almost' rectangle (Figure 6.15).

Figure 6.15   Rearranging circle sectors to resemble a rectangle

If we try again, but make the sectors even thinner, it becomes a closer approximation of a rectangle (Figure 6.16).

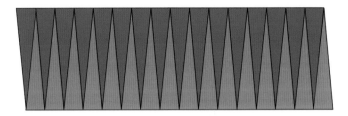

Figure 6.16   Thinner sectors make a closer approximation to a rectangle

And the thinner the sectors get, the closer we get to a rectangle. Assume we can get them infinitely thin … and we have our rectangle. The height is the length of the circle radius. The width is one half of the circumference of the circle (Figure 6.17).

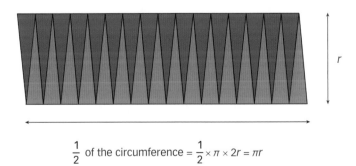

$$\frac{1}{2} \text{ of the circumference} = \frac{1}{2} \times \pi \times 2r = \pi r$$

$$A = \pi r \times r = \pi r^2$$

Figure 6.17   Thin sectors arranged to approximate a rectangle help us deduce the formula for the area of a circle

When teaching area of shapes, be sure to provide students with *all* of the side lengths as well as the perpendicular height. This will help you check whether students genuinely know what they're looking for, rather than just plugging in the two numbers provided in the question. Similarly, for circles, give a variety of measurements such as the circumference and the diameter rather than just the radius each time.

Volume

Whilst area is the space inside the boundary of a two-dimensional shape, volume is a measure of the space inside the boundary of a three-dimensional shape.

For any shape of constant width, the formula to calculate its volume is relatively straightforward and can be generalised to:

Area of cross section × depth of shape

Hence, the formulae for the shapes in Figure 6.18 are easily derived.

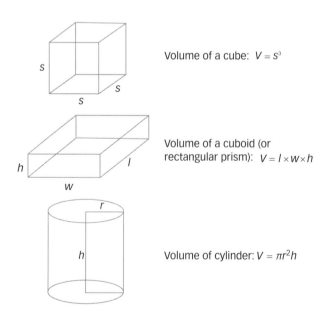

Volume of a cube: $V = s^3$

Volume of a cuboid (or rectangular prism): $V = l \times w \times h$

Volume of cylinder: $V = \pi r^2 h$

Figure 6.18   The volume of prisms is the area of a cross section multiplied by the depth of the shape

However, there are a few other shapes students are expected to be able to calculate the volume for, which do not have constant width. These formulae are a little trickier to derive.

The pyramid

The volume of a pyramid is calculated using the formula:

$$V = \frac{1}{3} \times \text{area of base} \times \text{height}$$

And is often written as:

$$V = \frac{1}{3} \times \text{length} \times \text{width} \times \text{height}$$

(Figure 6.19)

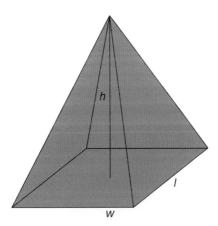

Figure 6.19   A labelled pyramid

But where does *a third* come from? The area of a triangle uses a half, so intuitively you may be thinking we should also use a half here, as we're dealing with a shape that looks very triangular. Let's take a closer look.

If we take a single, particular type of pyramid, we can in fact move towards a generalisation for this formula.

In Figure 6.20 you can see the trisection of a cube.

Figure 6.20   A trisected cube

Each pyramid is equal, there are three of them, and together they make a cube. Therefore, their volumes must each be:

$$\frac{1}{3} \times \text{length} \times \text{width} \times \text{height}$$

But this is only a single case and does not serve as a general proof.

However, if we were to stretch the pyramid in any dimension by a scale factor x the volume will simply adjust proportionately, and the formula will stay the same. This might be easiest to visualise by simply stretching the diagrams we just used (Figure 6.21).

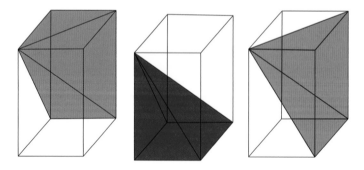

Figure 6.21   A trisected cuboid

Hopefully, you're now convinced that, at least for a pyramid that is formed using a right-angled side, the volume is always:

$$\frac{1}{3} \times \text{length} \times \text{width} \times \text{height}$$

Now, to generalise for any pyramid, imagine creating equally spaced horizontal slices across the pyramid (Figure 6.22).

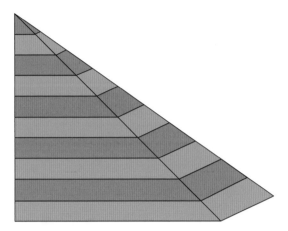

Figure 6.22   A horizontally sliced pyramid

By adjusting each layer, we get an approximation of a pyramid whose apex is perpendicular to the centre of its base.

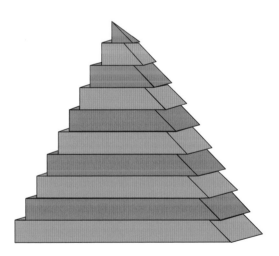

Figure 6.23   A demonstration of Cavalieri's Principle

By making the slices thinner and thinner, we get closer and closer approximations of a true pyramid, without any chunky 'steps' between layers.

If we were to make these slices infinitely thin, then the 'steps' between layers would essentially disappear completely, and we'd be left with a smooth-edged pyramid.

During this process, is the volume changing? It is not! This explanation is a simple interpretation of what is known as **Cavalieri's Principle** (Figure 6.23).

The cone

Cones have an identical volume formula to pyramids. Imagine a square-based pyramid and a cone side by side. Both have equal height, the cone has radius r and the side of the base of the pyramid is $r\sqrt{\pi}$.

This would mean that the base of the pyramid is πr^2, and therefore equal to the base of the cone (Figure 6.24).

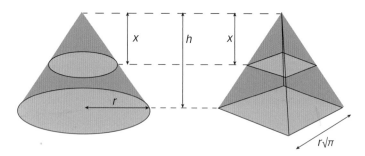

Figure 6.24   A cone and a pyramid with equal base and height

If we take any cross section of the cone, at a distance x from the apex (see Figure 6.24), then the radius of that cross section would be $\dfrac{x}{h}r$, and the side of the square cross section of the pyramid, at the same distance x from its apex, would be $\dfrac{x}{h}r\sqrt{\pi}$. Therefore, they are proportionately the same, and thus have equal volume. Hence, the formula for this cone must also be $\dfrac{1}{3}\pi r^2 h$.

Again, using Cavalieri's Principle, it can be shown that the volume of *any* cone can be found using the same formula.

The sphere

A nice proof for the volume of a sphere utilises our cone, our cylinder and a bit of the Pythagorean Theorem to great effect.

The formula for the volume of a sphere is:

$$V = \frac{4}{3}\pi r^3$$

Take a hemisphere, and place it at the bottom of a cylinder of equal radius and height (therefore the height can be labelled the same as the radius) (Figure 6.25).

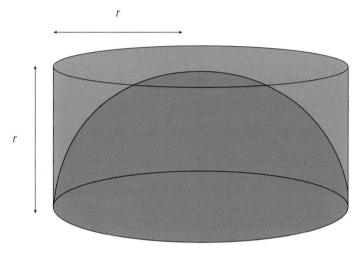

Figure 6.25   A hemisphere inside a cylinder with equal radius and height.

If we place a cone face down into the cylinder, again with radius r and height r, we have something like Figure 6.26.

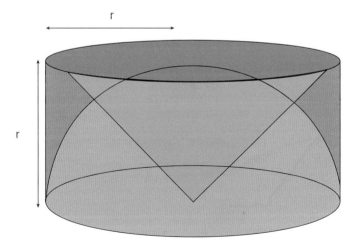

Figure 6.26   Derivation of the volume of a sphere

Now, if we took a thin horizontal slice of this cylinder, at any point above the base, at say, height h, then:

- The area of the slice of the cylinder will be πr^2 (because the cylinder is of uniform width).
- The area of the slice of the cone will be πx^2, where x is the radius of the cross section of the cone at that point.
- The area of the slice of the hemisphere will be πy^2, where y is the radius of the cross section of the hemisphere at that point.

If we imagine a horizontal slice near the base of the cylinder, it would look like Figure 6.27.

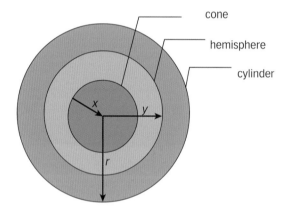

Figure 6.27   A horizontal cross section of a cone, sphere and cylinder

Let us now take a two-dimensional *vertical* slice at the same place as before, to see what's going on at this point (Figure 6.28). For simplicity, only one half of the cone is shown (ABC).

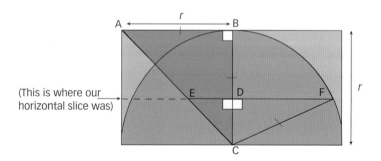

Figure 6.28   A vertical cross section of a cone, sphere and cylinder

Let:

$$x = DE$$

$$y = DF$$

We can see that triangle ABC and triangle EDC are similar isosceles triangles, and therefore CD = DE.

CF is also a radius, so CF = r.

We can also see that triangle CDF is a right-angled triangle. Therefore, using the Pythagorean Theorem:

$$CD^2 + DF^2 = CF^2 = r^2$$

Now, because we know that CD = DE, we can substitute it here and show that:

$$DE^2 + DF^2 = r^2$$

Multiply everything by π and we get:

$$\pi DE^2 + \pi DF^2 = \pi r^2$$

Recall that:

$$x = DE$$

$$y = DF$$

And so:

$$\pi x^2 + \pi y^2 = \pi r^2$$

Let's just make what we're saying clearer in our minds by going back to our two-dimensional horizontal cross section (Figure 6.29).

This must be true for all cross sections, and therefore the entire shape.

In other words, this is a true representation of the *volume* of the shapes.

Volume of hemisphere + volume of cone = volume of cylinder

Recall that the volume of a cylinder is $\pi r^2 h$, but our cylinder here has height r so we can write the volume of *this* cylinder as πr^3.

Algebraically then:

$$\text{Volume of hemisphere} = \pi r^3 - \frac{1}{3}\pi r^3$$

$$= \frac{2}{3}\pi r^3$$

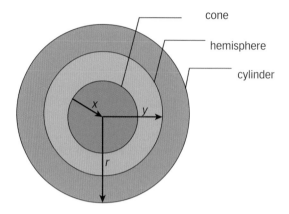

cone

hemisphere

cylinder

Figure 6.29 Derivation of the volume of a sphere

And since the hemisphere is only half of a sphere, we need to double this to get the volume of a sphere:

$$\text{Volume of a sphere} = \frac{4}{3}\pi r^3$$

Surface area

There is another set of formulae we teach students for the **surface area** of shapes. Surface area is just the area of the surface of a three-dimensional shape. Most surface area calculations simply involve calculating each face separately, often by visualising the net of the shape. For example, the cuboid (Figure 6.30) and the tetrahedron (Figure 6.31).

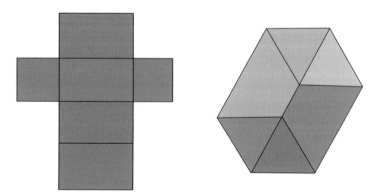

Figure 6.30 The net of a cuboid

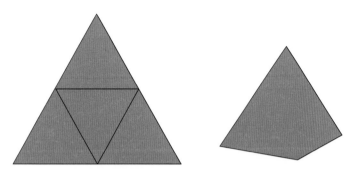

Figure 6.31   The net of a tetrahedron

Others are a little more complicated. We will focus primarily on the less intuitive formulae here.

Cylinders

$$\text{Surface area} = 2\pi rh + 2\pi r^2$$

If we unpick this formula, there are two distinct parts: $2\pi rh$ and $2\pi r^2$.

$2\pi r^2$ is easily identifiable as the area of two identical circles. This makes sense, as there are circles at both ends of the cylinder (assuming the cylinder is 'closed') (Figure 6.32). If it is specifically mentioned that the cylinder is 'open', then this part of the formula is omitted.

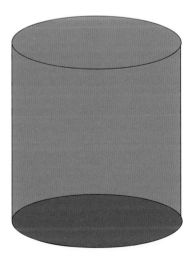

Figure 6.32   A cylinder

So how can we explain the first part of the formula, $2\pi rh$?
It's easiest if we look at the net of a cylinder (Figure 6.33).

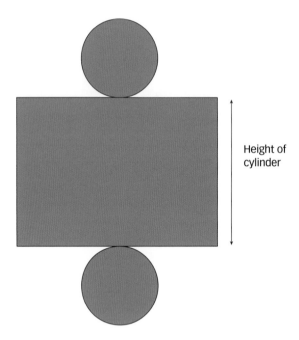

Height of
cylinder

Figure 6.33   The net of a cylinder

We can see that because the $2\pi r^2$ part of the formula relates to the two circles,
then $2\pi rh$ *must* relate to the area of the rectangle. With h as the height of the cylinder, we're left with the length of the rectangle, which must somehow equate to $2\pi r$.
    Well, you'll no doubt recognise $2\pi r$ as the formula for the circumference of a circle.
This is exactly why it is here too. The length of the rectangle must be equal to the circumference of the circle, as it wraps exactly around it when we create our cylinder.
    Hence, the full formula for the surface area of a cylinder is:

Area of rectangle (whose length is the circumference of the circle) +
area of base circle + area of lid (identical circle)

Or, put neatly and mathematically:

$$2\pi rh + 2\pi r^2$$

Which incidentally factorises nicely to:

$$2\pi r(h + r)$$

Cones

Cones are even stranger upon first inspection. The formula for the surface area of a cone is:

$$\text{Surface area} = \pi r s + \pi r^2 \text{ (Figure 6.34)}$$

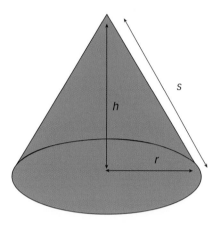

Figure 6.34   A labelled cone

Again, the πr^2 part of the equation is fairly obvious, it's the circle at the bottom of the cone. But how can we be sure that the curved surface is equal to $\pi r s$? Where does that come from?

The easiest way to figure this out, is to inspect the net of an open cone (Figure 6.35).

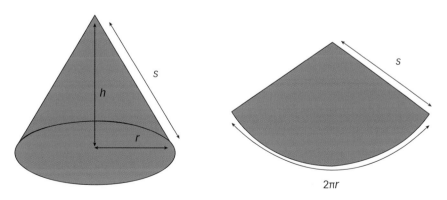

Figure 6.35   The net of a cone

If we now view the net of the cone as part of a much bigger circle, with radius s, we get something like Figure 6.36.

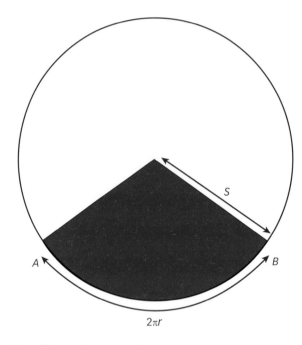

Figure 6.36 Derivation of the surface area of a cone

Now, the ratio of the area of the cone (the green part), to the area of this bigger circle is equal to the ratio of the arc AB to the circumference of the larger circle:

$$\frac{2\pi r}{2\pi s}$$

Which simplifies nicely to:

$$\frac{r}{s}$$

Therefore, the area of the sector (remember, this is the net of our cone) is:

$$\frac{r}{s} \times \pi s^2$$

$$= \frac{\pi r s^2}{s}$$

$$= \pi r s$$

Hence, the formula for the total surface area of a cone (including the circular base) is:

$$\pi rs + \pi r^2$$

Spheres

The surface area of a sphere is perhaps one of the most interesting formulae covered in the GCSE curriculum. Its simplicity is ultimately misleading, as its derivation is anything but straightforward.

The formula for the surface area of a sphere is:

$$4\pi r^2$$

In other words, the largest possible circle across the centre of the sphere will fit exactly over a quarter of it, and four of them will cover it entirely with nothing left over. The simplest derivation of this formula is similar in many ways to the derivation of the area of a circle that we looked at earlier.

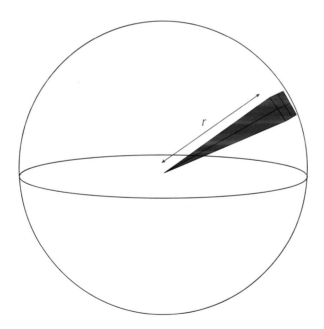

Figure 6.37   Approximating a sphere using pyramids

Imagine a sphere sliced into approximations of pyramids, four of which are shown in Figure 6.37. Each piece has height r, equal to the radius of the sphere. The pieces are not quite pyramids, as their base is part of the surface of the sphere, which is curved. However, if we made smaller and smaller slices, they would get closer and closer to approximations of pyramids (i.e. their bases would get flatter and flatter).

It's not too hard to imagine then, that the sum of the volume of all of these infinitesimally thin pyramids is in fact equal to the volume of the sphere, as the bases of the pyramids are so tiny, that they negate the curve of the sphere's surface. We're also assuming therefore, that the sum of the bases of the pyramids is equal to the surface area of the sphere.

Recall that the formula for the volume of a pyramid is:

$$\frac{1}{3} \times \text{area of base} \times \text{height of pyramid}$$

Remember that the height of our pyramids making up our sphere is equal to the radius of the sphere.

Recall that the volume of a sphere is given by:

$$\frac{4}{3}\pi r^3$$

Therefore,

$$\frac{1}{3} \times \text{surface area} \times r = \frac{4}{3} \times \pi \times r^3$$

$$\text{Surface area} \times r = 3 \times \frac{4}{3} \times \pi \times r^3$$

$$\text{Surface area} = 4\pi r^2$$

Unit conversions

There are a multitude of units of measurement. For most of them, conversions are relatively straightforward. Miles to metres, for example, is a simple case of measuring how many metres 'fit' into a mile. However, converting units of measurement when dealing with area or volume, is somewhat confusing at first glance. For example:

$$100 \text{ m}^2 = 1{,}000{,}000 \text{ cm}^2$$

But you'd be forgiven for thinking that intuitively it must be 10,000 cm² because there are 100 cm in a metre (and $100 \times 100 = 10{,}000$). However, this is unpicked relatively easily:

$$100 \text{ m}^2 = 10 \text{ m} \times 10 \text{ m} = 1000 \text{ cm} \times 1000 \text{ cm} = 1{,}000{,}000 \text{ cm}^2$$

Students can quite easily derive most unit conversions through the use of everyday charts, such as birthweight comparisons, child height projection charts, body mass index calculators, healthy eating guidelines, braking distances for cars and boiling points of liquids.

Some more unusual units of measure

A **barleycorn** is equal to 1/3 of an inch, still used today in measuring shoe sizes.

A **cable** is a nautical unit of 1/10 of a nautical mile, based on the length of an anchor chain.

A **cow's grass** is an old Irish unit used to measure the size of fields. Its size is roughly the size of an area of grass able to support a single cow.

A **cubit** (also **ell**) is a measure from the tip of the middle finger to the elbow, still used for hedge laying.

A **decametre** is a seldom-used unit meaning 10 metres.

A **digit** (also **finger**) is an ancient measure based on the breadth of a finger.

A **fathom** is an old unit of measure for the depth of water. It is equal to 6 feet.

A **hand** is equal to 4 inches and is used to measure the height of horses.

A **poppyseed** is about 1/4 of a barleycorn.

A **shackle** is 15 fathoms. Sections of anchor chain were joined by a physical shackle in the Navy (hence the name). This would allow sailors to count the shackles as they released more anchor chain into the ocean, and thus determine the depth of the water.

A **shaftment** is around 6½ inches in length, and refers to the distance between the tip of an outstretched thumb and the wrist. Shaftments were used to measure the length of poles and staves.

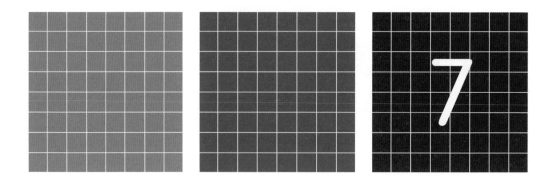

Algebra

We have used some algebra already in previous chapters, but here we will look in more detail at what algebra actually is, where it originated, what its purpose is, and why it's useful. It's often the part of mathematics that students worry about the most, perhaps because the expectation is that mathematics involves (and only involves) numbers. However, as we'll see, algebra is very powerful and incredibly important.

What is algebra?

Algebra is a branch of mathematics that uses not only numbers, but also symbols (usually letters) to *represent* numbers and relationships. Algebra enables us to generalise mathematical properties and definitively prove phenomena.

The name algebra is derived from the Arabic *al-jebr*, which means 'completion' or 'restoration'. The word appeared in what is generally considered the first book to introduce the concepts of algebra as a new branch of mathematics, written by a Persian mathematician named Muhammad ibn Musa al-Khwarizmi. You may notice al-Khwarizmi is very similar to the word 'algorithm', which in fact derives from his name.

The purposes of algebra

There are two main purposes for algebra at school. The first is the use of letters to mean an *unknown* number, albeit usually one that can be found. The second is to highlight a *relationship* between different things. Before we look at either of these, it is important to understand algebraic notation, which is summarised in Table 7.1 and Figure 7.1. We will predominantly use the letter b here, just to avoid confusion between x and the multiplication symbol $\times$.

Some algebraic notation

Table 7.1

Notation	Meaning
b	$1 \times b$
$3b$	$3 \times b$ (equal to $b + b + b$)
b^2	$b \times b$
$3b^4$	$3 \times b \times b \times b \times b$
$3bc$	$3 \times b \times c$
$(3b)^2$	$(3 \times b) \times (3 \times b)$
$\dfrac{3}{b}$	$3 \div b$
$\dfrac{b}{3}$	$b \div 3$

Note that it is conventional to write algebraic expressions involving more than one letter in alphabetical order. Hence, we would normally write abc and not cba. There are also some new key terms associated with algebra:

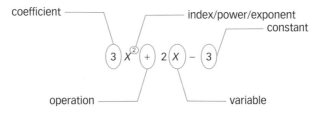

Figure 7.1 The technical language of algebraic expressions

Formula – a rule, such as $F = ma$ or $A = \pi r^2$. The plural can be written as either formulae or formulas.

Expression – a mathematical statement without an equals sign, such as $3b + 6$. Expressions can be simplified, but not solved.

Identity – an equation that is always true, regardless of what values are substituted for any variables used. For example, $b + b = 2b$.

Equation – a mathematical statement *with* an equals sign (note that the word *equation* is the noun, and *equal* is the adjective). Equations can be solved, unlike expressions. For example, $3b = 20$.

Variable – something that can change its value. In algebra, this is usually written as a letter. Be mindful though. Expressions and formulae both use variables; however, some equations use letters that are *unknowns*, such as $3b = 20$. Here, b does not vary, so calling it a variable is misleading.

Coefficient – literally means a 'co-worker', but in this context, it is the constant by which we multiply the variable.

Teacher tip

There is no real need to write letters in algebra. The basic premise is that symbols replace numbers. Students will be familiar with the idea of a question mark in an equation, such as $3 + ? = 8$ and algebra is really just an extension of this idea. However, be very careful not to misinterpret the purpose of algebra in the early stages. A common mistake is to redefine a quantity of objects algebraically, such as 3 bananas being replaced with '$3b$' and 2 apples being replaced with '$2a$'. This is *not* algebra. It is **codifying** and can be very misleading. For example, if we assume $3b = 3$ bananas, what would $3b^2$ mean? What would $3 \div b = 12$ mean? It quickly becomes nonsensical and far removed from real algebra.

Algebraic equations

Algebraic equations always contain an equals sign (=). Hence, they are showing that two things are equal, but with at least one unknown value. For example:

$$1 + b = 10$$

This is barely a step away from $1 + ? = 10$, which students are introduced to very early in their mathematical journey. The left side is equal to the right side, so the value of b must be something that, when added to 1, is equal to 10. Now this is a fairly trivial example, in fact we can solve it just by inspection: b is clearly 9. It is important though, even at this early stage, to understand *how* we can manipulate this equation in order to solve it. In other words, solving it *without* just looking at it. Also note that there is only one possible value of b. It is unlikely that students will encounter anything where b can be more than two possibilities when solving algebraic equations ($b^2 = 9$ for example, has two solutions); however, they can arise in some situations.

It is also important to keep the equation *true*, in other words, we cannot simply add or subtract things from one side only, or multiply some things and not others. Doing so will create an error. To visualise *why* this is, it's easiest to look at equations *without* algebra:

$$3 + 1 = 4$$

If we were to subtract 1 from the left side only, we would get (erroneously):

$$3 + 1 - 1 = 4$$
$$\text{or } 3 = 4$$

Clearly this isn't true! Whatever we apply to one side of the equation, we must apply to the other:

$$3 + 1 - 1 = 4 - 1$$
$$3 = 3$$

Now it is still true.

If we go back to our original equation then:

$$1 + b = 10$$

We can subtract 1 from *both* sides and it will remain balanced. In doing so, we'll also solve our equation:

$$1 + b - 1 = 10 - 1$$
$$b = 9$$

This of course seems like a very long-winded way of solving a very simple equation. However, this process is key to being able to confidently solve more complex equations later on. Be mindful that some students are keen to avoid looking so deeply at such a simple process because it is, at this point anyway, intuitive – it can be done in our heads without having to think about the processes behind the calculation. It is important to note here that from the very beginning, the value of b doesn't change. It is a hidden number, and that number will be the same at the beginning of our solution as it will be at the end.

Balance using manipulatives

When we visit algebra for the first time, it's important that balance becomes a well-established concept to maintain when solving equations. To help students, a visual representation of problems can often help. Figure 7.2 is a representation of:

$$b + 4 = 7$$
$$b + 4 - 4 = 7 - 4$$
$$b = 3$$

Figure 7.2 A visual representation of the solution to $b + 4 = 7$

What is fundamental, is that when we talk about solving equations, we avoid embedding the idea of things 'crossing over to the other side', or passing some kind of barrier which changes positives to negatives and vice versa. Such approaches are dangerously misleading, and only distance students from true understanding of what is being done to the equation. The idea of crossing sides implies all kinds of magical properties of maths that simply aren't there, and students often begin to assume other strange manipulations must also be valid, such as 'moving a multiplication to become a division'.

The perils of multiplication and division in algebraic manipulation

Keeping an equation balanced with addition and subtraction is relatively straightforward – we simply add (or subtract) the same thing to both sides and we keep the balance. Multiplication and division are a little more complicated though. If we multiply something by an amount, we must multiply *everything* by that amount to keep the balance.

Let's look at another example:

$$3b = 15$$

Here $3b$ means $b \times 3$, and as such, division (the inverse of multiplication) is the operation we need to solve the equation.

$$3b \div 3 = 15 \div 3$$
$$b = 5$$

If you're unsure as to why $3b \div 3 = b$, it's because anything divided by itself is 1, and as such $3b \div 3 = (3 \div 3) b = 1b$, but we don't write $1b$, we write b. It's just lazy convention. Why write two things next to each other when we can imply it by just writing one thing? Mathematicians love efficiency. If we can save a character, we'll save a character!

What if we have multiplication *and* addition? Consider this example:

$$3b + 3 = 18$$

What do we do first? Look what happens if we divide both sides by 3, but ignore the $+ 3$ term:

$$(3b \div 3) + 3 = 18 \div 3$$
$$b + 3 = 6$$
$$b = 3$$

It's hard to see if we've made an error, but if we substitute $b = 3$ back into our original equation:

$$3b + 3 = 18$$

We end up with:

$$(3 \times 3) + 3 = 18$$
$$12 = 18$$

Clearly this is not correct! Our error was that we did not divide **everything** by 3 when we did our initial division. The + 3 was left untouched, and because of this, it caused an error in our solution. This is a common error students make. Why *wouldn't* b = 3? It seems perfectly reasonable unless we substitute it back into our original equation – *which we always should do!* Again, visual explanations can help.

Figure 7.3 is a pictorial representation of:

$$3b + 3 = 18$$

$$\frac{3b + 3}{3} = \frac{18}{3}$$

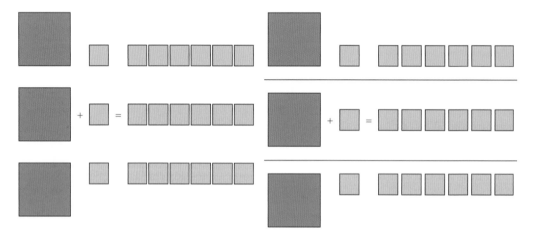

Figure 7.3   A visual representation of using division in algebraic equations

Teacher tip

When solving even the most basic of algebraic equations, it is a good idea to start off without any algebra at all, but just to play around with numerical equations. For example:

$$3 \times 4 = 12$$

Students could rearrange this equation to get 3 = 12 ÷ 4. It is much easier to see visually if the rearrangement is correct, and it helps instil the need to balance equations rather more intuitively than if we jump head first into algebra.

Solving linear algebraic equations

To solve an algebraic equation, we rely on keeping the equation balanced at all times, and undoing anything that has been *done* to the subject by means of *inverse operations*.

For example:

$$5b = 20$$

What has been *done* to b? It has been multiplied by 5. How do we undo multiplying something by 5? We do the *inverse*, which is to *divide* by 5. Keep it balanced by doing the same to both sides, and we get a nice answer of:

$$b = 4$$

But of course, things get more complicated, and we start to encounter equations such as this:

$$2b + 20 = 34$$

Now we have two things to deal with. b has been multiplied by 2, but we've also added 20 into the mix. Which should we deal with first? Why?

Reversing the order of operations

With relatively straightforward algebraic equations, a rule of thumb is to tackle things in the reverse order of operations. In other words, deal with addition and subtraction first, then multiplication and division, then brackets and indices. It's not always quite as simple as that, but it's a start. But why do we do that?

It's easiest to understand if we picture how the equation was formed from the subject in the first place.

Take our example of $2b + 20 = 34$. If we break that down, we're saying:

Take b, multiply it by 2, and then add 20. Your answer is equal to 34.

To undo this, we work backwards, i.e.

Subtract 20, divide by 2, and you have b.

What we're *not* saying is:

Take b, add 20, and multiply by 2. Your answer is equal to 34.

That would look like this:

$$2(b + 20) = 34$$

Which yields a very different answer of $b = -3$ rather than $b = 7$.

Students can visualise this easily with the aid of a 'number machine', which we'll use in the next example:

$$\frac{b}{3} - 5 = 20$$

Figure 7.4 shows this written as a number machine.

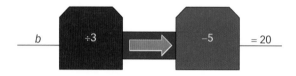

Figure 7.4   A number machine representing $\frac{b}{3} - 5 = 20$

So if we *reverse* this number machine, we'll get a nice solution (Figure 7.5).

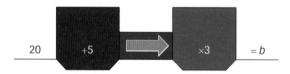

Figure 7.5   A number machine representing the solution to $\frac{b}{3} - 5 = 20$

It gets less obvious as we start to introduce *implied* brackets such as with this example:

$$\frac{b+3}{2} + 4 = 10$$

It may be tempting to subtract 4, then subtract 3, then multiply everything by 2. However, there is an implied pair of brackets:

$$\frac{(b+3)}{2} + 4 = 10$$

As such, our number machine would look like Figure 7.6.

Figure 7.6   A number machine representing $\dfrac{(b+3)}{2} + 4 = 10$

And again, our solution would work by working backwards (Figure 7.7).

Figure 7.7   A number machine representing the solution to $\dfrac{(b+3)}{2} + 4 = 10$

With a little experience, the need to think in this way becomes more intuitive and natural.

Before we move on, it should be noted that some algebraic equations have two solutions rather than one. How does that work?

Why does b^2 have two solutions, but b^3 have only one?

First, ask yourself what it means when we say b^2?

$$b^2 = b \times b$$

In other words, a number multiplied by itself.

So, if $b^2 = 36$, we're essentially saying a number, multiplied by itself is equal to 36. So far no surprises. However, there are in fact two numbers that multiply by themselves to equal 36.

6 is the obvious example, but the less obvious second answer is −6.

As we saw in Chapter 1, a negative number multiplied by another negative number produces a positive answer (can you remember why?). And so,

$$-6 \times -6 = 36$$

It is a perfectly acceptable answer, so we have two solutions for b, which we can write as follows:

$$b^2 = 36$$

$$b = \pm 6$$

Yet this doesn't happen when we deal with b^3. When we cube something, we multiply it like so:

$$b \times b \times b$$

This would in fact return a negative answer for a negative b, and a positive answer for a positive b, so there is only one possible solution.

If you continue with that logic, you'll realise that b^n will have two solutions if n is even, and only one solution is n is odd. (Remember that b can also be written as b^1.)

Solving simultaneous equations

At a more advanced level, students eventually begin to solve linear equations with *two* unknowns, usually written as x and y. It is impossible to solve an equation with two unknowns without a little more information. As such, problems involving two unknowns are usually in the format of *simultaneous* equations, whereby two separate equations involving the same two unknown values are given, and students must use *both* equations to solve the problem. One such example is shown below:

$$2x + y = 20$$

$$2x + 3y = 36$$

The standard approach to solving the problem above, is to eliminate one unknown. In this case, if we subtract one equation from the other, we eliminate x, allowing us to find the value of y easily. We will subtract the first equation from the second, so that y remains positive (otherwise we have more work to do, and we're lazy mathematicians, remember?):

$$(2x + 3y) - (2x + y) = 36 - 20$$

$$2y = 16$$

$$y = 8$$

Now we can substitute $y = 8$ into either of our original equations and find the value of x:

$$2x + 8 = 20$$

$$2x = 12$$

$$x = 6$$

Let's stop for a minute though. Earlier we emphasised the need for balance in equations, and that whatever we did to one side, we needed to do to the other, otherwise it became untrue. However, here we seem to be doing something else entirely. We're subtracting $2x + y$ from one side, and 20 from the other side. Why does that work?

The key to solving this puzzle is equality, and the subtle difference between things being equal and things being identical. Moving the algebra to one side for a moment, consider the equation below:

$$3 + 1 = 4$$

Now, what if I subtract 2 from one side, but I subtract $(1 + 1)$ from the other side?

$$3 + 1 - 2 = 4 - (1 + 1)$$

The balance is still preserved. However, the things I subtracted were not identical in appearance, although they had the same value. They were equal to each other. It is not dissimilar to subtracting a kilogram weight from one side of a scale, and a thousand individual grams from the other. They look different, but they are equal.

We're ready to bring algebra back in:

$$2x + 3y = 36$$

$$2x + y = 20$$

When I subtract equation 2 from equation 1, I'm subtracting $2x + y$ from the left-hand side, and I'm subtracting 20 from the right-hand side. But just like in the non-algebraic example above, these two things are equal in value. You may be wondering why we don't just subtract 20 from both sides, or subtract $2x + y$ from both sides, but the whole purpose of doing the operation is to eliminate one unknown (x or y). If we just subtract 20 from both sides (or $2x + y$) that objective is not met and we'll be no closer to solving the equations.

Multiplying out brackets and factorising

Multiplying out brackets is often a counter-intuitive process for students. This is due in part to the amount of emphasis we sometimes place on the order of operations. Without algebra, brackets are an indication of something that needs to be dealt with before anything else:

$$3 (2 + 4) = 3 (6) = 3 \times 6 = 18$$

The brackets used above must be completed before multiplying by 3. At least, that's how we teach it. However, 'must' is a bit misleading. We can in fact separate the brackets out as shown below:

$$3 (2 + 4) = 3 \times 2 + 3 \times 4 = 6 + 12 = 18$$

We still get to the same result, and we didn't break any rules. In fact, we just used the distributive property of multiplication. It may seem pointless at first to do this, as it's quicker and more efficient to just multiply 3 by 6. However, when we switch to algebra, and terms are unknown to us, this distributive property is essential to progress. For example we could have something like this:

$$3 (b + 4) = \ldots$$

We can't do anything inside the brackets when we have two terms that are not alike – in this case a known 4 and an unknown b. However, using the distributive property of multiplication we can still rewrite this as:

$$3 (b + 4) = 3 \times b + 3 \times 4 = 3b + 12$$

If students have never experienced the distributive property of multiplication used in this way before, *without* algebra, then understandably, the whole concept *with* algebra can seem very unintuitive.

The concept can be extended to double brackets (and any other quantity of brackets):

$$(2 + 3) (4 + 5) = (2 + 3) \times 4 + (2 + 3) \times 5 = 2 \times 4 + 3 \times 4 + 2 \times 5 + 3 \times 5$$
$$= 8 + 12 + 10 + 15 = 45$$

Using algebra:

$$(b + 3) (b + 5) = (b + 3) \times b + (b + 3) \times 5 = b \times b + 3 \times b + b \times 5 + 3 \times 5$$
$$= b^2 + 3b + 5b + 15$$
$$= b^2 + 8b + 15$$

There are several different strategies to multiply out brackets such as the grid method:

$$(b + 3)(b + 5)$$

	b	$+3$
b	b^2	$+3b$
$+5$	$+5b$	$+15$

$$= b^2 + 8b + 15$$

Or a simple matching activity to ensure all things have been multiplied by each other (Figure 7.8).

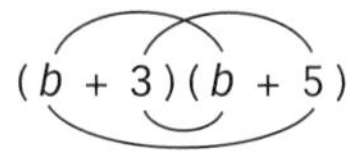

$$(b + 3)(b + 5)$$

Figure 7.8   Matching to ensure all things have been multiplied by each other

Teacher tip

Often this method is referred to as the *crab* method or *smiley face* method. Both names distract away from what is happening mathematically. *The emphasis should be on what is happening, not what it looks like!*

Despite these approaches looking different, they are all doing exactly the same thing as in our first example.

Factorising

The process of *factorising* looks a lot like the *reverse* of multiplying out brackets. The word itself is the verb form of 'factor' meaning, mathematically, *multiplicative contributions to an end product* (etymologically similar to 'factory' incidentally).

Factorising without algebra has been covered earlier in this book; recall that the factors of 20 are 1, 2, 4, 5, 10 and 20.

We could therefore *factorise* 20 as any of the following:

$$1 \times 20$$

$$2 \times 10$$

$$4 \times 5$$

These are each known as *factor pairs* because not only are they factors, but as a pair, they multiply to equal the original number.

While 4 and 2 are factors of 20, they are not a factor pair of 20, because they don't multiply together to equal 20.

We could also factorise 20 as:

$$2 \times 2 \times 5$$

Note that this is also referred to as *prime factorisation* because we only used prime numbers. We can also say that we've written 20 as a *product of its prime factors*.

Algebraically, the principle is exactly the same. We're trying to rewrite an algebraic expression as a product of its factors. The difficulty, however, is that, contrary to the factorisation of integers, we're unlikely to get pretty single terms multiplied by other nice single terms. It's more likely that we'll end up with less intuitive, messy things.

Let's take a simple example to start things off:

$$4b + 12$$

The terms $4b$ and 12 have a common factor of 4. This indicates to us that we can factorise the expression, that is, 4 multiplied by *something* will be equal to our expression:

$$4(something) = 4b + 12$$

So 4 is part 1 of our factor pair, but what is the 'something'?

Well, using the $4b + 12$ part to help us, we can deduce that:

$$4(b + 3) = 4b + 12$$

Because:

$$4b + 12 = 4 \times b + 4 \times 3 = 4(b + 3)$$

Hence, $4(b + 3)$ is a factorisation of $4b + 12$. The product in this case is $(4b + 12)$ and the factor pair is 4 and $(b + 3)$.

You may be thinking 'Wait a minute, 4 is a factor of 12, but $b + 3$ is absolutely *not* a factor of 12, so how is this right?'.

Well, you're right! $(b + 3)$ isn't a factor of 12. It's a factor of $(4b + 12)$. The difference is subtle, but for students it can be a difference between understanding what is happening, and seeing this whole thing as a weird rule that you just have to memorise.

Again, the concept can be extended to double brackets.

For example:

$$b^2 + 7b + 10$$

Can be factorised as:

$$(b + 5)(b + 2)$$

In other words, $(b + 5)$ and $(b + 2)$ is a factor pair of $b^2 + 7b + 10$.

Solving quadratic equations

Things get a lot trickier when students are introduced to quadratic equations (equations in the form $ax^2 + bx + c$). Not only do these equations have *two* solutions, they're also made more difficult when we have 'something x^2' alongside 'something x', such as this:

$$2x^2 + 3x = 14$$

Here, we almost have two unknowns, which as we've seen, would be impossible to solve without more information. Fortunately, whilst we do have two separate things, they are at least linked to each other. There are a variety of ways to solve quadratics. We can factorise, 'complete the square' or use the quadratic formula, which is a rather ugly beast, but it gets the job done. We'll have a look at each of these methods in turn, and as always, figure out why they work.

Completing the square

The way to solve quadratic equations known as 'completing the square' was a precursor to the popular quadratic formula we will visit shortly. The phrase 'completing the square' is a literal description of the method, which utilises a pictorial representation of a quadratic equation, involving, you guessed it, a square. In fact the word *quadratic* literally means 'made square'. The method is often refined down to an algorithm seemingly disassociated with logic, which goes something like:

> To complete the square, take the whole number over to the right of the equals sign, then take half of the coefficient of the x-term, square it, and add that to both sides of the equation. Factorise the left-hand side and solve.

Using an example, let's for a moment explore this method with no conceptual groundwork:

$$x^2 + 4x - 21 = 0$$

Take the whole number over to the right of the equals sign ...

$$x^2 + 4x = 21$$

Then take half of the coefficient of the x-term, square it, and add that to both sides of the equation:

$$x^2 + 4x + \left(\frac{4}{2}\right)^2 = 21 + \left(\frac{4}{2}\right)^2$$

$$x^2 + 4x + 4 = 25$$

Factorise the left-hand side:

$$(x + 2)(x + 2) = 25$$

And solve:

$$x + 2 = \pm 5$$

$$x = 3 \text{ or } x = -7$$

If you substitute those values back into $x^2 + 4x - 21 = 0$, you'll see that it really does work; however, a lot of people will have absolutely no idea why.
Here's why:

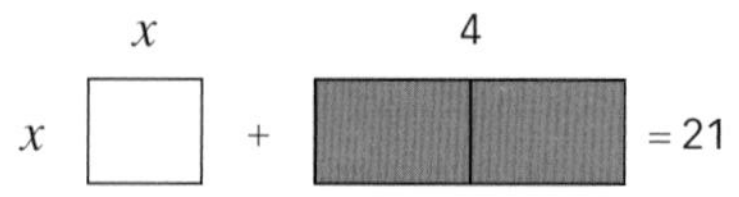

Figure 7.9 A visual representation of $x^2 + 4x = 21$

Using algebra tiles, we are representing x^2 as a square x by x, and $4x$ as a rectangle of length 4 and height x (Figure 7.9). The line dividing the $4x$ rectangle in two is to highlight this rearrangement (Figure 7.10).

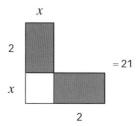

Figure 7.10 Creating a partial square using $x^2 + 4x = 21$

This new L shape is starting to take the form of a square, although it needs ... completing (Figure 7.11).

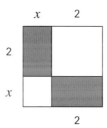

Figure 7.11 Completing the square using $x^2 + 4x$

The additional large white square has an area of $2 \times 2 = 4$ (units are irrelevant), and we have *added* it on, therefore we need to add an equal amount to the other side of our equation to keep it balanced (Figure 7.12).

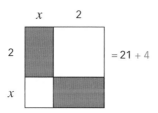

Figure 7.12 Balancing the completion of a square using $x^2 + 4x + 4 = 21 + 4$

Hence:

$$(x+2)(x+2)=25$$

When our equation involves *subtracting*, such as:

$$x^2 - 10x = 11$$

Then our goal is to create a smaller square, rather than a larger one (Figure 7.13).

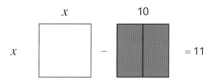

Figure 7.13   A visual representation of $x^2 - 10x = 11$

Here, as we are subtracting, we need to *subtract* the red rectangles from the white square (Figure 7.14).

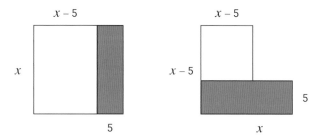

Figure 7.14   Creating a square with $x^2 - 10x$ leaves a 5 × 5 square

To maintain the shape of the white square, we have ended up with a little of the red rectangle left over (Figure 7.15).

Figure 7.15   Completing the square for $x^2 - 10x = 11$

Hence:

$$(x-5)(x-5) = 36$$
$$x = 11 \text{ or } x = -1$$

Solving by plotting

We can also solve quadratic equations by plotting them. If we take the example $x^2 + 2x - 3 = 0$ and plot $y = x^2 + 2x - 3$, we get the following, shown in Figure 7.16.

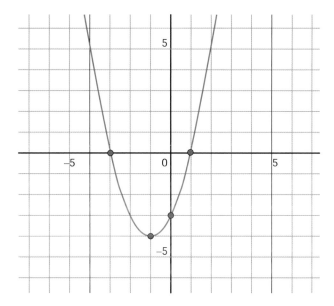

Figure 7.16 Plotting a quadratic equation to find solutions

Which has roots at $x = 1$ and $x = -3$ (those are the points where $x^2 + 2x - 3 = 0$). This method works nicely if our roots are integers, but it gets difficult to remain accurate if our solutions are fractions, as we're relying a lot on being able to read off the x values from the curve.

Where does the quadratic formula come from?

Rather than derive the formula from $ax^2 + bx + c = 0$, let's work backwards from it:

$$x = \frac{-b \pm \sqrt{b^2 - 4ac}}{2a}$$

$$x = -\frac{b}{2a} \pm \frac{\sqrt{(b^2 - 4ac)}}{2a}$$

$$x + \frac{b}{2a} = \pm \frac{\sqrt{(b^2 - 4ac)}}{2a}$$

$$\left(x + \frac{b}{2a}\right)^2 = \frac{b^2 - 4ac}{4a^2}$$

$$x^2 + \frac{bx}{a} + \frac{b^2}{4a^2} = \frac{b^2}{4a^2} - \frac{4ac}{4a^2}$$

$$x^2 + \frac{bx}{a} + \frac{b^2}{4a^2} = \frac{b^2}{4a^2} - \frac{c}{a}$$

$$x^2 + \frac{bx}{a} = -\frac{c}{a}$$

$$ax^2 + bx = -c$$

$$ax^2 + bx + c = 0$$

You may notice this is an application of completing the square.

Sequences

In mathematics, sequences are ordered number patterns. There are many types, but within the curriculum there are four specific categories of sequences: linear (also known as arithmetic), quadratic, geometric and 'Fibonacci style'. The latter sounds made up, but it means any sequence of the form $F_{n+2} = F_n + F_{n+1}$, or in more familiar terms, *add the two previous terms together to get the next term*. This of course requires you to know the first two terms, otherwise it's useless. It can also produce some rather counter-intuitive sequences. The Fibonacci sequence itself is quite straightforward:

$$0, 1, 1, 2, 3, 5, 8, 13, \ldots$$

However, this 'Fibonacci style' sequence goes all over the place:

$$-2, 1, -1, 0, -1, -1, -2, -3, \ldots$$

Fibonacci was a 12th-Century Italian mathematician, who famously created the Fibonacci sequence as an answer to a problem about increasing rabbit populations.

The sequence itself was used in India long before Fibonacci was born, but it was then referred to as the Virahanka numbers.

Linear sequences

A linear sequence is one that increases or decreases by the same amount with each sequential term. For example, we may add 3 each time, or subtract 6 each time, but whatever we do, we do it every time. Arguably, the most simple example of a linear sequence is basic counting in 1's.

$$1,2,3,4,5, \dots$$

Here each new term increases by 1.
    If we look at the 2× table:

$$2,4,6,8, \dots$$

You'll notice we're simply increasing by 2 each time. We call this a **common difference** of 2.
    If we map each term against the sequence number, which we'll call n, then we get:

n	1	2	3	4	5
term	2	4	6	8	10

Our sequence can be generalised, using the number n, in the sequence by the formula $2n$, that is, if you give me a number n, I can give you the term in the sequence at that point, using the formula $2n$.
    Similarly, the 3× table will have an nth term of $3n$ and the nth term of the 4× table is $4n$, and so on.
    What is the 17th term of my $4n$ sequence? Well, n is 17, so the 17th term is $4 \times 17 = 68$.
    Other linear sequences are a little more complicated, but not by a lot:

$$3,5,7,9,11, \dots$$

If we map each term against the sequence number, n:

n	1	2	3	4	5
term	3	5	7	9	11

You'll notice that again we're increasing by 2 each time, the same as the 2× table. However, we have a different starting point. There is a *shift*. This can be seen on a number line (Figure 7.17).

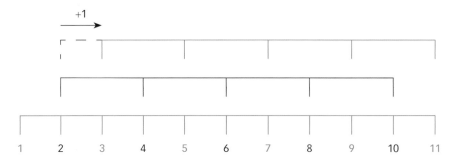

Figure 7.17 Visualising the 'shift' in a linear sequence

Hence, the *n*th term for this sequence is $2n + 1$.
Why does that work?
If we look at each term for the generic sequence $an + b$, we get:

n	1	2	3	4	5
$an + b$	$a + b$	$2a + b$	$3a + b$	$4a + b$	$5a + b$

As you can see, the difference between each term is a, hence to find the coefficient of *n* for our *n*th term, we use the difference between terms, then substitute it into $an + b$ to find b (Figure 7.18).

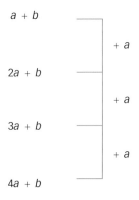

Figure 7.18 Finding the difference between terms for a linear sequence

Note, if we generalise linear sequences, they are of the form $an + b$, which looks a lot like $mx + c$ for linear graphs, because it's almost exactly the same, just using different letters to represent the same things. The key difference is that for $an + b$, n must be a natural number.

Quadratic sequences

A quadratic sequence is defined by having the form $an^2 + bn + c$; again, this is no different from $ax^2 + bx + c$, we're just using n instead of x, and n must be a natural number.

The simplest quadratic sequence is n^2:

n	1	2	3	4
term	1	4	9	16

Note that these sequences do not progress by a fixed amount each time (they do not increase in a linear fashion), so now it's a bit more difficult to figure out the elusive nth term.

We often teach a method that goes something like:

Find the difference between each term, then find the second difference. Halve the second difference to determine the coefficient of n^2, then find the shift.

Once again, we're provided with a magical formula with no grounding in common sense or understanding. And once again it works … well, almost.

Anything of the form $an^2 + c$ works:

n	1	2	3	4
term	3	9	19	33

The second difference is constant, and it's 4.
Half of 4 is 2, so $a = 2$:

$$2n^2 + c$$

When $n = 1$, $2n^2 = 2$ but our term is 3, hence we need to add 1, and therefore $c = 1$.
So, finally, our nth term is $2n^2 + 1$, which is correct.

We'll see how this algorithm works shortly, but first let's look at where it doesn't work. Consider the sequence $n^2 + 2n + 3$:

n	1	2	3	4
term	6	11	18	27

The second difference is 2, so we're dealing with n^2 (so far so good), but our shift is not linear. We're not dealing with a simple 'then add 3'. We have the additional complication of $2n$, which stops our algorithm working. There are ways to get around this, but this whole mess would be much easier if we just understood what we were doing!

Take the generic form of a quadratic equation: $an^2 + bn + c$.

n	1	2	3	4
$an^2 + bn + c$	$a(1)^2 + b(1) + c$	$a(2)^2 + b(2) + c$	$a(3)^2 + b(3) + c$	$a(4)^2 + b(4) + c$
term	$a + b + c$	$4a + 2b + c$	$9a + 3b + c$	$16a + 4b + c$

Observe the first and second differences between each term (Figure 7.19).

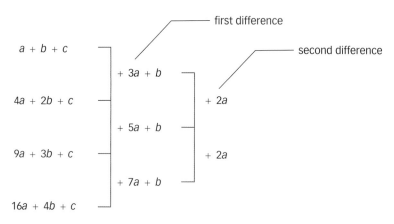

Figure 7.19 Finding the difference between terms for a quadratic sequence

You can see that the second difference is $2a$, hence the need to *halve* the second difference to find a, the coefficient of an^2.

Once we know a, we can substitute it into our first difference to find b.
Once we know b, we can substitute both a and b into our first term, and find c.
Now it makes sense!

Geometric sequences

A geometric sequence is very similar to an arithmetic sequence, but instead of increasing (or decreasing) by a fixed amount, the sequence is increased (or decreased) by the same *multiplier* each time. This means we'll be dealing with a formula of the structure ar^{n-1}. That probably seems a bit of a leap, so let's look at the idea in a bit more depth:

First, we'll rename our multiplier as our *common ratio*, r. That is, the ratio between two consecutive terms. It's still the same thing, but that's why it's written as r. Imagine our starting number is 2, and our common ratio (multiplier) is 3. Then our sequence will build up as follows:

$$2, 2 \times 3, 2 \times 3 \times 3, 2 \times 3 \times 3 \times 3$$

Which we can rewrite as:

$$2 \times 3^0, 2 \times 3^1, 2 \times 3^2, 2 \times 3^3$$

If we map that against n:

n	1	2	3	4
term	2×3^0	2×3^1	2×3^2	2×3^3

You can see that 3 rises to the power of $(n-1)$ for each iteration.

So if we generalise our starting number as a, then the general formula for a geometric sequence is:

$$ar^{n-1}$$

All that's left then is to understand how to derive the nth term of a given geometric sequence. So here's one:

$$4, 8, 16, 32$$

Our first term is 4, so straight away we have our a.

$$a = 4$$

Our *common ratio* is our multiplier, and we can find that by dividing any term by the immediately preceding term:

$$\frac{8}{4} = 2$$

So our common ratio is 2:

$$r = 2$$

Hence, our nth term is:

$$4 \times 2^{n-1}$$

Inequalities

Inequalities are things that are *not equal*. In mathematics, we have a variety of symbols that essentially mean *not equal to* but are also a bit more specific. These are:

$\neq$ not equal to

$<$ less than

$\leq$ less than or equal to

$>$ greater than

$\geq$ greater than or equal to

These symbols make more sense with actual letters:

$a \neq b$ (a is not equal to b)

$a < b$ (a is less than b)

$a \leq b$ (a is less than or equal to b)

$a > b$ (a is greater than b)

$a \geq b$ (a is greater than or equal to b)

We could use numbers too, rather than letters; however, the $\leq$ and $\geq$ symbols only make sense when used algebraically.

The names for these symbols are, rather disappointingly, the 'less than' symbol and the 'greater than' symbol. Whilst these symbols are relatively straightforward, particular attention should be paid to the properties of inequalities. There are equivalent symbols for number lines too (Figure 7.20).

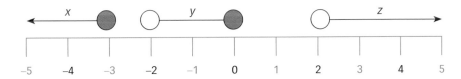

Figure 7.20   Plotting inequalities on a number line

In the figure, we have represented the following visually:

$$x \leq -3$$
$$-2 < y \leq 0$$
$$z > 2$$

The empty and filled-in circles are to differentiate between $<$, $>$ and $\leq$, $\geq$ respectively.

Properties of inequalities

The transitive property

$$\text{If } a \geq b \text{ and } b \geq c \text{ then } a \geq c$$

No surprises here. If a is greater than or equal to b, and b is greater than or equal to c, then a is also greater than or equal to c.

The converse property

$$\text{If } a \geq b \text{ then } b \leq a$$

Again, this feels intuitive, but it may need to be taught explicitly, as students can be presented with an inequality that looks like this:

$$5 \leq x \leq 8$$

In this case, reading left to right would yield '5 is less than or equal to x, which is less than or equal to 8'.

Whilst that's true, the message here is that 'x is greater than or equal to 5 and less than or equal to 8.'

But to appreciate that shift in focus from the 5 to the x, we need to be comfortable with the converse property of inequalities.

Addition and subtraction properties

For any real numbers:

$$\text{If } a \geq b, \text{ then } a + c \geq b + c$$

This can be understood clearly on a number line (Figure 7.21).

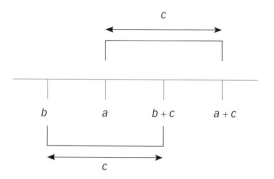

Figure 7.21 Addition properties of inequalities

Multiplication and division properties

For real numbers a and b, and where $c > 0$:

$$\text{If } a \geq b \text{ then } ac \geq bc$$

For real numbers a and b, and where $c < 0$:

$$\text{If } a \geq b \text{ then } ac \leq bc$$

This is possibly the property that confuses students the most. Probably because without the use of real numbers, it is harder to spot why doing it incorrectly makes no sense.

If we take for example:

$$5 > 3$$

And we multiply by a number that is greater than zero, say 4:

$$5 \times 4 > 3 \times 4$$
$$20 > 12$$

It still makes perfect sense. However, if we multiply by a negative number, *without* altering our 'greater than' symbol:

$$5 \times -2 > 3 \times -2$$
$$-10 > -6$$

This is not true. Negative 10 is definitely *not* greater than negative 6. Hence, the inequality symbol needs to be reversed. It's much easier to see with real numbers.

We can also use inequalities to specify regions on plotted graphs. For example, $y > 2x$ would refer to the region *above* the line $y = 2x$, whereas $y \geq 2x$ would refer to the region above *and including* the line $y = 2x$. We can differentiate between the two using a dotted line (for >) and a solid line (for ≥) (Figure 7.22):

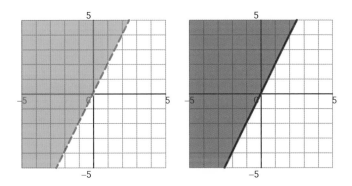

Figure 7.22   Plotting inequalities

Some interesting Vedic maths tricks

Vedic maths is a method of performing seemingly complex mental calculations quickly using shortcuts (that sadly negate understanding completely if taught in isolation), but here we'll look at how three curious tricks work using the power of algebra.

Trick 1: Checking if a number is divisible by 9

To check if an integer is exactly divisible by 9, we can add up all the digits together. If they sum to a multiple of 9, the original number is exactly divisible by 9.
e.g.:

$$4509$$

$$4 + 5 + 0 + 9 = 18 = 9 \times 2$$

$$\therefore 4509 \text{ is exactly divisible by 9}$$

$$\left(\frac{4509}{9} = 501 \right)$$

Why does that work?
Take a four-digit number (you can apply this idea to any number of digits) whose digits are *abcd*:

$$1000a + 100b + 10c + d$$
$$(999a + a) + (99b + b) + (9c + c) + d$$
$$= 999a + 99b + 9c + a + b + c + d$$

Clearly the first three terms are divisible by 9, so all that is left is $a + b + c + d$, i.e. the sum of the digits.

Trick 2: Squaring a number that ends in 5

To square any number that ends in 5, remove the last digit (a 5), multiply the remaining number by (itself + 1), then square the last digit and place it (25) at the end:

$$125^2$$
$$(12)(12 + 1) = 156$$
$$5^2 = 25$$
$$\therefore 125^2 = 15,625$$
$$45^2$$
$$(4)(4 + 1) = 20$$
$$\therefore 45^2 = 2025$$

Why does that work?

$$(10x+5)^2$$
$$= 100x^2 + 100x + 25$$
$$= 100(x)(x+1) + 25$$

Trick 3: Checking divisibility by 7

To check if a number is divisible by 7, double the last digit and subtract it from the number made by the remaining digits. If the answer is exactly divisible by 7, then the original number divides by 7.

e.g.:

$$672$$
$$67 - (2 \times 2) = 63$$

63 is exactly divisible by 7

$\therefore$ 672 is exactly divisible 7

$$\left(\frac{672}{7} = 96 \right)$$

Why does that work?

Let our number be:

$$100a + 10b + c$$

Then:

$$10a + b - 2c = 7x$$

Multiply by 10:

$$100a + 10b - 20c = 70x$$

Add 21c

$$100a + 10b + c = 70x + 21c$$
$$100a + 10b + c = 70x + 7(3c)$$

$\therefore$ $100a + 10b + c$ is divisible by 7.

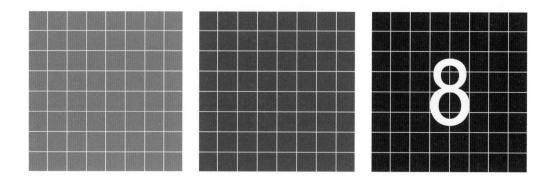

Statistics and Probability

In this chapter we will look closer at the branches of mathematics known as statistics and probability. We will look at the different ways in which data can be presented and understood, why they are useful and the relative merits of each method. We will also look at the history of probability as a field of mathematics, and how the rules of probability calculation have been derived.

Statistics is the practice of collecting, presenting, analysing and understanding data. The word statistics stems from the German word *Statistik*, meaning the 'science of state', but the field itself has existed for centuries. The beginnings of the science of data collection were in the form of record keeping, such as population and wealth censuses – which we know existed in ancient Egypt and China.

At school, statistics is concerned primarily with the different ways in which we can present data, and analyse information presented to us – rather than the collection methods themselves (although this is not excluded entirely). Students are usually presented with a rather bland table of data, and required to present the data in some kind of more exciting chart to help them extrapolate patterns and inferences that seemed hidden before.

Here we will look at each of the key types of standard charts students are expected to use to present and summarise data, and try to better understand why they are useful.

Frequency tables

A frequency table is one of the first data summarisation techniques that students are exposed to. Students are expected to be able to both read *from* a table of information, and to create one from existing data. This simple technique to summarise data may seem dull and pointless, but it is in fact incredibly useful, and introduces some important concepts relating to statistics. Frequency tables are just one example of data presentation methods collectively known as **frequency distributions**.

Why are frequency tables useful?

The purpose of a frequency table is simple – it allows for the categorisation of data, which in turn makes information easier to summarise. By tabulating data in this way, we are grouping them and making them more obviously *quantifiable* (measurable).
   If we consider the following scenario and subsequent data collection:

Student A wants to know his friends' favourite colours. He asks them all in turn, and receives the following responses:

Blue, blue, black, green, purple, blue, orange, red, yellow, pink, blue, green, purple, red, red.

As presented above, the data are hard to make much sense of, other than that we have a list of responses. We may have spotted straight away that blue is the most popular colour; however, imagine Student A had 500 friends. it's doubtful then that we'd be able to spot any emerging patterns quite so easily.
   Now, if we tabulate the responses in a frequency table, you can see instantly that blue is the most popular colour choice from the sample (Table 8.1).

Table 8.1   A simple frequency table

Colour	Frequency
Black	1
Blue	4
Green	2
Orange	1
Pink	1
Purple	2
Red	3
Yellow	1

Just for illustration, imagine again that 500 people were asked. That would be a couple of pages full of responses if we just wrote a list. However, it would fit in just as small a table as the one above, and would be much easier to analyse in its tabulated form. Note that even though we often use terms such as 'number of responses' instead of 'frequency' for our second column heading, the meaning is the same. Frequency simply means the number of times something occurs.

Bar charts

The first known use of a bar chart was by a Scottish engineer called William Playfair in 1786. Playfair is considered the founder of graphical methods of statistics, and is also credited as the creator of the pie chart and line graph. The bar chart is introduced early on in a child's schooling, and again is an example of a **frequency distribution** summary. Here, using a pair of axes (x and y) the height of each bar represents the frequency (again, very often this is not referred to as frequency, but rather the '*number of* "something"') and the x-axis label is dependent on what data are being represented:

Note that we must include labels, a suitable **scale** such that each interval is the same size, and a suitable title (Figure 8.1). Without these, interpreting the data would be impossible.

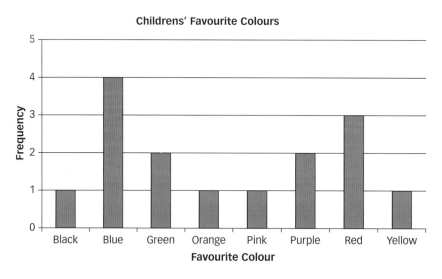

Figure 8.1 A bar chart

Bar charts do not necessarily have to be vertical either (Figure 8.2).

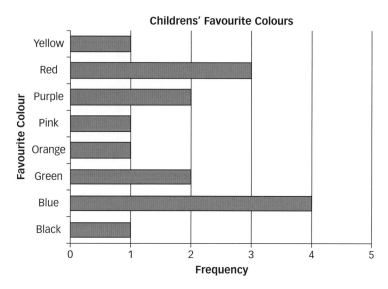

Childrens' Favourite Colours

Figure 8.2   A horizontal bar chart

Note that a bar chart has gaps between each bar to help emphasise that they are not related categories. In other words, each category is **discrete**. If we have no gaps between each bar, then the suggestion is that the categories are **continuous** such as in a histogram (see later).

Pie charts

The name pie chart derives, unsurprisingly, from its uncanny similarity to a delicious pie. Here, frequencies are distributed using 'pie slices'. Mathematically speaking, these slices are derived as proportionate circle sectors. This may seem like a rather complicated way of representing data compared with a bar chart, which does the same job. That's because it is. Furthermore, it's much easier to compare data on a bar chart than on a pie chart. See Figure 8.3 for an example.

From the pie chart, it's not overly clear which team scored the most goals.

Statisticians are not fans of the humble pie chart, as it is difficult to compare each discrete frequency, compare one pie chart with another, and, perhaps most annoyingly, the pie chart becomes fairly useless as soon as there are more than a small handful of sections to analyse. For example, the pie chart in Figure 8.4 is fairly useless.

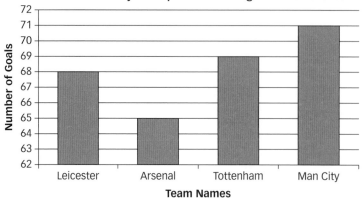

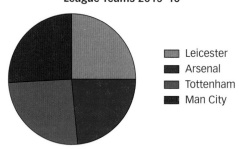

Figure 8.3   Comparing the same data in a bar chart and a pie chart

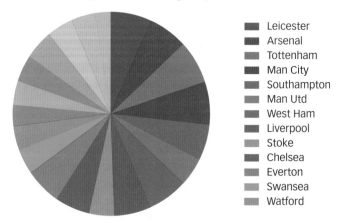

Figure 8.4   Pie charts can be difficult to interpret accurately

Why are pie charts popular?

Despite the flaws of pie charts, they are stubbornly defiant and remain a very popular choice to represent data amongst media outlets and businesses – probably because they make it very easy to see the highest frequencies when there are only a few slices. It can also feel a little exciting when looking at one, as the largest slice can appear to be literally engulfing the others like Pac-Man.

Number of Games Won by Pac-Man Characters

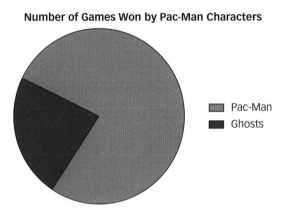

■ Pac-Man
■ Ghosts

Figure 8.5   Pie charts highlight significant differences between frequencies well

Converting data into a pie chart

To create a pie chart takes a little more mathematical prowess than a bar chart. Data should be tabulated so that they are grouped correctly. Then frequencies need to be converted into proportions of 360° (our central angle of our pie chart), which can be calculated using $\dfrac{\text{frequency}}{\text{total frequency}} \times 360$.

Finally, we need to mark these angles onto the circumference of our circle and draw our slices.

Teacher tip

Don't be shy about pointing out the flaws of pie charts. It will make lessons on the topic more interesting, and students deserve to understand the advantages and disadvantages of each method of data representation. Statistics is one of the few topics in mathematics that students will be exposed to throughout their life beyond schooling, and a critical eye is no bad thing.

Line charts

A line chart is usually used to present successive recorded data points over time, known as a **time series** (Figure 8.6). Unlike bar charts and pie charts, line charts do not always represent frequency distribution and proportionality. More often they are used to mark data points, in a similar manner to scatter diagrams (see later).

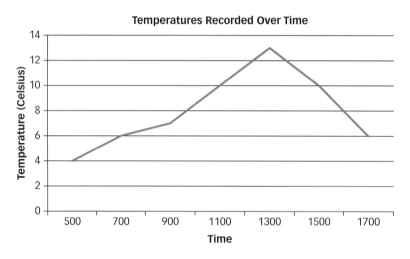

Figure 8.6   An example of a line chart

Notice that the lines do not have to begin at the *y*-axis, and so the line can 'float'. Also notice that the data points are joined with **straight lines**, not with a **smoothed line**.

Why do we use straight lines to join data points?

Smooth lines (which will appear curvy) should only be drawn when intermediate values (those between the known data points) are believed to fall on the curve. In fact, by plotting straight lines we are explicitly saying that we *don't* know any intermediate values between data points. By drawing smoothed lines we're also in real danger of encouraging misinterpretations of our data. Consider an example for the same data (Figure 8.7).

The smoothed lines imply the data are in places where they simply haven't been measured. It's not a good idea!

Yes, But Why? Teaching for Understanding in Mathematics

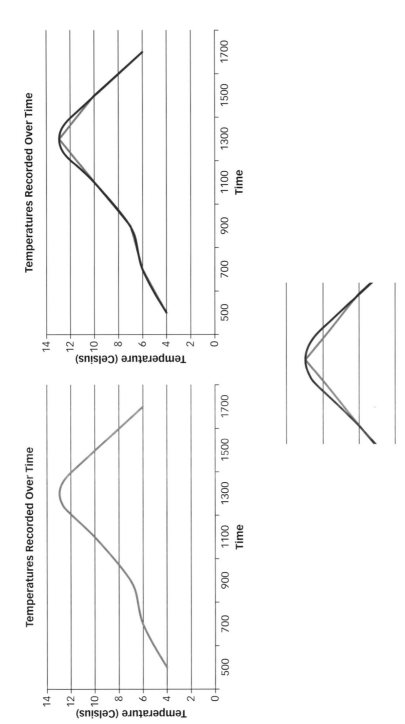

Figure 8.7 Smoothing a line chart can be misleading

Scatter diagrams

Scatter diagrams, also known as scatter *plots*, are used to display two paired variables plotted against each other. For example, height and shoe size, or grades across two different subjects. Scatter diagrams are a good way to identify relationships between two variables, known as *correlations*. The first known use of a scatter diagram was by English statistician Sir Francis Galton in 1888. The word *correlation* stems from the Latin *cor* meaning 'together', and *relatio* meaning 'relation'. This is important, as the emphasis in correlation should really be on things *moving together*, rather than any inference regarding *why* they move together. This leads us to a popular phrase *correlation does not imply causation*. As a brief example, if we (fictionally) mapped the number of super hero films released per year against the number of people going to universities in the UK (Figure 8.8),

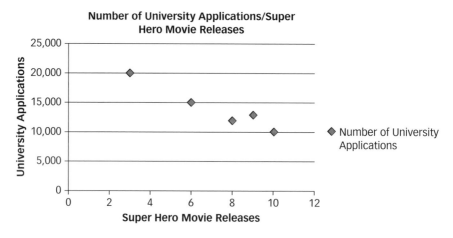

Figure 8.8   Correlation does not imply causation

we would be rather foolish to assume that we could improve the uptake of university applications by releasing fewer super hero movies.

There are three general trends associated with scatter diagrams. Positive, negative and no correlation (Figure 8.9).

Note that the positive/negative idea of correlation is exactly the same as the positive/negative direction of the gradient of lines (gradients are covered in depth in Chapter 9).

If we have any kind of linear correlation in our scatter diagram, we can then add to the diagram a more concrete linear relationship using a **line of best fit** (Figure 8.10).

Yes, But Why? Teaching for Understanding in Mathematics

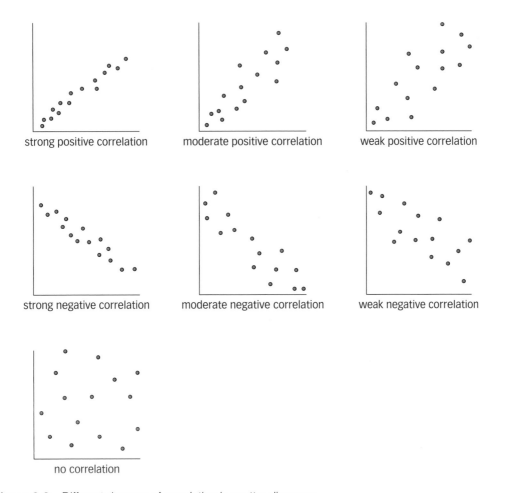

Figure 8.9 Different degrees of correlation in scatter diagrams

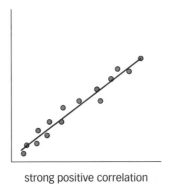

strong positive correlation

Figure 8.10 An example of a line of best fit

A line of best fit allows us to predict with reasonable accuracy any intermediate values between our data points. This may seem a little at odds with our reasoning for not using smoothed lines for line charts earlier; however, the line of best fit is not perceived as actual readings, but predictions of where they may lie. Whereas smoothing in a line chart implies deviations *are* actual readings.

Lines of best fit are a bit problematic in that determining *where* to place them is somewhat unclear.

For example, which of the two lines in Figure 8.11 is a 'better' line of best fit?

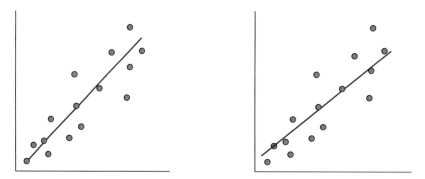

Figure 8.11 A line of best fit is not entirely accurate

A line of best fit should be constructed to minimise vertical deviations whilst also maintaining a roughly equal measure of data points either side of it (vertically). Sounds easy right? Not really. If we use those instructions as a guide, they don't really help us with some cases (Figure 8.12).

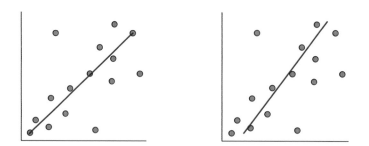

Figure 8.12 Outliers can make lines of best fit harder to plot

Here we need to be mindful of **outliers** which don't seem to fit alongside the **cluster**. An outlier is a data point that does not seem to fit with the general pattern of data.

Rest assured there are more mathematical methods to construct a line through the data (known as a regression line); however, they are not required at this level.

Yes, But Why? Teaching for Understanding in Mathematics

Stem and leaf diagrams

A stem and leaf diagram (plot) is simply a different type of frequency table, where every data measure is displayed in ascending order, and grouped into classes, with an appropriate key (Figure 8.13).

Dataset: {61, 61, 62, 66, 68, 75, 75, 76, 79, 79, 80, 81, 81, 84, 92, 98, 98, 99, 100, 100}

stem	leaf
6	1 1 2 6 8
7	5 5 6 9 9
8	0 1 1 4
9	2 8 8 9
10	0 0

Key: 6 | 1 = 61 marks

Figure 8.13   A stem and leaf diagram

Stem and leaf diagrams are particularly useful to compare two sets of data back to back, allowing for a simple comparison of both overall distribution, and distribution across a smaller sub-group (i.e. a shared stem). The visual appearance of the data displayed in this way also makes it easy to spot asymmetry within either dataset (Figure 8.14).

Class A		Class B
leaf	stem	leaf
2 1	6	1 1 2 6 8
5 5 4 2	7	5 5 6 9 9
8 1 0	8	0 1 1 4
9 9 9 9 8 8 7 7	9	2 8 8 9
0 0 0	10	0 0

Key: 6 | 1 = 61 marks

Figure 8.14   A back-to-back stem and leaf diagram

Histograms

Histograms were developed by an English mathematician called Karl Pearson in around 1910, although it's unclear why he gave them the name *histogram*, which may simply mean 'historical diagram'. A histogram is effectively a bar chart for continuous data, rather than discrete data. Continuous data are data that can take any value within a given range, such as temperature or time. There are no 'gaps' in temperature. 34°C and 35°C do not have a gap between them, one rolls seamlessly into the other (34.1, 34.2, 34.3, 34.31, etc.). Thus, the bars themselves have multiple differences to their bar chart compatriots. First, each bar represents a *range* rather than an individual entity. Second, the areas of the rectangular bars have purpose. The *areas* of each range represent their frequencies, which allows for flexibility in the width of each bar, and lets us identify the densest data range (i.e. the *range* with the highest frequency) quite easily. Histograms are used to help identify patterns of data *distribution*.

To reflect the continuous nature of the data, and to help differentiate a histogram from a bar chart, the bars in a histogram have *no gaps* between them.

Let's look at the process of constructing a histogram, to try and better understand them.

Why do we use frequency density?

It may seem odd that we use frequency density at all in histograms – histograms without frequency densities are not difficult to read. Consider the process of grouping data (technically referred to as **data binning**). It's usually already done in exam questions, but it is the process of sorting data into class widths. For example, imagine we are studying the number of birds seen feeding from a bird feeder over the course of 25 minutes (I'm sure someone somewhere does this ...?). We need to decide what our time intervals are going to be for our table. Should we just use 5-minute slots (Table 8.2)?

Table 8.2   A grouped frequency table

Time interval	Frequency of birds
$0 < x \leq 5$	4
$5 < x \leq 10$	0
$10 < x \leq 15$	10
$15 < x \leq 20$	12
$20 < x \leq 25$	5

These would be equally distributed, but perhaps we don't see any birds between the 5th minute and the 10th minute. That would look odd in a histogram with uniform column widths, as we'd have a gaping hole between bars (Figure 8.15).

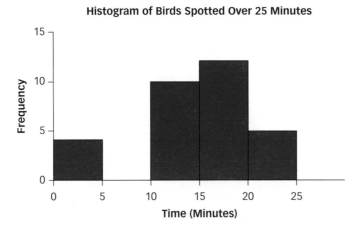

Histogram of Birds Spotted Over 25 Minutes

Figure 8.15   A histogram with uniform column widths

So maybe we want to group all of that time together (Table 8.3).

Table 8.3   A grouped frequency table with different sized groupings

Time interval	Frequency of birds
$0 < x \leq 5$	4
$5 < x \leq 15$	10
$15 < x \leq 20$	12
$20 < x \leq 25$	5

We're beginning to see *why* data ranges for histograms may sometimes be unequal. It's not just for the sake of it!

More generally, wider class widths are often used for low frequency densities to reduce focus on them, and conversely using narrower class widths for high frequency densities will *increase* focus on them, helping highlight (and increase the precision of) high frequency densities in the data distribution.

Our problem now though is that one of our bars will be *wider* than the others, otherwise the *x*-axis data will not be evenly distributed. As one bar is wider, it will look disproportionate to the others (Figure 8.16). How are we going to adjust the chart to cater for this disproportionate size?

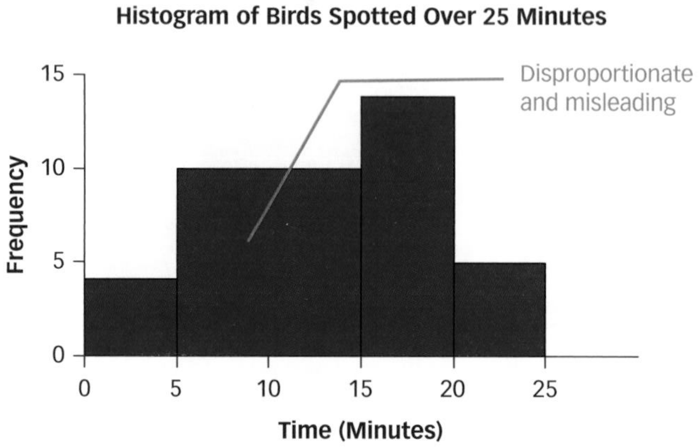

Histogram of Birds Spotted Over 25 Minutes

Figure 8.16 An erroneous histogram. Altering column widths alone is misleading

The solution to these issues is the concept of **frequency density**. It allows us to proportionately adjust the heights of bars of different widths so that they are on a level playing field. This in turn means that the **areas** of the bars now represent their frequencies, not just their heights.

Note, there is no need to convert *frequency* to *frequency density* **if** the class widths are all equal in size.

Calculating frequency densities

The formula for frequency density is:

$$\text{Frequency density} = \frac{\text{frequency}}{\text{class width}}$$

This formula effectively makes the size of each bar proportional to its frequency (Table 8.4).

Yes, But Why? Teaching for Understanding in Mathematics

Table 8.4 Frequency density allows for histogram bars to be proportionate

Time interval	Frequency of birds	Frequency density
$0 < x \leq 5$	4	0.8
$5 < x \leq 15$	10	1
$15 < x \leq 20$	12	2.4
$20 < x \leq 25$	5	1

We can now plot the histogram with the classes on the x-axis and the frequency density on the y-axis (Figure 8.17).

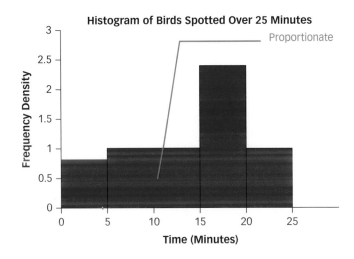

Figure 8.17   A corrected histogram to cater for different bar widths

Averages

Whilst there are a few more diagrams to discuss, they are all related to the concept of averages. There are several different types of average, but in general these are all methods of finding a measure of **central tendency** – that is, a measure that can be used to show what a *typical* data value looks like within the set. The three most common types of average used are the median, mode and mean. Each of these tells us a different thing about our dataset, and each has specific advantages and disadvantages which we will look at in turn.

Median

The median is literally the middle value. Median stems from the Latin *medianus*, which translates as 'of the middle'. In order to determine the middle value, we logically need to have our dataset in order, which when tabulated it usually is; however, as raw data it often isn't:

2 3 4 7 9 1 2 3 8

For the dataset above, the middle is *not* 9, despite it being right in the middle of the list.

The dataset needs to be in order (ascending or descending, the middle stays the same!):

1 2 2 3 3 4 7 8 9

Now it's in order, and the median is 3. In other words, for this dataset, the central value is 3.

If we have a dataset with an *even* number of things in it:

1 2 2 3 3 3 4 5 6 7 8 9

the middle is in fact two numbers (3 and 4 in this case).

It may seem counter-intuitive that a dataset of 9 things has a definite middle, whereas a dataset of 8 things does not. That's simply because we're used to thinking about even numbers being exactly divisible by 2. Dividing by 2 feels like the right thing to do to find the middle, and so the two things get a little confused with each other. But if a group of objects is divided exactly by 2, then there's no middle value left over.

So what do we do if we have two middle numbers? Simple – we find the middle of *those* two numbers. We do this by adding them together and dividing by 2 – which feels clearer on a number line (Figure 8.18).

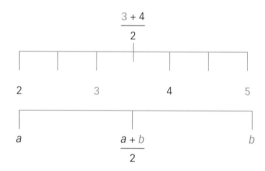

Figure 8.18 Finding the median of an even data set requires finding the middle of the middle two values

Yes, But Why? Teaching for Understanding in Mathematics

So the median of our second dataset is 3.5, which is in the middle of 3 and 4.

Be mindful of using the term 'middle' though, as students could incorrectly assume we're referring to the middle of the range. Consider the dataset {1, 9, 10}. The median is 9, but 9 is not 'in the middle' of 1 to 10, it's in the middle of {1, 9, 10}.

Why is the median useful?

Finding the median of a dataset is useful for when you have a dataset with **outliers**. Outliers will not distort the median; however, they do distort the **mean**. The median is not appropriate in other scenarios, such as trying to determine the average lap time of an athlete, as it would effectively ignore all the lap times except for the middle one.

The mode

The mode is the most common value (or values) in a dataset. In other words, the value(s) with the highest frequency. Sometimes there simply is no mode, as with this dataset: {1, 2, 3, 4, 5}, and other times there are several modes, e.g. {1, 1, 2, 2, 3, 3, 4}.

Why is the mode useful?

Finding the mode of a set of data is useful in scenarios where the frequency of a number is important. For example, in retail, a manager would want to know their most popular product, or a researcher might want to know what the most popular responses were in a survey. The mode is also the only measure of central tendency that can be used for non-numerical data.

The mean

The mean of a dataset is a little more complicated than either the mode or the median; however, it is the most common type of measure of central tendency. It is also technically called the *arithmetic mean*.

To calculate the mean, we take the sum of all the data, and divide it by the number of measurements.

For example, for the dataset {5, 15, 10, 10, 5}, we calculate the mean as follows:

$$\frac{5 + 15 + 10 + 10 + 5}{5} = 9$$

But that only explains how to calculate it. What does 9 actually *tell* us?

A nice way to envisage what is happening here is to draw each of these numbers as rectangles. The mean is taking each of these numbers, and evening them out (without adding or subtracting any additional quantity to the dataset) (Figure 8.19).

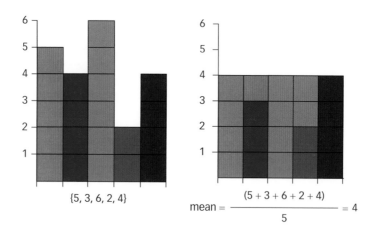

Figure 8.19 The mean is a measure of central tendency

Why is the mean useful?

Calculating the mean of a dataset is useful to gain what is arguably the best sense of typicality amongst a dataset, as it does not ignore any of the data. However, that is also its downfall, because it will use outliers within the calculation, which can skew the result. It is therefore arguably more accurate as a measure of central tendency when used with a dataset that has a small **range**.

Consider these two datasets. Set A has no outliers, but Set B does. Look what happens to the mean:

$$\text{Set A} = \{1, 2, 2, 3, 3, 4\}$$
$$\text{Mean} = \frac{1 + 2 + 2 + 3 + 3 + 4}{6} = 2.5$$
$$\text{Set B} = \{1, 2, 2, 3, 3, 25\}$$
$$\text{Mean} = \frac{(1 + 2 + 2 + 3 + 3 + 25)}{6} = 6$$

Set B has a mean that is higher than 5 out of the 6 numbers in the set. Whereas Set A has a mean that closely reflects what a *typical* value looks like.

Anscombe's quartet

Statistician Francis Anscombe highlighted the effects of outliers on the mean of a dataset in 1973 with his famous quartet of scatter diagrams showcasing the enormous variance of data spread that can result in the same (or very nearly the same) mean (Figure 8.20).

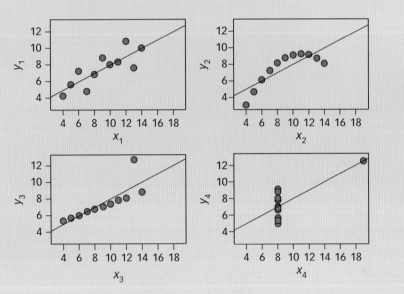

Figure 8.20   Anscombe's quartet highlights the effects of outliers on the mean of a dataset

Finding the mean, median and mode of grouped data

Whilst finding different averages of a raw dataset is relatively straightforward, it becomes less so when we look at tabulated data.

For example, consider the following dataset:

$$\{1, 1, 1, 2, 4, 6, 6, 6, 8, 10, 13, 13, 15, 15, 15, 16, 23, 25\}$$

We can easily calculate the mean: $\dfrac{180}{18} = 10$.

The modal values are 1, 6 and 15.

The median is $\dfrac{10 + 8}{2} = 9$.

However, if our dataset was displayed as in Table 8.5, we can only *estimate* each type of average, as we can't tell what each actual data value is.

Table 8.5   We can only *estimate* the mean from a grouped frequency table

Class	Frequency
1–5	5
6–10	5
11–15	5
16–20	1
21–25	2

We can only *estimate* each type of average, as we can't tell what each actual data value is. We only know that 5 of the data values lie between 1 and 5, another 5 lie between 6 and 10, and so on. Here we begin to play with *likelihood*.

If we were to assume all of our data values were at the bottom end of each class (i.e. 1, 6, 11, 16 and 21), then it's likely that our mean estimate would be too low. Similarly, if we were to assume all of our data values were at the top end of each class, then our mean would probably be too high. Hence, we go for the safe middle ground of each class. We may be a bit high for some, or a bit low for others, but it won't be as dramatically different (in theory, remember we're just talking about likelihoods) as the two extremes.

This is why we use the midpoints of each class to estimate the mean of data in a grouped frequency table (Table 8.6).

Table 8.6   We can use midpoints to generate an estimate of the dataset

Class	Midpoint	Frequency
1–5	3	5
6–10	8	5
11–15	13	5
16–20	18	1
21–25	23	2

At this point we would now use these estimations to work out our mean, median and mode. In other words, we're assuming (for the purpose of estimation) that our dataset is:

$$\{3, 3, 3, 3, 3, 8, 8, 8, 8, 8, 13, 13, 13, 13, 13, 18, 23, 23\}$$

For which we can easily calculate an estimate for the mean, median and mode. However, with the exception of the estimated mean, students are only required to find the modal and median *class*, rather than specific values.

There are other methods to calculate an estimate for each of these types of average, and they lead us back nicely to our remaining types of statistical chart.

Cumulative frequency diagrams

A cumulative frequency diagram is a statistical chart that maps the cumulative frequency of a dataset against each individual measure or class. It can be used to find **percentiles**, including the lower quartile (the 25th percentile), median (50th percentile) and upper quartile (75th percentile) (Figure 8.21).

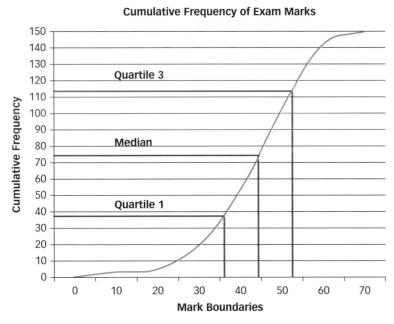

Figure 8.21 A cumulative frequency diagram highlights the spread of data

The term cumulative frequency is literally a running accumulation of the frequencies, i.e. a running total. Hence, to find the 50th percentile (the median), we simply find the halfway point between 0 and the total cumulative frequency. Half of the

50th percentile will give us the 25th percentile (the lower quartile, Q1), and the two summed together give us the 75th percentile (the upper quartile, Q3). They are usually S-shaped (an **ogive**, which is thought to derive from French and effectively means 'curved' or 'arched'), highlighting low frequencies at the top and bottom end of the distribution, and higher distribution in the middle – which may sound familiar, as it echoes the famous bell curve of normal distribution (Figure 8.22).

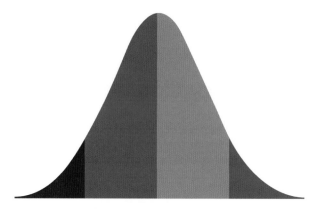

Figure 8.22 A bell curve

Unlike line charts, the curve for a cumulative frequency diagram should not 'float' because that would imply that we know where within the first class the first measure is. It should begin at the x-axis at the lowest data value – not necessarily at $(0,0)$. Similarly, when plotting the diagram, the data point for each class should be plotted at its maximum value, rather than the middle or beginning of the class boundary. This is for similar reasons – we do not want to imply that we know where within the class boundaries each data point is, when all we really know is that by the end of the class boundary, there have been x data measures (where x is the frequency).

Measures of spread

Quartiles are a measure of *spread* rather than central tendency. Measures of spread help verify the validity of measures of central tendency. For example, if data have a large spread, then the mean is considered less accurate than if the spread is small. Another method of measuring the spread of data is to find the **range** by subtracting the lowest data value from the highest data value. This gives a quick indication of how useful the mean would be; however, it doesn't give any real indication of the underlying distribution of the data. Quartiles also divide data into quarters to allow for focused distribution analysis. For example, quartiles could be used as a way of determining entry requirements to courses or to distribute grades in an exam.

Quartiles (and percentiles in general) are also used to track the weight and height of babies over time in comparison to national trends.

There is a further use of quartiles at school, and that is to calculate the **interquartile range** by subtracting the upper quartile from the lower quartile. This is a way to look at the dispersion of the central 50% of data.

Box plot diagrams

A box plot diagram (also referred to as a box and whisker plot) is a diagram that explicitly highlights the range, dispersion and quartiles of a dataset. The range is indicated by the 'whiskers' and the quartiles are indicated by the sides of the box (quartiles 1 and 3) and the vertical line going across the box (quartile 2 – the median) (Figure 8.23).

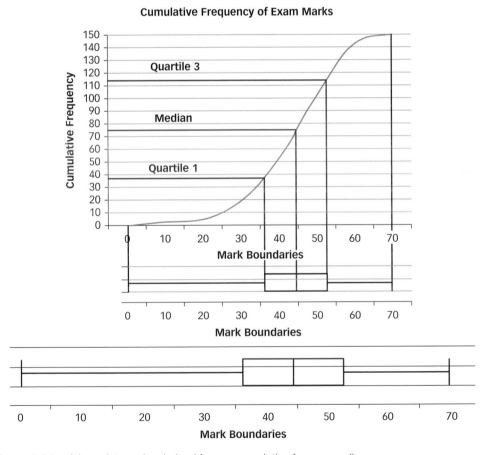

Figure 8.23   A box plot can be derived from a cumulative frequency diagram

Why are box plots useful?

A box plot diagram is a simple summary of data. It allows for quick reference to the quartiles and range, and hence is a visually efficient depiction of the spread and distribution of a dataset. Furthermore, box plot diagrams can show several datasets all within one diagram, to allow easy comparisons to be made (Figure 8.24).

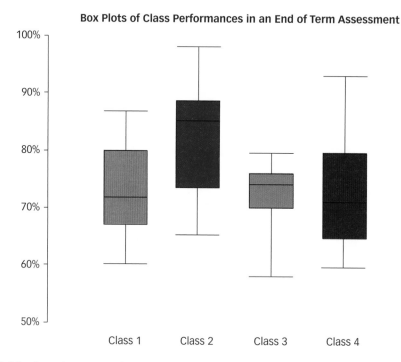

Box Plots of Class Performances in an End of Term Assessment

Figure 8.24   Box plots are useful to compare distributions of data

Probability

Probability is an area of mathematics focused on the relative likelihood of events. Probability theory dates back to around 1650, when mathematicians Pierre de Fermat and Blaise Pascal began studying a shared problem about making informed choices during gambling. Before that, probability had not been formally studied in mathematics; however, gambling itself dates back much earlier than the 1600s.

The basic premise of probability is that if a set of possible outcomes are deemed equally likely to occur, then the probability of one of those outcomes *actually* occurring is:

$$\frac{1}{\text{total number of outcomes}}$$

A familiar example is the rolling of a fair die (the implication therefore is that all outcomes are equally likely). There are six possible outcomes, each is equally likely (there is no **bias**) and therefore, the *probability* of rolling a 4 is $\frac{1}{6}$. Furthermore, the *only* possible outcomes are rolling 1, 2, 3, 4, 5 or 6. This is known as our **sample space**, which we can write in set notation as {1, 2, 3, 4, 5, 6}.

Teacher tip

Be cautious with sample spaces. If I rolled two dice and summed their total, my sample space could be written as {2, 3, 4, 5, 6, 7, 8, 9, 10, 11, 12}, but those outcomes are *not* equally likely. A more useful way to write it would be as a **sample space diagram** (Table 8.7).

Table 8.7 A sample space diagram

	1	2	3	4	5	6
1	2	3	4	5	6	7
2	3	4	5	6	7	8
3	4	5	6	7	8	9
4	5	6	7	8	9	10
5	6	7	8	9	10	11
6	7	8	9	10	11	12

Note that probability is usually written as a fraction (sometimes as a decimal), and that probabilities lie on a likelihood scale between 0 and 1 (Figure 8.25).

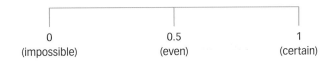

| 0 | 0.5 | 1 |
| (impossible) | (even) | (certain) |

Figure 8.25 A likelihood scale

Therefore, the probability of any outcome cannot be lower than 0 or greater than 1. If you're wondering why, then ask yourself how anything can be more likely than certain (probability = 1), or less possible than impossible (probability = 0).

We can write this mathematically as:

$$0 \le P(\text{E}) \le 1$$

Where $P(\text{E})$ simply means the probability of an event, E.

Teacher tip

It is tempting when discussing likelihood scales for the first time, to ask students about the likelihood of a range of events. Be mindful here that relatively concrete examples of throwing dice are often mixed with much more subjective likelihoods such as weather and habitual behaviours (e.g. 'I will eat lunch at 12:30 tomorrow'). More subjective probabilities can prompt really interesting and important discussions about likelihood, but students may interpret any conclusions or opinions as having a mathematical underpinning beyond simple informed guesswork. It's also a good idea to get into the habit of writing $P(\text{event})$ from the very beginnings of student journeys into probability. For example, when talking about the probability of getting a 2 on a die, we should write on the board '$P(2) =$'.

We can extend this idea further, in that the sum of *all* possible outcomes is also 1. That is, it is certain that one of the possible outcomes will happen. Using our example of rolling a die, the probability that we get 'a number between 1 and 6' is certain, i.e.:

$$P(\text{number between 1 and 6}) = 1$$

Recall that the probability of rolling a specific number between 1 and 6 was $\frac{1}{6}$, and we can see that all these outcomes do in fact sum to equal 1:

$$\frac{1}{6} + \frac{1}{6} + \frac{1}{6} + \frac{1}{6} + \frac{1}{6} + \frac{1}{6} = 1$$

Therefore, with a bit of maths, we can find the probability of an event *not* occurring:

$$P(\text{not E}) = 1 - P(\text{E})$$

Again, this hasn't come out of nowhere. If we continue with our original die, recall that the probability of rolling a 4 was $\frac{1}{6}$, therefore the probability of *not* rolling a 4, is the probability of rolling anything else. There are 5 other possibilities, all of which have a probability of $\frac{1}{6}$ that they occur, so:

$$\frac{1}{6} + \frac{1}{6} + \frac{1}{6} + \frac{1}{6} + \frac{1}{6} = \frac{5}{6}$$

Which is the same as $1 - \frac{1}{6}$.

Probabilities involving a combination of events

Probabilities get a little more complicated when we start to look at the occurrence of two or more events.

Consider the following example:

Joe rolls a fair die twice, what is the probability that he rolls two even numbers?

We can calculate the probability of rolling an even number in both instances. There are three even numbers out of six possible outcomes on our first roll, so that's $\frac{1}{2}$, and the second roll we have the same again, so that's also $\frac{1}{2}$.

But that doesn't tell us the probability overall of rolling two even numbers. What do we *do* with these two probabilities we've identified? If we add them, we get '1'. But that doesn't make sense. The probability of rolling two even numbers is intuitively *not* certain (i.e. 1).

Instead then, we multiply them together. Therefore, the probability of rolling two consecutive even numbers is $\frac{1}{2} \times \frac{1}{2} = \frac{1}{4}$.

If we look at a sample space diagram, this becomes even more intuitive (Table 8.8).

Table 8.8   Sample space diagram for rolling consecutive numbers

Odd	Even
Odd	Odd
Even	Even
Even	Odd

Note, we could have made a sample space diagram from all possible number outcomes, but in essence we're not interested in *what* number we get, just whether it's odd or even. Both approaches result in the same conclusion – that the probability of getting two even numbers consecutively when rolling a die is $\frac{1}{4}$. When outcomes are unaffected by one another, such as these, we refer to them as **independent** events. As such, we are discussing the probability of independent events.

Our general formula for so-called 'and' outcomes for independent events is:

$$P(A \text{ and } B) = P(A) \times P(B)$$

In simple terms, this means the probability of two events, A and B both occurring, is equal to the probability of event A occurring, multiplied by the probability of event B occurring.

The other rule about independent events is:

$$P(A \text{ or } B) = P(A) + P(B)$$

We've already stumbled across this rule before, when we logically deduced why:

$$P(\text{not } E) = 1 - P(E)$$

To reiterate:

$$P(\text{not } 4) = 1 - P(4) = \frac{5}{6} = \frac{1}{6} + \frac{1}{6} + \frac{1}{6} + \frac{1}{6} + \frac{1}{6}$$

Notice that $P(\text{not } 4) = P(1,2,3,5, \text{or } 6)$.

There are also times when we study the probability of **dependent** events, in other words, when the outcome of the first event affects the outcome of the second.

The probability of an event, A, *given that another event, B, has occurred* is known as conditional probability.

Conditional probability

We can write this as $P(A|B)$.

This is usually played out as drawing cards or objects from bags *without replacement*. Hence, the denominator of each fractional probability would differ:

Find the probability that two cards drawn from a deck, *without replacement*, are both Aces.

In this example, once a card is drawn, the number of cards remaining has changed. Furthermore, once an Ace is drawn, the number of Aces remaining has also changed:

$$\frac{4}{52} \times \frac{3}{51} = \frac{12}{2652} = \frac{1}{221}$$

It's a good idea to refer back to number lines or likelihood scales even at this more advanced level, so that students can truly appreciate just how unlikely $\frac{1}{221}$ is (Figure 8.26).

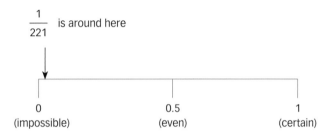

Figure 8.26 The probability of an event can be contextualised on a likelihood scale

Venn diagrams

A common organisational tool used in probability (and other areas of mathematics, such as finding the highest common factor of two numbers) is the Venn diagram. Named after their creator, Yorkshire born John Venn, they consist of a number of intersecting shapes (usually circles) such that all possible combinations are displayed (e.g. Figure 8.27).

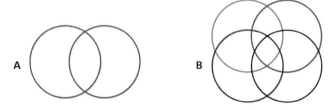

Figure 8.27 A Venn diagram (left) and an Euler diagram (right)

In the figure, A is a Venn diagram; however, B is not, as there is no section that comprises only the blue and green circle, or the red and black circle. The second diagram is known as an Euler diagram, which is very similar, and predates the Venn diagram. Euler diagrams also depict the relationship between sets; however, they are not restricted to the need to explicitly show every possible combination of groupings, regardless of whether there is a relationship there or not. Figure 8.28 highlights the difference for sets {a,b}, {b,c} and {d}.

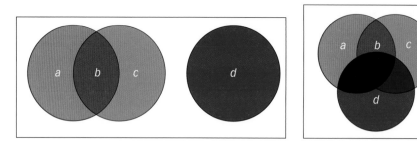

Figure 8.28 The difference between an Euler diagram (left) and a Venn diagram (right)

Set notation for Venn diagrams is the same as for probability theory (Figure 8.29).

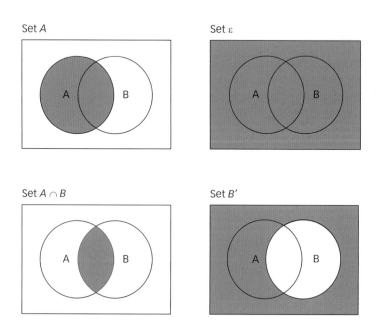

Yes, But Why? Teaching for Understanding in Mathematics

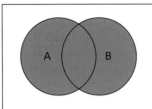

Set $A \cup B$

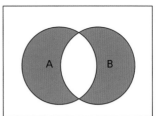

Set $A \cup B - A \cap B$

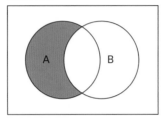

Set $A \cap B'$

Figure 8.29   Set notation and corresponding Venn diagrams

Curious facts about probabilities and statistics

- The probability of two players on a football pitch sharing a birthday is more than 1/2 (assuming 11 players each, and a referee). You can prove it by finding the probability of players not having the same birthday:

$$\frac{365}{365} \times \frac{364}{365} \times \frac{363}{365} \times \ldots \times \frac{343}{365} = 0.491 (3dp)$$

Hence, the probability that two people *do* share a birthday is approximately:

$$1 - 0.491 = 0.509 = 50.9\%$$

(Continued)

- John Venn was the grandchild of John Venn, and had a son called John Venn who became the Vice Chancellor of Cambridge University.
- The Monty Hall Problem is a famous example of a counter-intuitive probability conundrum:

  o Imagine you are on a game show. Three closed doors are presented to you. Behind one is a prize. The remaining doors have goats behind them. The host allows you to pick a door. He opens one you didn't choose, to reveal a goat. You then have the opportunity to change your mind about your own door. If you change your mind and swap doors, you are more likely to win the prize.

- The concept of a median was developed in 1599 by Edward Wright, who wanted to determine the variation in compass readings in navigation.
- The word average derives from the distribution of financial losses to owners of damaged wooden boats. The word stems from the French *avarie* meaning 'damage to ship'.
- Sicherman dice are a pair of dice that have the exact same probability of totalling 2–12 as a pair of normal dice, but their faces are: {1, 2, 2, 3, 3, 4} and {1, 3, 4, 5, 6, 8}. You can prove this yourself using a sample space diagram (Table 8.9).

Table 8.9 A sample space diagram of the outcomes for Sicherman dice

+	1	2	2	3	3	4
1	2	3	3	4	4	5
3	4	5	5	6	6	7
4	5	6	6	7	7	8
5	6	7	7	8	8	9
6	7	8	8	9	9	10
8	9	10	10	11	11	12

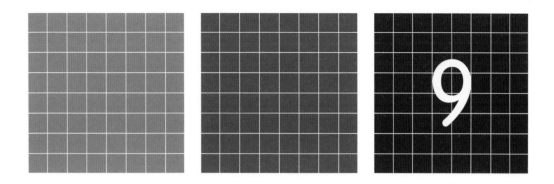

Functions and Linear Graphs

We have already looked at graphs and charts in Chapter 8, and algebraic equations in Chapter 7, but now it's time to delve a little deeper and look at graphing equations. We'll start with a look at the concept behind coordinates themselves, before moving onto what we mean by linear *equations*.

Cartesian coordinates

Two-dimensional coordinates are a set of numbers that describe a point on a plane. A coordinate pair corresponds to the horizontal (x) and vertical (y) distance from the **origin (0,0)** (Figure 9.1).

The origin is simply a reference point where the x-axis and y-axis intersect. The y coordinate is also known as the **ordinate**, whilst the x coordinate is also known as the **abscissa** (meaning the cut-off point of a line).

We can move from two-dimensional coordinates to three dimensions by simply adding a third parameter: (x, y, z); in fact, we can have as many as we want, but after three dimensions we venture into the realm of theoretical planes rather than real ones.

The name Cartesian is derived from the creator of the system, 17th-Century French mathematician René Descartes (although the system was independently created by Pierre de Fermat as well). The Cartesian coordinate system was revolutionary when it was conceived, as it seamlessly fused both algebra and geometry.

SAGE would like to acknowledge that most figures in this chapter were created with GeoGebra (www.geogebra.org).

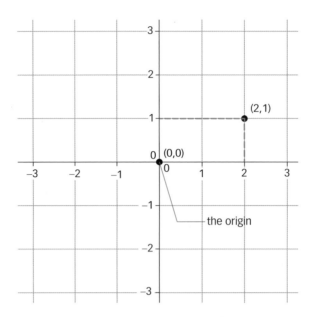

Figure 9.1 Coordinates are horizontal and vertical distances from the origin

Linear equations

A plotted *linear* equation will always be a straight line. This is fairly easy to remember, as the term *linear* literally means 'arranged in a straight line'. It's a very simple relationship between two variables: x and y. The line does not bend or change angle at any point – it just keeps going straight.

Why does a linear equation never change angle?

The line created by an equation is really an infinite set of coordinates, with each single coordinate dictated *by* the equation. The simplest example is the equation $y = x$. It's very easy to plot a single pair of coordinates for this equation. Just take any value of x or y (from – infinity to + infinity… Let's start with $x = 1$):

$$x = 1$$

Now our equation dictates that y is equal to x, therefore, y must *also* be 1.

So there we have it, our first coordinate is (1,1). It's not overly exciting yet, but there's still time.

But one coordinate simply isn't enough. We can't draw a straight line from one coordinate, can we? Well, actually we can, but it could go in any direction at all (within two dimensions!), and the line will almost certainly not match the equation $y = x$. So we need at least *two* coordinates to get the line $y = x$ drawn. Let's go for $(-3,-3)$ just to delve into negative coordinates for fun.

It is plotted in Figure 9.2.

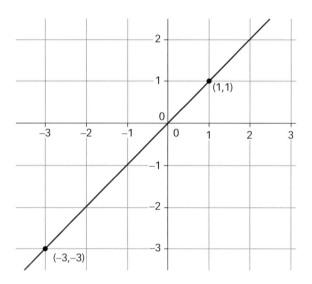

Figure 9.2 A linear graph can be drawn from a minimum of two coordinates

Our line is a set of infinite coordinates! Pick any point on that line, and you'll have an x coordinate, and an identical y coordinate, due to the equation being $y = x$. The relationship never changes, because the equation never changes, and so the line never changes angle. Note that in two dimensions, we have four **quadrants**, which are the four areas surrounding the origin $(x, y), (-x, y)(-x, -y), (x, -y)$.

In three dimensions, we have eight **octants**.

Take a look at Figure 9.3. Is this a **linear graph**?

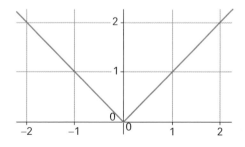

Figure 9.3 An example of a piecewise linear graph

Well, it's straight, at least in separate segments. Sadly, it doesn't fit into our linear graph club, because it's not entirely a single straight line. Instead, this type of graph is referred to as a **piecewise linear graph**. In other words, each segment (piece) is linear.

We're almost finished with $y = x$. Figure 9.4 shows the plotted graph of $y = -x$ (in red) alongside $y = x$ (in green).

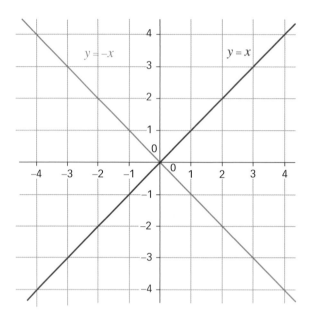

Figure 9.4   The plotted graphs of $y = x$ and $y = -x$

But why does using $-x$ seem to rotate the line around by 90°?

How are reflections created in linear graphs?

We should probably ascertain where that reflection lies before we go any further. Is it across the x-axis or the y-axis? It seems to be *both* in our example. Let's try $y = x + 1$ (green) and $y = -x + 1$ (red) instead (Figure 9.5). (We'll come back to the other one later.)

You can see that the line is clearly reflected *across the y-axis* in this example. Curious. Why does that happen?

Well it becomes clear when we go back to looking at the coordinates for each equation, and draw from our knowledge of negative numbers.

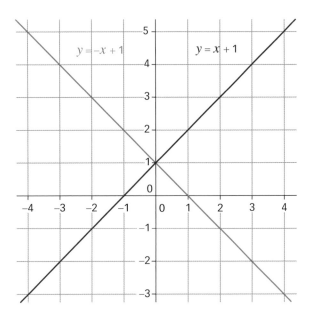

Figure 9.5   The plotted graphs of $y = x+1$ and $y = -x+1$

For $y = x + 1$, we have coordinates such as (2,3). But for $y = -x + 1$, the same y coordinate (3) would be paired with $x = -2$, in other words (−2,3) (Figure 9.6).

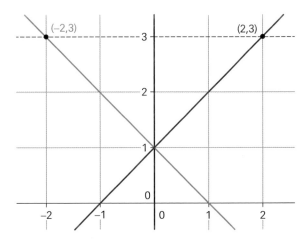

Figure 9.6   Reflected coordinates across the y-axis

Notice that for any shared y coordinate, the two equations will produce corresponding x coordinates that are the positive/negative opposites of one another. When plotted on a pair of axes, this will place the x coordinate equidistant from the y-axis, albeit on the 'other side', i.e. 2 to the right of the y-axis for (2,3) and 2 to the left of the y-axis for (−2,3).

So how can we reflect the line in the x-axis?

Sticking with $y = x + 1$, which is shown in Figure 9.7, if we take the coordinate (0,1) on the line, then a reflection of this coordinate in the x-axis would yield a coordinate of (0,−1). The x intercept of $y = x + 1$ has the coordinate (−1,0), and a reflection in the x-axis would yield the exact same coordinate (because $y = 0$ at this particular point).

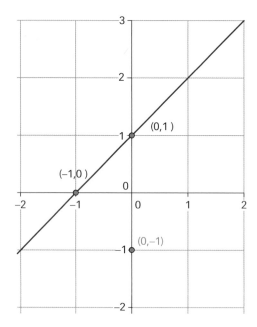

Figure 9.7 Determining the reflection of $y=x+1$ in the x-axis

So now we have two coordinates to find the equation of the *reflection* of $y = x + 1$. We can calculate the equation of the line, but conveniently in this instance our coordinates already give us the x and y intercepts, so we can shortcut straight to the equation, which must be $y = -x - 1$.

Notice that $y = -x - 1$ can be written as $y = -(x + 1)$. So by putting the original equation in brackets, and sticking a negative in front of it, we seem to reflect the line across the x-axis!

Yes, But Why? Teaching for Understanding in Mathematics

Figure 9.8 highlights both cases.

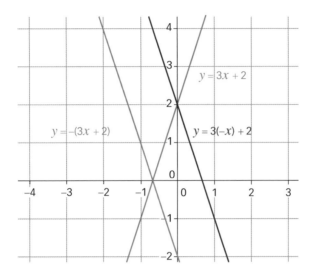

Figure 9.8 Reflections in both the *x*-axis (blue and red) and *y*-axis (red and green)

It turns out that all linear equations are reflected in the *x*-axis by multiplying the original equation by −1 and all linear equations are reflected in the *y*-axis by substituting any instance of *x* with −*x*.

We're clearly in need of some new terminology to represent these relationships mathematically. Let's start looking at **functions**.

What's the difference between an equation and a function?

We have been talking about the equations of lines up to this point. However, the time has come to start using the term **function**. A function differs from an equation in that it is an input/output mechanism rather than a single-value solution. A function matches each *x* value to only one *y* value.

For example, $x + 2 = 10$ is an *equation* because it is only concerned with a single *x* value. Whereas, $y = x + 2$ is an example of a *function* because there is no 'solution' per se here – it is simply a relationship that maps every *x* value to a single *y* value.

But we've been talking about **linear equations** this whole time. Are they really functions? Is there a difference?

What is the difference between a linear equation and a linear function?

We're in danger of getting confused at this point. Rest assured the path ahead is clear. Most linear equations can also be considered to be linear *functions*. However, a few cannot. Our definition of a function has not changed. A function *matches each x value with only one y value*. So $y = 2x$ can be described as a linear equation *and* a linear function. However, $x = 3$ is an example of a linear equation that is *not* a linear function, as the value $x = 3$ has multiple (infinite!) y values (Figure 9.9).

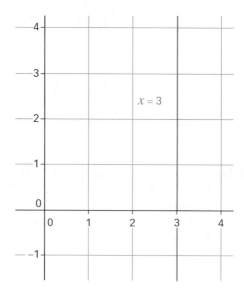

Figure 9.9   The linear equation $x = 3$ is not a linear function

As with most things mathematical, our definition is quite rigorous, and therefore $y = 3$ *can* be described as a linear function because *each x value is matched with only one y value* (Figure 9.10).

It doesn't matter that the y value is the same for each x value. It matters that each x value has only one y value. The difference is subtle, but enough to allow one thing into the club, but not the other. Now some functions have **asymptotes** (a straight line that a curve nears as it tends to infinity – the word means 'not falling together') such as $f(x) = \dfrac{1}{x}$ (Figure 9.11).

Is that a function? There's clearly a value of x (i.e. $x = 0$) that doesn't have an equivalent y value. In order therefore for it to be considered a function, we must give it a **domain**. In other words, a set of numbers for which it *is* a function, and

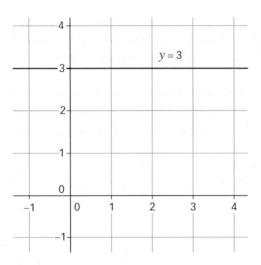

Figure 9.10 The linear equation $y = 3$ is also a linear function

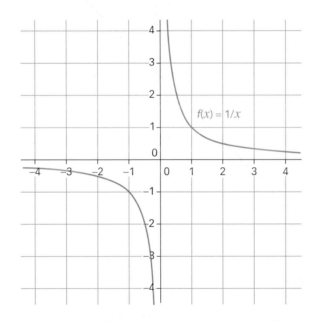

Figure 9.11 The linear equation $y = 1/x$ is only a function within a specified domain

thus *exclude* the values for which it is not. In this case, the domain is $R - \{0\}$ (all the real numbers, except for zero).

Now that we've got functions nicely defined, let's adjust our definition of a reflection in the *y*-axis.

We no longer need to say $y = -$(original equation), we can now simply say $-f(x)$. Furthermore, instead of saying $y = $ (substitute '$-x$' for all instances of 'x' in original equation) we can say $f(-x)$. Phew! In summary then:

$-f(x)$ will reflect $f(x)$ across the x-axis

$f(-x)$ will reflect $f(x)$ across the y-axis

Just to round that off nicely, if we go back to our example of $y = x$ and $y = -x$, where the two lines reflected both in the x-axis *and* the y-axis (Figure 9.4).

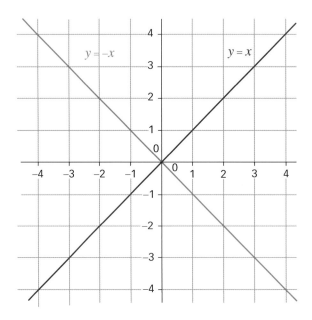

Figure 9.4 The plotted graphs of $y = x$. and $y = -x$

We can now understand why!

If $f(x) = x$

Then $-f(x) = -x$

And $f(-x) = -x$

So $-f(x)$ gives us the same line as $f(-x)$ in this case. Hence, the reflection is in both axes.

And as if we weren't all exhausted enough at this point, there are a whole bunch of other function transformations to consider ...

1. f(ax)

Before we get into this, let's figure out what we mean by $f(ax)$:

$$\text{Let } f(x) = 2x^2 + 5$$

We'll use $a = 3$ for $f(ax)$. In other words, then:

$$f(3x) = 2(3x)^2 + 5$$

So we can say that $f(ax)$ means 'In your equation, replace any instances of x with ax'.

How will $f(3x)$ affect how the function looks? Well, we're essentially saying that whatever inputs we *had* for each value of x in $f(x)$, we're now going to use numbers three times larger instead. So when $x = 5$ for $f(x) = 2x^2 + 5$, originally we'd have $y = 2(5)^2 + 5$, but now we're going to have $y = 2(3 \times 5)^2 + 5$.

The overall effect of this is that the graph will appear narrower, or steeper if it's linear (see Figures 9.12 and 9.13). It's easiest to see why with a small table of values (Table 9.1).

Table 9.1 A table of values

Function	$x = 1$	$x = 2$	$x = 2$
$f(x) = 2x^2 + 5$	$y = 2(1)^2 + 5 = 7$	$y = 2(2)^2 + 5 = 13$	$y = 2(3)^2 + 5 = 23$
$f(3x) = 2(3x)^2 + 5$	$y = 2(3 \times 1)^2 + 5 = 23$	$y = 2(3 \times 2)^2 + 5 = 77$	$y = 2(3 \times 3)^2 + 5 = 167$

The value of y for each x coordinate is much higher for $f(3x)$ than $f(x)$, hence the apparent narrowing towards the y-axis.

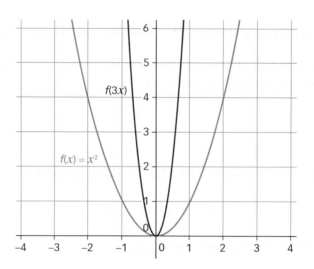

Figure 9.12 $f(3x)$ creates a narrowing effect on a quadratic function

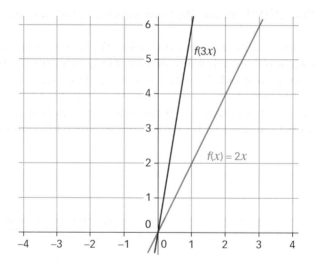

Figure 9.13 $f(3x)$ creates a steepening effect on a linear function

2. af(x)

This simply means $a \times f(x)$. Hence, if $f(x) = x^2 + 2$, and we let $a = 2$, then:

$$af(x) = 2(x^2 + 2) = 2x^2 + 4$$

So it looks narrower (we now have $2x^2$ instead of x^2), and we start further up the y-axis because we're adding 4 to every x value, rather than 2. So the lowest point on the y-axis will be increased by $4 - 2 = 2$ (Figure 9.14).

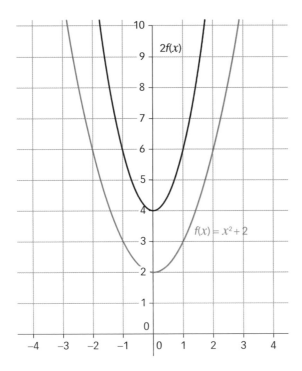

Figure 9.14 $2f(x)$ multiplies $f(x)$ by 2

Note that if our y-intercept is negative, the function will move further *down* the y-axis rather than up.

3. $f(x \pm a)$

This one throws everyone off kilter for fairly obvious reasons. Let's take $f(x + a)$ for example, and use $a = 2$ in this instance. Because we're writing $f(x + 2)$ the logical conclusion would be that our function is going to move towards infinity on the x-axis (in other words, go right by adding 2). Well that seems crystal clear, apart from it *doesn't* go right. It goes *left* (Figure 9.15)!

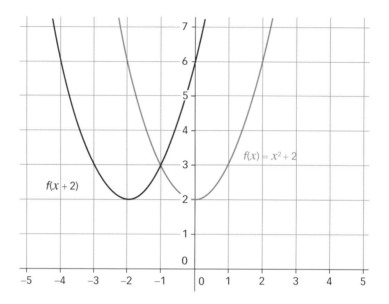

Figure 9.15 $f(x+2)$ moves *f(x)* left by 2

So what's going on there then?

Why does f(x + a) move left instead of right?

Well, once again a look at an example makes things a lot clearer.
Let's take $f(x) = x^2 + 2$ as shown in Figure 9.15.

$$\text{Then } f(x+2) = (x+2)^2 + 2$$

Time for a quick table (Table 9.2).

Table 9.2 Substituting into the function

Function	$x = 1$	$x = 2$	$x = 3$
$f(x) = x^2 + 2$	$y = (1)^2 + 2 = 3$	$y = (2)^2 + 2 = 6$	$y = (3)^2 + 2 = 11$
$f(x+2) = (x+2)^2 + 2$	$y = (1+2)^2 + 2 = 11$	$y = (2+2)^2 + 2 = 18$	$y = (3+2)^2 + 2 = 27$

The tricky part is getting your head around the fact that $f(x+2)$ is referring to the *y values* being greater (we're adding 2 onto each value of *x* that we're pumping into our function, but the *x* value for the coordinate pair isn't changing!). The effect of doing that is that the value of y for each coordinate pair is going to be 2 units further along the plotted function than it would have been originally. From our table, our y value isn't supposed to be 11 until $x = 3$, but because we're racing ahead by putting a value greater than x into our equation, we get there earlier (at $x = 1$ in this case) (Figure 9.16).

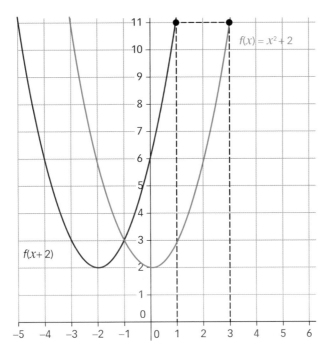

Figure 9.16 $f(x+2)$ reaches y coordinates 2 units earlier than $f(x)$

That also explains why $f(x-a)$ goes right instead of left. We are arriving at the original y values *later* because we're putting a value *less* than x into our equation each time when using $f(x-3)$.

4. $f(x) \pm a$

This one is more intuitive. $f(x)+a$ simply means that I'm going to apply the function to get my y value out, then add a to my y value.

In other words, for $f(x) = x^2 + 2$, if I put $x = 0$ in, I get $y = 2$ out. However, if I use $f(x)+2$, I put $x = 0$ in, I get 2 out *but then add 2*. So my final y value for $x = 0$ is $y = 2 + 2 = 4$.

The effect of this can be seen in Figure 9.17, but put simply, if I'm adding 2 to every y value, then it's going to appear higher up the y-axis by 2.

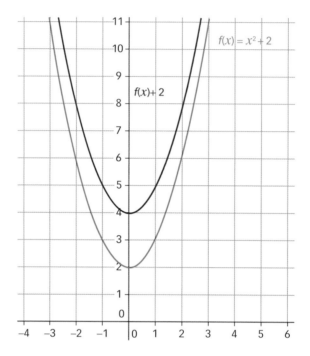

Figure 9.17 $f(x)+2$ moves $f(x)$ 2 units up the y-axis

The same applies for $f(x)-a$: y values will be lower by a for each corresponding x value. Hence, the plotted function will appear lower on the y-axis by a.

Inverse functions

An inverse function has the notation $f^{-1}(x)$ and denotes the mapping of y to x instead of x to y.

For example, if $f(x) = 2x - 1$, then $f^{-1}(x) = \dfrac{x+1}{2}$ because:

$$x = 2y - 1$$
$$2y = x + 1$$
$$y = \frac{x+1}{2}$$

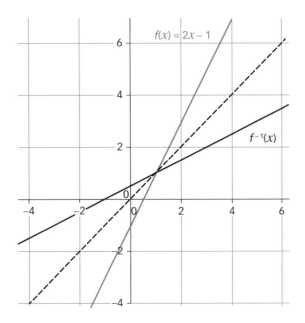

Figure 9.18 $f^{-1}(x)$ reflects $f(x)$ across the line $y = x$

You may notice that all inverse functions are in fact a reflection of the original function in the line $y = x$ (see Figure 9.18).

An inverse function is principally the same as an inverse operation. In other words, one *undoes* the other. For each coordinate pair (a,b) therefore, the inverse function will map to (b,a) – which has the effect of reflecting across $y = x$.

Composite functions

A composite function is a function composed of (surprise!) two or more other functions.

For example, let $f(x) = 3x$ and $g(x) = 2x^2 + 1$.

A composite function could take the form of $f(g(x))$.

What this means is that we're going to apply the function $f(x)$ to the function $g(x)$. We will replace all instances of x in $f(x)$ with $2x^2 + 1$:

$$g(x) = 2x^2 + 1$$

$$f(x) = 3x$$

$$f(g(x)) = 3(2x^2 + 1)$$

$$f(g(x)) = 6x^2 + 3$$

Similarly, we could create the composite function $g(f(x))$ where we will replace all instances of x in the function $g(x)$ with $3x$:

$$g(f(x)) = 2(3x^2) + 1$$

$$g(f(x)) = 18x^2 + 1$$

We can even create composite functions of a single function:

$$f(x) = 2x^2 + x$$

$$f(f(x)) = 2(2x^2 + x)^2 + (2x^2 + x)$$

$$f(f(x)) = 8x^4 + 8x^3 + 2x^2 + 2x^2 + x$$

$$f(f(x)) = 8x^4 + 8x^3 + 4x^2 + x$$

We don't really need all these confusing brackets either. We can write $f(f(x))$ as $ff(x)$ to make things a little easier.

Why do different types of function take different shapes?

This may seem like an odd question, but have you ever wondered *why* a quadratic function produces a **parabola**? Or *why* a cubic function creates such a strange shape? Let's look at the ways in which a function alters the rate of change, and how that affects the general appearance of our plots.

Linear functions $y = mx + c$

This is a straightforward one (pun intended). Everything changes at the same *rate* proportionately. This results in a nice straight line. No turns, no curves.

Quadratic functions $y = ax^2 + bx + c$

With quadratic functions, the y values for evenly spaced corresponding x values don't ascend or descend linearly – i.e. by the same amount between every iteration. With quadratic equations, the rate at which the y value changes against corresponding x values is referred to as 'quadratic growth'. Quadratic growth creates curvature, and in the case of a quadratic equation, that growth will peak or trough depending on whether we are dealing with ax^2 or $-ax^2$. In both instances, the process of squaring ensures that at some point in the function, the curve will start to pinch to a vertex, then the y values will come back on themselves to create a parabola. This is for two reasons. The first is that as x gets closer to zero, the difference between x and x^2 becomes very small. Furthermore, as x becomes negative, then x^2 will be positive (because of the properties of negative numbers), which is why the curve turns to become a parabola. For example, for a simple case like $y = x^2$:

x	−2	−1	0	1	2
y	4	1	0	1	4

The visual appearance of these y values going back on themselves is that of a parabola. Parabola means 'set side-by-side'.

Cubic functions $y = ax^3 + bx^2 + cx + d$

Note that a cubic equation looks oddly similar to a parabola. In fact, it behaves almost exactly like a parabola, but where a parabola comes back on itself (because of the properties of negative numbers), a cubic function will *not* act in the same way. To clarify, imagine the simple function $f(x) = x^3$.

At $x = 1$, the y value would be $(1)^3$, which is still 1. Now consider $x = -1$. When we *square* this, it becomes positive 1, and hence, the y value here will be the same as when $x = 1$. However, we aren't squaring it. We're *cubing* it. So:

$$(-1)^3 = -1 \times -1 \times -1 = -1$$

Hence, we *don't* get the same value of y as we did when $x = 1$.

That at least explains simple cases. But what about the function $f(x) = x^3 - 2x^2$ in Figure 9.19? Why does that start to come back on itself then change its mind?

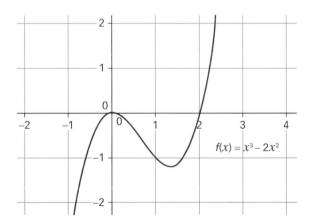

Figure 9.19 Cubic functions can change direction several times

The key here is that the $\left(-2x^2\right)$ part of the equation is bringing the value of y *lower* when x is positive, until the value of x is sufficiently large enough to make $x^3 > 2x^2$.

x^3 will always trump $-ax^2$, once the coefficient a is less than the value of x.

Exponential functions $y = k^x$

Exponential functions grow *exponentially*, and are so called because x is the *exponent* within the function (recall that exponent is a synonym of *power* and *index number*). The most common example of exponential growth/decay at GCSE is compound interest in banking.

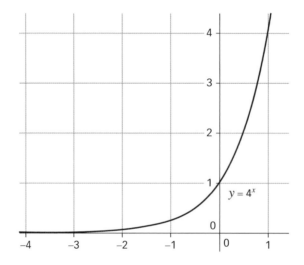

Figure 9.20 Exponential functions get very steep very quickly

Exponential growth clearly 'accelerates' quite quickly (Figure 9.20), which makes sense, as we increase the value of the exponent (x) then the equivalent y value will get very big very quickly. Consider the function $f(x) = 4^x$:

x	1	2	3	4	5	6
$f(x) = 4^x$	$4^1 = 4$	$4^2 = 16$	$4^3 = 64$	$4^4 = 256$	$4^5 = 1024$	$4^6 = 4096$

Similarly $f(x) = 4^{-x}$ gets very small very quickly:

x	1	2	3	4	5	6
$f(x) = 4^{-x}$	$4^{-1} = \dfrac{1}{4}$	$4^{-2} = \dfrac{1}{16}$	$4^{-3} = \dfrac{1}{64}$	$4^{-4} = \dfrac{1}{256}$	$4^{-5} = \dfrac{1}{1024}$	$4^{-6} = \dfrac{1}{4096}$

Gradients of linear graphs

We have described the angles of linear graphs previously, but we should really be talking about the **gradient** of the line. The gradient is the mathematical term for the *slope* of the line. Figure 9.21 shows various lines with different gradients.

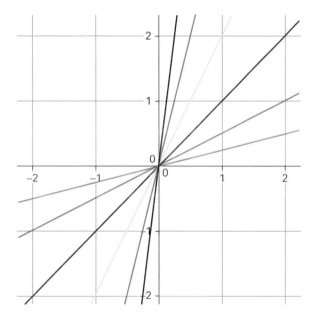

Figure 9.21　The gradient of a line is a measure of its slope

Knowing the gradient of a line helps us predict what it will look like before we even start plotting it. For example, a line with a gradient of 0 will be horizontal, parallel to the x-axis, and a line with gradient equal to 1 will be at a 45° angle to the x-axis.

Extending this logic, you can see why linear functions with the *same* gradient (which can be identified by the coefficient of x) will be *parallel* when plotted (Figure 9.22).

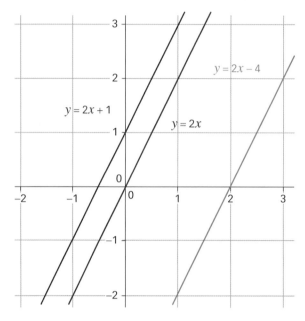

Figure 9.22   The gradient is m in $y = mx + c$

Here's a puzzler though: the gradient of a line parallel to the y-axis is *undefined*. Figure 9.23 is the graph of $x = 3$.

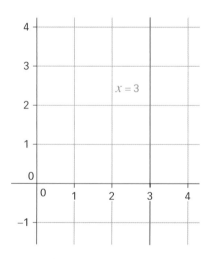

Figure 9.23   What is the gradient of $x = 3$?

Yes, But Why? Teaching for Understanding in Mathematics

Why is the gradient of a line parallel to the *y*-axis undefined?

To understand why the gradient for any equation of the form $x = a$ (where a is a number, not a variable), we first need to appreciate how the gradient of a line is calculated. The equation for the gradient of a line is $m = \dfrac{y_2 - y_1}{x_2 - x_1}$ (there are other variations). Straightforward enough, until you have either a line parallel with the *x*-axis or a line parallel with the *y*-axis. In these two cases, one of our numbers to put into our equation will be zero.

Consider the line $y = 3$ (Figure 9.24).

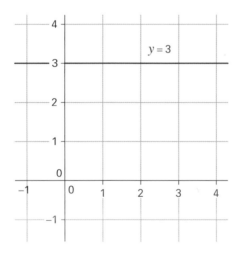

Figure 9.24 What is the gradient of $y = 3$?

Let us take two coordinates to work with, say (1,3) and (4,3).

Substitute them into our equation $m = \dfrac{y_2 - y_1}{x_2 - x_1}$ and we get: $\dfrac{3-3}{3-4} = 0$. Hence, the gradient of this line is *zero*.

You're probably figuring the next one out already. Going back to our previous example, the line $x = 3$, again we can take two coordinates on the line, say (3,5) and (3,10), and put them into the same equation to find the gradient:

$$m = \left(\frac{5 - 10}{3 - 3} \right) = \dots$$

Oh. We seem to be dividing by zero. If you recall from Chapter 1, dividing by zero simply isn't done in maths. Hence, this time the gradient is 'undefined'. Incidentally, if you're wondering what the maximum value for a gradient is (seeing as 0 is horizontal, and 1 is 45°), you may be initially surprised to know there isn't one!

There is no reason why you can't have a line of equation $y = 999999x$, for example (the gradient of which, would be 999999). Lines such as this become painfully close to vertical, but never quite get there. To the naked eye, there is very, very little difference in the slope of a line once you pass a gradient of 100 or so.

Of course, you can spot the gradient and y-intercept of a line quite easily once you know the formula $y = mx + c$. But where did that come from?

Why is m the gradient, and c the y-intercept in $y = mx + c$?

This can be shown with a single handy diagram (Figure 9.25).

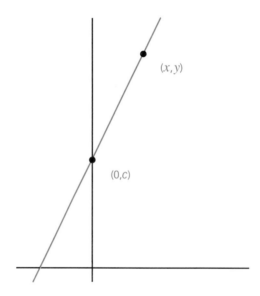

Figure 9.25 Deriving the formula $y = mx + c$

Let m be the gradient of the line, then:

$$m = \frac{y - c}{x - 0}$$

$$mx = y - c$$

$$y = mx + c$$

Yes, But Why? Teaching for Understanding in Mathematics

You might be wondering why we don't just use angles to describe the slope of a line, but imagine the inconvenience of determining an angle of a line from a given equation. You'd have to plot a pair of points, draw a right-angled triangle and start some trigonometry. Nobody has time for that!

However, we can use triangles to help us find the general formula for perpendicular lines.

Perpendicular lines

The way to identify or create equations of perpendicular lines is that the gradient of one line must be the **negative reciprocal** of the other. Put simply, this means:

$$y = mx + c$$

$$y = \left(-\frac{1}{m}\right)x + d$$

These formulae are generalisations of a pair of perpendicular lines ($m \neq 0$). Knowing, and knowing *why* are two different things, so let's prove that it's true.

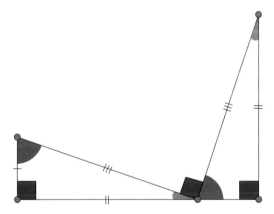

Figure 9.26 Creating similar triangles with two perpendicular lines

Study Figure 9.26. It should become clear that the two triangles are congruent, and that the red, blue and green angles sum to 180°, hence the two hypotenuses are **perpendicular** to each other. Now, if we map this diagram onto a coordinate grid (Figure 9.27):

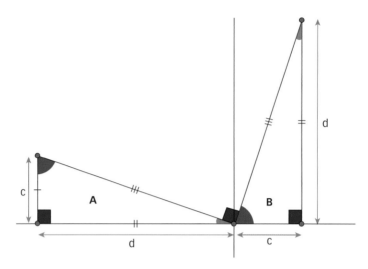

Figure 9.27 The negative reciprocal of the gradient of a line is the gradient of a perpendicular line

the gradient of the hypotenuse of triangle B is $\dfrac{d}{c}$, and the gradient of the hypotenuse of triangle A is $-\dfrac{c}{d}$ (Figure 9.28).

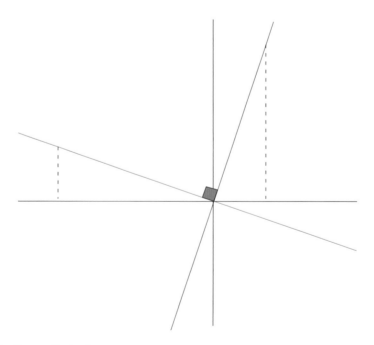

Figure 9.28 Perpendicular lines

Yes, But Why? Teaching for Understanding in Mathematics

Cast your mind back to the beginning of the chapter. We pondered why $y = x$ looked like a 90° rotation of $y = -x$. You can see now just from their equations that they are indeed perpendicular lines, and that the equation $y = -x$ can be rewritten as $y = -\frac{1}{1}x$, hence the gradient is the negative reciprocal of $y = x$.

Finding intercepts

Intercepts are simply the points within a plotted function where it intercepts (touches, or crosses through) the x-axis or the y-axis. Linear graphs can have an x-intercept, a y-intercept or (usually) both (Figure 9.29).

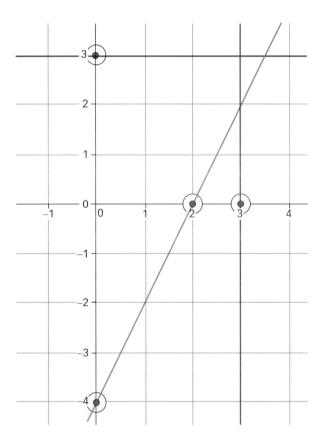

Figure 9.29 Linear graphs can have either or both of an x- and y-intercept

Finding the y-intercept is straightforward, it's simply c in the equation $y = mx + c$.

Finding the x-intercept is also relatively simple, we just substitute $y = 0$ into the function, e.g. $y = 2x + 2$ has an x-intercept when:

$$0 = 2x + 2$$
$$2x = -2$$
$$x = -1$$

so the x-intercept is at $(-1, 0)$.

Quadratic functions, however, can have zero, one or two x-intercepts (Figure 9.30).

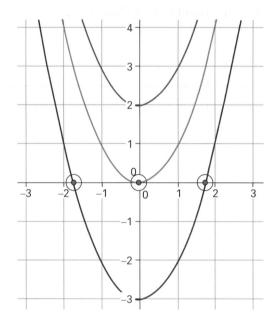

Figure 9.30   Quadratic graphs can have zero, one or two x-intercepts

For quadratics it is a little trickier to find the x-intercepts from a function's equation, but the same principle applies.

$$y = ax^2 + bx + c$$

c is still the y-intercept, and putting y equal to zero will find the roots of x (the x-intercepts) – *if they exist!* This will of course require solving a quadratic equation, by, for example, using the quadratic formula, factorising or completing the square.

Yes, But Why? Teaching for Understanding in Mathematics

In fact we can be even smarter, and find how many solutions exist by looking at a specific part of the quadratic equation referred to as the *discriminant*.

$$x = \frac{-b \pm \sqrt{b^2 - 4ac}}{2a}$$

Specifically, if:

$b^2 - 4ac = 0$ there is one solution (therefore one x-intercept)

$b^2 - 4ac > 0$ there are two solutions (therefore two x-intercepts)

$b^2 - 4ac < 0$ there are no solutions (therefore zero x-intercepts)

Why does that work?

Let's look at each case in turn:

Case 1

$$b^2 - 4ac = 0$$

If this is true, then the quadratic formula will become:

$$x = \frac{-b \pm 0}{2a} = \frac{-b}{2a}$$

Which will only yield one solution.

Case 2

$$b^2 - 4ac > 0$$

If this is true, then the quadratic formula will produce two solutions for

$$x = \frac{-b \pm \sqrt{b^2 - 4ac}}{2a}$$

Because we get two solutions for any square root of a positive number (as indicated by the presence of the $\pm$ symbol in the equation).

Case 3

$$b^2 - 4ac < 0$$

If this is true, then we cannot take a square root of a negative number (without using complex numbers, which we're not going to do), hence there are no *real* solutions.

Finding the turning point (vertex) of a quadratic

There are several ways to determine the turning point (vertex) of a quadratic function. The first combines our knowledge of completing the square, and function transformations.

We need to first appreciate that $y = x^2$ has a vertex at (0,0) (Figure 9.31).

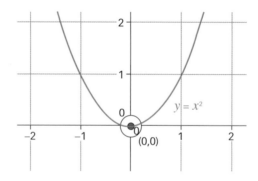

Figure 9.31 $y = x^2$ has a turning point at (0,0)

Let's look now at a more complicated example. We'll use $y = x^2 + 6x + 5$ as our example. By completing the square, I can rewrite that as $y = (x+3)^2 - 4$.

Using our knowledge of transformations, then the vertex must have moved *left 3* (the '+3' bit) and *down 4* (the '–4' bit) from the origin so the vertex for $y = x^2 + 6x + 5$ is the point (0–3,0–4) = (–3,–4) (Figure 9.32).

The process works for any quadratic equation, no matter how complicated:

$$y = 3x^2 + 18x + 10$$

Complete the square:

$$y = 3(x+3)^2 - 17$$

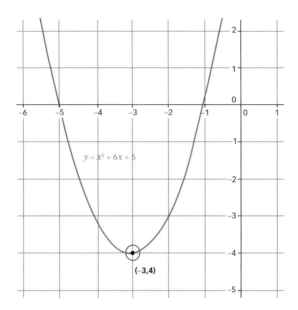

Figure 9.32 $y=x^2+6x+5$ has a turning point at $(-3,4)$

So the vertex is a transformation of $(0,0)$ left 3, and down 17. It must be at $(-3,-17)$ (Figure 9.33).

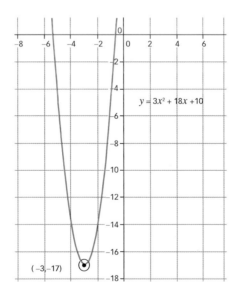

Figure 9.33 $y=3x^2+18x+10$ has a turning point at $(-3,-17)$

But there's an even more impressive way to do it than that!

Using symmetry to determine turning points

Appreciate that all parabolas have a line of symmetry about the vertex (Figure 9.34).

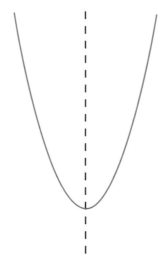

Figure 9.34   Quadratics have a line of symmetry

By factorising the first two terms of a quadratic function (i.e. $ax^2 + bx$) we can find two symmetrical points on the curve. Finding the midpoint of these two coordinates will find the x value of the turning point of the parabola. Plug that into your function to get the corresponding y value, and hey presto, you have the coordinates of your turning point. Let's do that then:

$$y = 3x^2 + 9x + 5$$

Factorise the first two parts of the equation:

$$y = 3x(x + 3) + 5$$

$y = 5$ when $x = -3$ and also when $x = 0$, hence we have two symmetrical points on our curve, namely $(-3, 5)$ and $(0, 5)$. We also know our curve is 'U-shaped' as we have ax^2 rather than $-ax^2$.

As a diagram then, we have Figure 9.35.

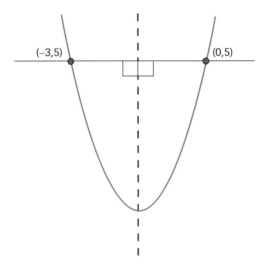

Figure 9.35 Finding the midpoint of two coordinates with the same *y* value

We don't know yet what the depth of the curve is between the two coordinates; however, we can calculate that the x coordinate must be midway between -3 and 0, therefore $x = -1.5$.

Substitute that into $y = 3x^2 + 9x + 5$:

$$y = 3(-1.5)^2 + 9(-1.5) + 5$$
$$y = -1.75$$

Therefore, the coordinates of the turning point of $y = 3x^2 + 9x + 5$ are $(-1.5, -1.75)$.
Very clever!

Vectors

To close this chapter, we'll look at the concept of vectors. A vector is rooted in physics, and is a measure of direction and magnitude (distance). We can 'plot' them to indicate both of these measures. Figure 9.36 shows a vector, $\boldsymbol{a}$.

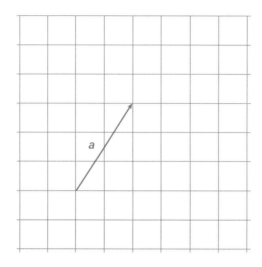

Figure 9.36 The vector $a = \begin{pmatrix} 2 \\ 3 \end{pmatrix}$

You can see it has a direction, and a size (Figure 9.37). We can represent these as a **column vector:**

$$a = \begin{pmatrix} 2 \\ 3 \end{pmatrix}$$

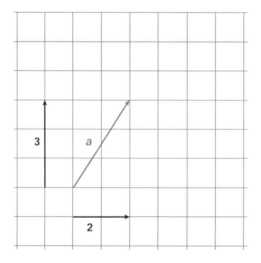

Figure 9.37 The construction of vector $a = \begin{pmatrix} 2 \\ 3 \end{pmatrix}$

You'll notice the general form of a vector is:

$$\binom{x}{y}$$

Be mindful here, as the 'plotting' is a little misleading. We can move that vector wherever we want, and it is still the same vector. It is *not* constrained by coordinates. It is effectively a set of instructions that determine a point relative to a starting point.

When the arrow is in a different direction, we clearly need to change our notation somehow to reflect that. This inevitably leads to us changing whether x or y are positive or negative (Figure 9.38):

$$b = \binom{1}{2} \quad c = \binom{1}{-2} \quad d = \binom{-1}{-2} \quad e = \binom{-1}{2}$$

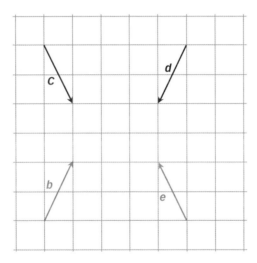

Figure 9.38   Vectors change direction depending on whether their x or y value is positive or negative

In fact we can represent the negative of a vector by multiplying both the x and y values by −1.

For example, take a vector:

$$m = \binom{4}{8}$$

$$-m = \binom{-4}{-8}$$

(Figure 9.39).

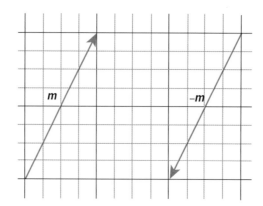

Figure 9.39 A negative vector points in the opposite direction

We can also create **resultant** vectors by adding or subtracting two vectors together. Below is the addition of vectors **f** and **g** (Figure 9.40):

$$\begin{pmatrix} 2 \\ 6 \end{pmatrix} + \begin{pmatrix} 4 \\ -2 \end{pmatrix} = \begin{pmatrix} 2+4 \\ 6+-2 \end{pmatrix} = \begin{pmatrix} 6 \\ 4 \end{pmatrix} = h$$

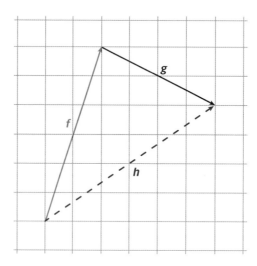

Figure 9.40 The resultant vector **h** is created from the addition of vectors **f** and **g**

The subtraction of vectors can be visualised as follows:

$$a - b = a + (-b) = c$$

For example, take two vectors, a and b such that:

$$a = \begin{pmatrix} 2 \\ 4 \end{pmatrix}$$

$$b = \begin{pmatrix} 3 \\ 1 \end{pmatrix}$$

Let $a - b = c$ (Figure 9.41). Then:

$$c = \begin{pmatrix} -1 \\ 3 \end{pmatrix}$$

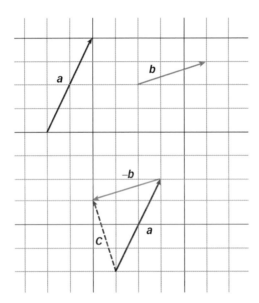

Figure 9.41 The resultant vector c is created from subtracting vector b from vector a

Multiplication of vectors by a scalar quantity

A scalar quantity has magnitude and, unlike vectors, has no associated direction (the measurement of **temperature** is a *scalar* quantity, for example). We can multiply vectors (which have magnitude *and* direction) by a scalar quantity – which will affect the vector's magnitude, but its direction will remain the same:

$$3 \times \begin{pmatrix} 1 \\ 2 \end{pmatrix} = \begin{pmatrix} 3 \times 1 \\ 3 \times 2 \end{pmatrix} = \begin{pmatrix} 3 \\ 6 \end{pmatrix}$$

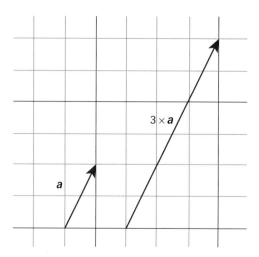

Figure 9.42 Multiplying a vector by a scalar quantity does not change its direction

The **resultant** vector has a different magnitude, but the direction is exactly the same (Figure 9.42).

Some fun functions that create pictures

The heart (Figure 9.43): $x^2 + \left(y - \sqrt{|x|}\right)^2 = 1$

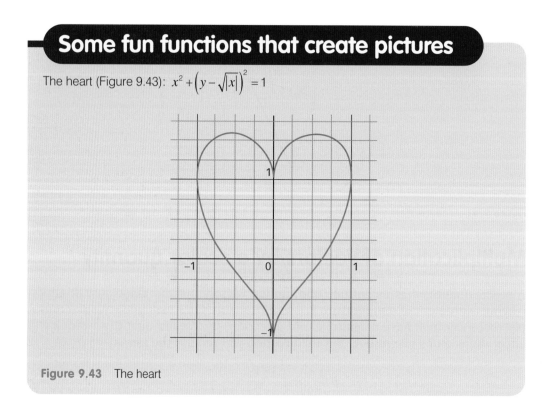

Figure 9.43 The heart

Yes, But Why? Teaching for Understanding in Mathematics

The squircle (Figure 9.44): $x^4 + y^4 = r^4$

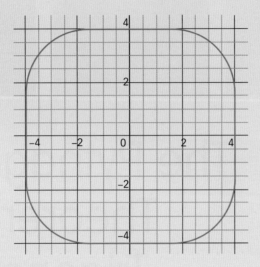

Figure 9.44   The squircle

The quadrifolium (Figure 9.45): $\left(x^2 + y^2\right)^3 = 4x^2y^2$

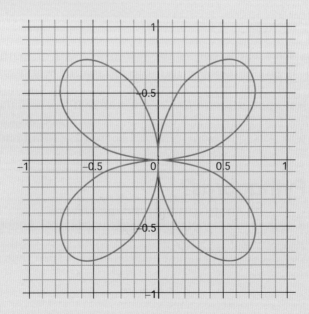

Figure 9.45   The quadrifolium

The Pythagorean Theorem and Trigonometry

The Pythagorean Theorem is one of my favourite areas of mathematics that is taught in school. It gives a glimpse into the fascinating world of mathematics – perhaps more so than most other topics. It also has a rich and interesting history coupled with a clear application to the 'real world' that has benefited both ancient and modern civilisations since its discovery. But when was it discovered? Who discovered it first? Why was Pythagoras afraid of beans? Let's find out.

Who was Pythagoras?

Pythagoras was a Greek mathematician, born on the Island of Samos around 570 BC. He is credited with proving the Pythagorean Theorem, which states that there is a relationship between the sides of all right-angled triangles such that:

$$a^2 + b^2 = c^2$$

Where a and b are the shorter 'legs' of the triangle, and c is the hypotenuse (longest side).

SAGE would like to acknowledge that most figures in this chapter were created with GeoGebra (www.geogebra.org).

Pythagoras is one of the earliest named mathematicians in history. He lived so long ago that very little is actually known about him, and much of what is said about him is disputed. He founded a secretive society, the Pythagoreans, in Croton, Italy, who dedicated their lives to the study of astronomy, philosophy and, of course, mathematics. The Pythagoreans also lived very much as a kind of cult, with a particular way of life and followed a set of rules and conservative principles by which to conduct themselves, known as the golden verses. The knowledge they possessed was largely communicated orally, rather than written, and they attributed all discoveries to Pythagoras, the master of their group. So, in theory, he may have been accredited with things he himself did not discover. We will never know. Legend has it that Pythagoras was afraid of beans. If you just laughed out loud, you're not alone. The legend seems to have basis in two stories: one is that at the time of his death, he was chased to a bean field, and declared he'd rather die than run through the beans – and was promptly killed. The other is that he is often quoted as saying 'Keep your hands from beans'. It all seems very odd, however there is a seemingly more plausible explanation. Beans were used to vote in ancient times – they were placed in large cups as votes for one thing or another, and then spilled out and counted (hence the phrase 'Spill the beans'), so even if the quote is true, it may well have been about abstaining from politics rather than sitting down to eat the ancient equivalent of baked beans on toast. Other sources, however, claim that the banning of the bean was linked to health issues, and yet other sources claim certain beans were considered sacred. And so we get a glimpse of how unreliable all of these stories are, although students will no doubt be fascinated by the idea of a fear of beans leading to the murder of arguably the most famous mathematician of all time.

The Pythagorean Theorem

For any right-angled triangle, with legs a and b, and hypotenuse c:

$$a^2 + b^2 = c^2$$

An arguably more useful (if slightly more complicated) interpretation of the theorem is that given any triangle with vertices A, B and C, the angle C is a right angle if the area of the square of the side c, opposite C, is equal to the sum of the squares of a and b.

This subtle shift moves us away from using the theorem to derive side lengths, and towards the idea of proving a triangle is a right-angled triangle. The latter was (and is) a far more useful (and utilised) application of the theorem when used in agriculture, architecture and engineering.

Incidentally, the word hypotenuse is derived from the Greek *hypoteinousa* meaning 'supporting line'.

Let's look at one of the most popular interpretations of the theorem (Figure 10.1).

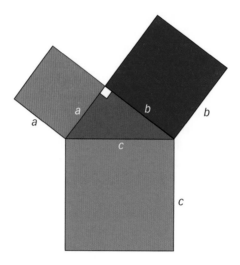

Figure 10.1　The 'Bride's Chair' diagram

This is often referred to as the 'Bride's Chair' proof. Curiously, the diagram alone isn't a proof at all. Furthermore, it's based on a proof that came *after* the one accredited to Pythagoras. This proof is attributed to Euclid, and looks more accurately like Figure 10.2.

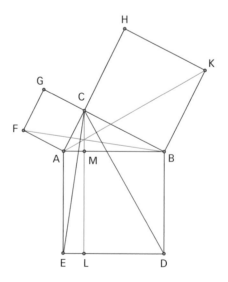

Figure 10.2　Euclid's Pythagorean proof

If we compare the two triangles ACE and AFB (shown in Figure 10.3), they are in fact identical (congruent).

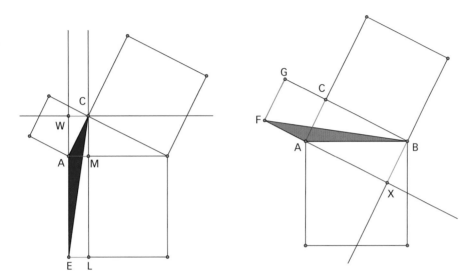

Figure 10.3 The two coloured triangles are congruent

Here's how we know:

Comparing the two diagrams in Figure 10.3, it is clear that AC = AF, AB = AE and ∠CAE = ∠BAF (if you're struggling to visualise that the angles are identical, think of it like this: both are the sum of ∠BAC and 90°). Hence, we have congruent triangles (by demonstrating they have two identical side lengths and enclosing angle, which we usually abbreviate as SAS).

We can also determine that the *area* of these identical triangles is equal to half of the square ACGF, which is *also* equal to the rectangle AELM.

Take a look at the blue triangle in Figure 10.3. Its area is $\frac{1}{2}$ × base × height. If we tilt the diagram (Figure 10.4):

We can see that the base is FA, and the height is XB.

We can also see that XB = AC.

Therefore, we can write the area of the blue triangle as:

$$\frac{1}{2} \times FA \times AC$$

Which is clearly half of the area of the square ACGF.

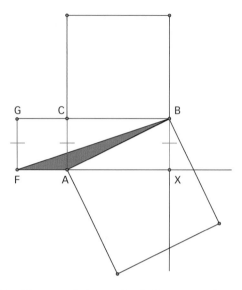

Figure 10.4 The area of the blue triangle is equal to half the area of the square ACFG

Now consider the green triangle, again, tilted (Figure 10.5).

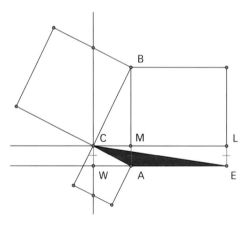

Figure 10.5 The area of the green triangle is equal to half the area of the rectangle AELM

The base is AE, and the height is WC.
WC = AM, so the triangle is half of the area of the rectangle AELM.
Remember the green and blue triangles are congruent, hence we can deduce that:

$$\frac{1}{2} \text{area(ACGF)} = \frac{1}{2} \text{area(AELM)}$$

Therefore, area(ACGF) = area (AELM)

In other words, the blue and green sections in Figure 10.6 are equal in area.

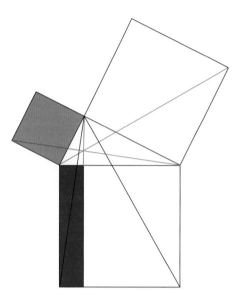

Figure 10.6   The two shaded areas are equal

We can repeat the same process using the other side of the diagram to show that the area of the second square, CBKH, is equal to the remaining section of the square of the hypotenuse, namely the rectangle LDBM (Figure 10.7).

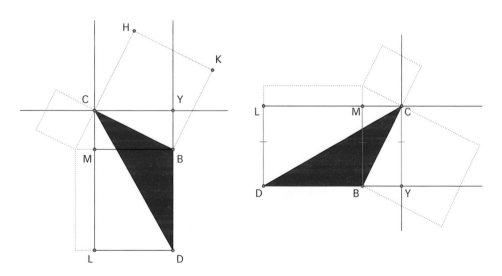

Figure 10.7   The area of the square CBKH is equal to the area of the rectangle LDBM

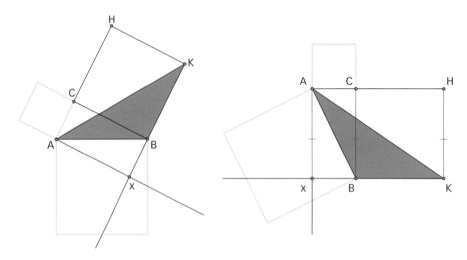

Figure 10.7 (Continued)

When we combine all of this, we can show that the squares of the legs of the right-angled triangle are equal to the square of the hypotenuse (which is the Pythagorean Theorem) (Figure 10.8).

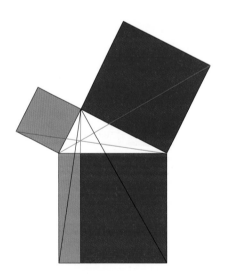

Figure 10.8 Euclid's proof of the Pythagorean Theorem

It's not the simplest of proofs, and hundreds of other proofs are in existence – so why do we use the Bride's Chair diagram so much? It's likely that it's because it is

Yes, But Why? Teaching for Understanding in Mathematics

a simple diagram that nicely demonstrates what we are referring to when we talk about a^2, b^2 and c^2, and what bits are equal to other bits. It's not difficult to assume c^2 is roughly equal to $a^2 + b^2$ using the diagram. Especially if we put in a few extra lines (Figure 10.9).

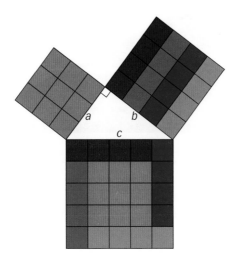

Figure 10.9   An intuitive visual explanation of the Pythagorean Theorem

For those looking for simpler proofs, here are a few of my favourites, which require no additional skills to understand beyond those we teach in the curriculum:

- Proof by dissection (Figure 10.10)

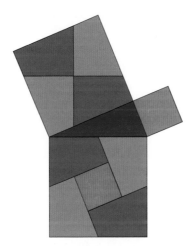

Figure 10.10   A proof by dissection by Henry Perigal

- Proof by similar triangles (Figure 10.11)

Figure 10.11   A proof using similar triangles

Here we have three similar triangles (you may be thinking there's only two, but ABC is one as well!).

As they are all similar,

$$\frac{AB}{AC} = \frac{BD}{BC} = \frac{AD}{AB}$$

Also

$$\frac{BC}{AC} = \frac{BD}{AB} = \frac{DC}{BC}$$

$$\text{Using } \frac{AB}{AC} = \frac{AD}{AB}$$

We can multiply everything by $(AC \times AB)$:

$$(AB)^2 = AC \times AD$$

Now using

$$\frac{BC}{AC} = \frac{DC}{BC}$$

We can multiply everything by $(\text{AC} \times \text{BC})$:

$$(\text{BC})^2 = \text{AC} \times \text{DC}$$

If we add those two expressions together, then:

$$(\text{AB})^2 + (\text{BC})^2 = \text{AC} \times \text{AD} + \text{AC} \times \text{DC}$$
$$(\text{AB})^2 + (\text{BC})^2 = \text{AC}(\text{AD} + \text{DC})$$

Look back at the diagram to remind yourself that $\text{AC} = \text{AD} + \text{DC}$.
Hence:

$$(\text{AB})^2 + (\text{BC})^2 = (\text{AC})^2$$

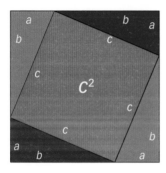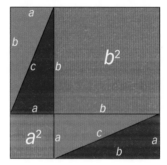

Figure 10.12 The proof attributed to Pythagoras

To finish, it seems only fair to include the proof attributed to Pythagoras (Figure 10.12).

You can see from both diagrams, that the outline square has an area of $(a+b)^2$.

In the left diagram, the space not occupied by the triangles is c^2 and, whilst we've rearranged the triangles in the diagram on the right, the total area remains the same, and the space not occupied by the triangles is $a^2 + b^2$. We can therefore deduce that $c^2 = a^2 + b^2$.

In fact, if you think carefully about the construction of $a^2 + b^2 = c^2$, you may come to realise that you don't even need squares at all. You just need similar shapes (Figure 10.13).

As long as each shape is similar, and shares a side with the sides of the original triangle, it always works because any shape has an area dependent on the square of any line segment *of* that shape.

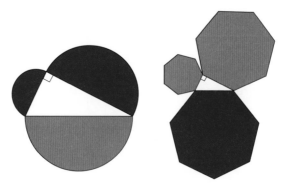

Figure 10.13   The principle behind the Pythagorean Theorem remains true as long as each shape is similar.

Earliest known uses of the Pythagorean Theorem

Leaving the name 'Pythagorean Theorem' behind for a moment, the applications and understanding of the relationship between the sides of a right-angled triangle were in fact known to other civilisations long before Pythagoras put his name to it with a definitive proof.

Versions of it can be found in ancient Chinese, Babylonian, Egyptian and Indian artefacts. However, the first formalised general proof of the theorem is attributed to Pythagoras, and so it is his name that continues to be associated with it.

Pythagoras and the equation of a circle

We also use the Pythagorean Theorem to prove the equation of a circle with centre (0,0) in coordinate geometry (Figure 10.14). The formula is:

$$x^2 + y^2 = r^2$$

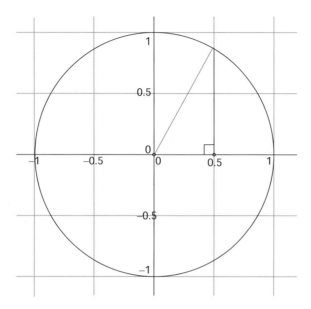

Figure 10.14   The Pythagorean Theorem explains the formula for a circle in coordinate geometry

You can see that the radius at any single point is calculated using the x and y coordinates as they form a right-angled triangle, with the radius as the hypotenuse. The more general formula, $(x-a)^2 + (y-b)^2 = r^2$ for circles without centre (0,0), simply translates the circle back to the origin.

Trigonometry

The word trigonometry literally means 'triangle measurement'. More specifically, trigonometry is concerned with the measure of the internal angles of triangles, and the calculation of the lengths of their sides. The mnemonic SOHCAHTOA (Sin(θ) = opposite divided by hypotenuse, Cos(θ) = adjacent divided by hypotenuse and Tan(θ) = opposite divided by adjacent) is one of the few elements of mathematics that seems to stay with students into adulthood, etched into memory. But what *are* the trigonometric functions sine, cosine and tan? What do they mean and where do they come from? How are they related to one another? To appreciate the origins of these fundamental elements of trigonometry, we should first talk a little about an Indian mathematician called Aryabhata.

Aryabhata was around in the 5th Century AD, and was the first mathematician to tabulate the values of half-chords of circles, which later became known as the Table of Sines. This table, included within his epic work known as the *Aryabhatiya* still exists today.

Now, it may seem strange that anyone would want to create a table of half-chords, but in ancient times, mathematicians used a variety of trigonometric tables as reference books, which were used to estimate distances that cannot be measured directly (using properties of similar triangles). For example, one could simply scale up the proportions of a triangle in the correct book, and one would be able to calculate accurately the lengths of sides required for a building of similar proportions.

One of those books was a book of chords, which make handy triangles (Figure 10.15).

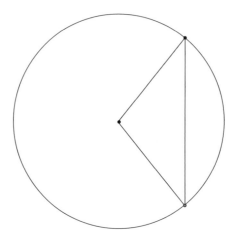

Figure 10.15 Chords form an isosceles triangle when their end points are joined back to the centre of the circle

Aryabhata went one step further with his table, based on the half-chord (Figure 10.16).

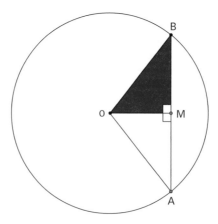

Figure 10.16 Aryabhata created a table of half-chords

Now we have a right-angled triangle (green) instead of an isosceles triangle. So if we imagine dragging point B around the circle, at every point, ∠MOB is changing, as are the lengths OM and MB. However, BO will forever be the radius of the circle, and will stay fixed in length (Figure 10.17).

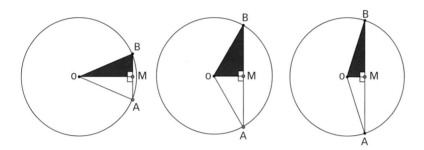

Figure 10.17 Moving the points A and B around the circumference will not affect the line BO which is a radius

Moving forward, if we take this idea of half-chords, and apply it to the unit circle, of which the radius is conveniently 1, then everything gets easier. There is no longer a need to think about ratios between the length of the hypotenuse and the side opposite the angle, as the hypotenuse is simply 1. If we also place the unit circle on a coordinate grid with its centre at the origin (Figure 10.18), you might notice that the 'sine' value for any half-chord (the red line) triangle – the base of which lies along the x-axis – is in fact the y coordinate of where the hypotenuse (radius) touches the edge of the circle (point A in Fig. 10.18). Our half chord is at an angle 36.87° (2 d.p.), hence:

$$\sin(36.87°) \approx 0.6$$

(It's not quite exact, because the angle is rounded to two decimal places.)

Furthermore, whilst the hypotenuse of any of these half-chord triangles never changes (it's always the radius, so it's always 1 in a unit circle), there is a second length that is always changing – the horizontal side of the triangle in line with the x-axis. This length is in fact the complementary sine, or cosine value. This length corresponds to the x coordinate where the triangle vertex with an interior angle of 90° sits (point B on the diagram).

Hence:

$$\cos(36.87°) \approx 0.8$$

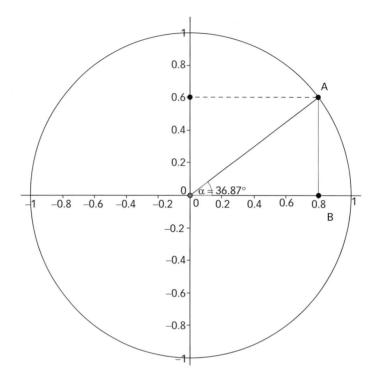

Figure 10.18 A half chord on a unit circle

Why is cosine called the *complement* of sine?

Sine and cosine are intrinsically linked, as the value of cosine for an angle, is exactly the same as the value of sine for the **complementary** angle (Figure 10.19).

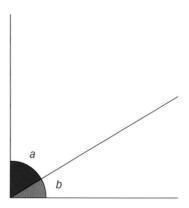

Figure 10.19 Complementary angles

Yes, But Why? Teaching for Understanding in Mathematics

This is perhaps easiest to understand with a visualisation (Figure 10.20).

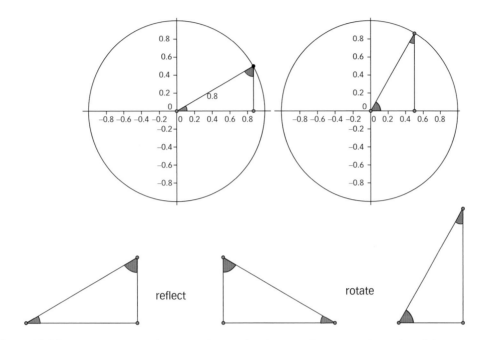

Figure 10.20   The sine value of an angle is equal to the complementary sine value of the complementary angle

And you can see for yourself in trigonometric tables that the cosine of an angle is equal to the sine of its complement (Table 10.1).

Table 10.1   Some exact values for Sine and Cosine

	30°	45°	60°
Sin	$\dfrac{1}{2}$	$\dfrac{\sqrt{2}}{2}$	$\dfrac{\sqrt{3}}{2}$
Cos	$\dfrac{\sqrt{3}}{2}$	$\dfrac{\sqrt{2}}{2}$	$\dfrac{1}{2}$

You can hopefully visualise too, that at 45° we have an isosceles triangle as our half chord.

Origins of the word sine

Much like the word 'surd', sine is the product of mistranslation. It was known as *jiba* in Arabic, meaning 'half-chord'. However, this was mistranslated into Latin as *sinusi* meaning 'bosom'. So whilst the literal translation of surd means deaf, but shouldn't, the literal translation of sine means bosom, and also shouldn't!

Tan

The word tan is short for *tangent*. As in, *tangent to the circle*. Tangent means 'to touch', and has the same roots as *integer* meaning 'untouched', or 'whole'. If we extend the sides of our half-chord triangle, such that the side opposite our angle at the origin becomes a tangent to the unit circle, then we can begin to understand the trigonometric function tan (Figure 10.21).

In fact, the hypotenuse of this larger, but similar triangle, is the derivation of the *secant* function, which comes into play in A-Level mathematics.

Anyway, the function tan is the length DE in the unit circle diagram for angle θ (Figure 10.21).

The trigonometric ratios

We can use properties of similar triangles to derive the trigonometric ratios. In Figure 10.22, the triangle ABC is a right triangle with a right angle at angle ACB and a hypotenuse of length 1 (it's a unit circle).

The larger triangle ADE is similar to ABC.

Hence:

$$\frac{BC}{AB} = \frac{DE}{AD}$$

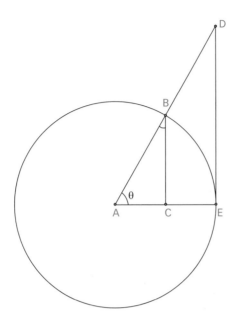

Figure 10.21 Tan refers to a tangent line

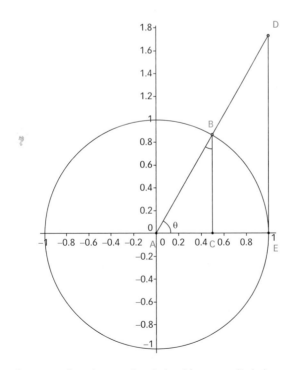

Figure 10.22 The trigonometric ratios can be derived from a unit circle

We know AB is the radius of the unit circle, which is 1, so:

$$\frac{BC}{1} = \frac{DE}{AD}$$

We also know that BC = sin θ, so:

$$\sin\theta = \frac{DE}{AD}$$

or, more familiarly:

$$\sin\theta = \frac{\text{opposite side}}{\text{hypotenuse}}$$

Furthermore,

$$\frac{AC}{AB} = \frac{AE}{AD}$$

We know AB = 1, and we know AC = cos θ, hence:

$$\cos\theta = \frac{AE}{AD}$$

or:

$$\cos\theta = \frac{\text{adjacent side}}{\text{hypotenuse}}$$

And finally,

$$\frac{DE}{AE} = \frac{BC}{AC}$$

AE is also a radius, hence AE = 1, and DE = tan θ, so:

$$\tan\theta = \frac{BC}{AC}$$

or:

$$\tan\theta = \frac{\text{opposite side}}{\text{adjacent side}}$$

Now that we've derived our trig ratios, let's go back and look at a table of trig values for various angles (Table 10.2).

Table 10.2   Trigonometric values for various angles

	0°	30°	45°	60°	90°
Sin	0	$\dfrac{1}{2}$	$\dfrac{\sqrt{2}}{2}$	$\dfrac{\sqrt{3}}{2}$	1
Cos	1	$\dfrac{\sqrt{3}}{2}$	$\dfrac{\sqrt{2}}{2}$	$\dfrac{1}{2}$	0
Tan	0	$\dfrac{\sqrt{3}}{3}$	1	$\sqrt{3}$	Undefined

There are a few values in the table that stand out as slightly odd, namely the zeroes and the 'undefined'. At this point in the book, you'll hopefully be able to spot that when something is 'undefined' in maths, it's usually related to dividing by zero. Let's take a closer look.

At 0°, we simply have no triangle to work with, we just have a single line (Figure 10.23)

Figure 10.23   sin (0°) = 0

However, that line is the radius, and therefore is 1. Hence, the cosine value is 1. It may be easier to visualise if we imagine we moved from 0 degrees to 5 degrees, then we have a very, very slim triangle, and the sine value would be a tiny amount above zero, and the cosine value would be a tiny amount below 1. If we squash that triangle flat into a single line, then the cosine length becomes 1, and the sine value becomes zero.

Similarly, at 90° we have a single line once again. This time, if we step back 5°, to 85°, we can see that it is the sine value this time that is approaching 1, and the cosine value is approaching zero (Figure 10.24).

Figure 10.24 tan (90°) is undefined

However, the tangent value is 'undefined' rather than zero. If we think back to our trigonometric ratios:

$$\tan \theta = \frac{\text{opposite side}}{\text{adjacent side}}$$

which is $\frac{1}{0}$ in this case. We're dividing by zero, which, as mentioned throughout the book, is classed as undefined.

The sine and cosine rules

These are easy to derive now that we've got our heads around sine, cosine and tan. Let's look at the sine rule first.

The sine rule (for any triangle):

$$\frac{a}{\sin A} = \frac{b}{\sin B} = \frac{c}{\sin C}$$

This rule is used to find any missing angle or side, given you know either

a) two sides and a corresponding opposite angle;
b) one side and any two angles (you can derive the third) (Figure 10.25).

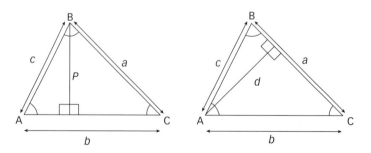

Figure 10.25 Deriving the sine rule

Using Figure 10.25, you can see that we're reinterpreting triangle ABC as two right-angled triangles, by using a perpendicular line from a point to a side.

For triangle ABC then:

$$\sin A = \frac{p}{c}$$

$$p = c \sin A$$

Similarly:

$$\sin C = \frac{p}{a}$$

$$p = a \sin C$$

We now have two expressions for p, hence:

$$a \sin C = c \sin A$$

Divide by $(\sin A \times \sin C)$:

$$\frac{a}{\sin A} = \frac{c}{\sin C}$$

Now, using the diagram on the right:

$$\sin B = \frac{d}{c}$$

$$d = c \sin B$$

Similarly:

$$\sin C = \frac{d}{b}$$

$$d = b \sin C$$

We now have two expressions for d, hence:

$$b \sin C = c \sin B$$

Divide by $(\sin C \times \sin B)$:

$$\frac{b}{\sin B} = \frac{c}{\sin C}$$

We have already shown that:

$$\frac{a}{\sin A} = \frac{c}{\sin C}$$

So altogether we can see:

$$\frac{a}{\sin A} = \frac{b}{\sin B} = \frac{c}{\sin C}$$

The cosine rule (for any triangle):

$$a^2 = b^2 + c^2 - 2bc\cos A$$

The cosine rule is used to find either a side or an angle, given you know either:

a) two side lengths and the angle between them (to find the missing side length);
b) three side lengths and no angles (to find an angle).

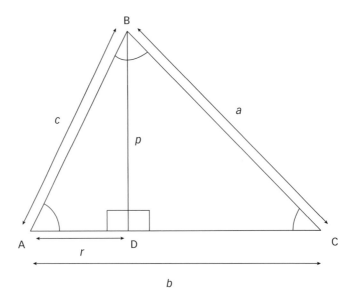

Figure 10.26   Deriving the cosine rule

Going back to our trusty diagram (Figure 10.26), using the Pythagorean Theorem for triangle BCD:

$$p^2 + (b - r)^2 = a^2$$
$$p^2 + b^2 - 2br + r^2 = a^2$$

Using the Pythagorean Theorem for triangle ABD:

$$p^2 + r^2 = c^2$$
$$p^2 = c^2 - r^2$$

Yes, But Why? Teaching for Understanding in Mathematics

We can now substitute this new expression for p:

$$c^2 - r^2 + b^2 - 2br + r^2 = a^2$$
$$a^2 = b^2 + c^2 - 2br$$

Using our trigonometric ratios, we can also find a different expression for r:

$$\cos A = \frac{r}{c}$$
$$r = c\cos A$$

We can now substitute this expression for r:

$$a^2 = b^2 + c^2 - 2bc\cos A$$

The area of a triangle using sine

$$\text{Area} = \frac{1}{2} \times ab \times \sin C$$

Again, we're using trigonometry for non-right-angled triangles, but really we're converting them into a pair of right-angled triangles (Figure 10.27).

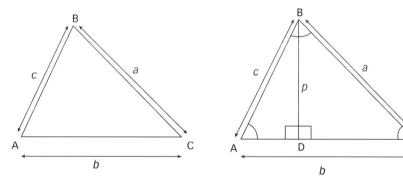

Figure 10.27   Deriving the area of a triangle using sine

Using triangle BCD:

$$\sin C = \frac{\text{opp}}{\text{hyp}} = \frac{p}{a}$$
$$p = a\sin C$$
$$\text{Area}(ABC) = \frac{1}{2} \times \text{base} \times \text{height} = \frac{1}{2} \times b \times a\sin C$$
$$\text{Area}(ABC) = \frac{1}{2}ab\sin C$$

The graphs of sine, cosine and tan

Now that we're familiar with the origins of $\sin(x)$, $\cos(x)$ and $\tan(x)$, their respective graphs will begin to make more sense. Let's take a look at sine and cosine first (Figure 10.28).

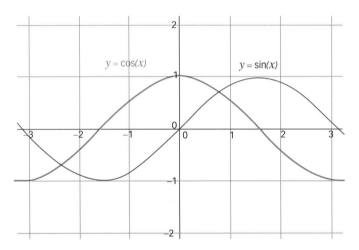

Figure 10.28   Plotting the graphs of sine and cosine

You'll notice that the waves go no higher than 1. That's because the measurements are taken from inside a unit circle, with radius 1.

In fact, if we superimpose the unit circle onto our graphs, you can see that the cosine curve wraps beautifully around the top of it (Figures 10.29–10.32).

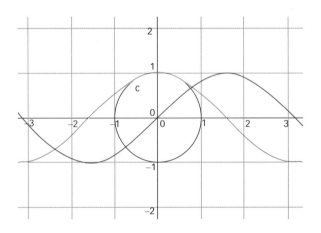

Figure 10.29   The graphs of sine and cosine and a unit circle

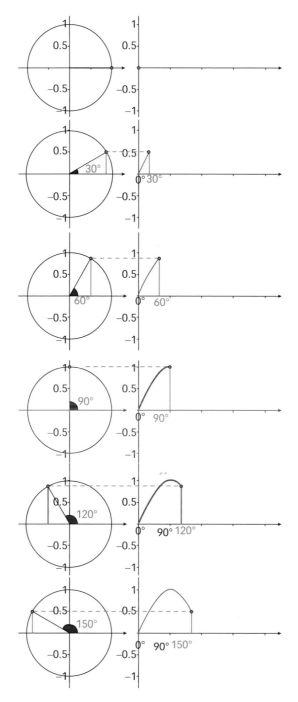

Figure 10.30 How the graph of Sine is created

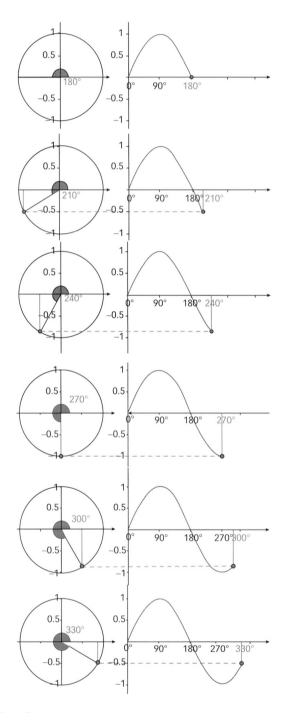

Figure 10.30 (Continued)

The cosine wave is constructed in much the same way, albeit that the reading taken is the other leg of the triangle.

The graph of tan is similarly formed, using a measure of the triangle constructed using the tangent to the circle as previously discussed. It is most obvious in Figure 10.31 at tan30°, where the entire triangle is clearly visible.

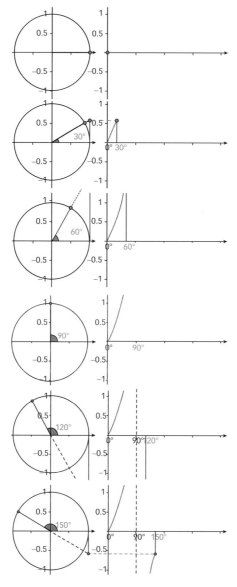

Figure 10.31 The graph of tan is formed using a measure of the triangle constructed using the tangent to the circle

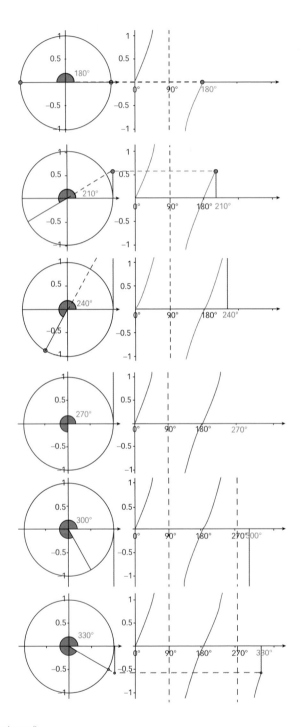

Figure 10.31 (Continued)

Yes, But Why? Teaching for Understanding in Mathematics

Interesting proofs based on the Pythagorean Theorem

The Vecten configuration

If you join the remaining vertices of the squares we looked at for the Bride's Chair Pythagorean Proof, the new triangles are all of equal area to the area of the original triangle. This is in fact true for any triangle whatsoever, not just right-angled triangles.

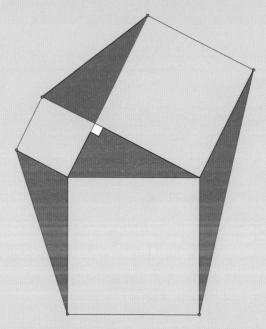

Figure 10.32   The Vecten configuration

So in Figure 10.32, the area of each red triangle is equal …

Grebe's theorem

Grebe's Theorem is a continuation of the Vecten configuration. By extending the sides of the squares from the Bride's Chair to form a new triangle, you create two similar triangles that are homothetic. That is, the new, large triangle is an enlargement of the original triangle, with a centre of enlargement A – the point at which lines passing through corresponding vertices meet (Figure 10.33).

(Continued)

(Continued)

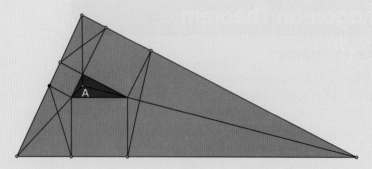

Figure 10.33   Grebe's theorem

Spiral of Theodorus

The Spiral of Theodorus is a spiral constructed entirely of right-angled triangles as shown in Figure 10.34. Theodorus of Cyrene was a Greek mathematician around the year 5 BC. The spiral is constructed using a sequence of triangles with height 1, and each triangle base is the hypotenuse of the previous iteration.

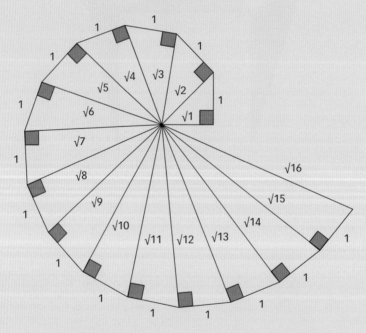

Figure 10.34   Spiral of Theodorus

Index

Yes, But Why? Teaching for Understanding in Mathematics